ASEAN-CANADA
FORUM 2008

ASEAN

Studies Centre

Institute of Southeast Asian Studies

Report No. 9

ASEAN-CANADA
FORUM 2008

ISEAS

INSTITUTE OF SOUTHEAST ASIAN STUDIES

Singapore

First published in Singapore in 2010 by
ISEAS Publishing
Institute of Southeast Asian Studies
30 Heng Mui Keng Terrace
Pasir Panjang
Singapore 119614
E-mail: publish@iseas.edu.sg
Website: bookshop.iseas.edu.sg

The responsibility for facts and opinions in this publication rests exclusively with the contributors and their interpretations do not necessarily reflect the views or the policy of the publisher or its supporters.

ISEAS Library Cataloguing-in-Publication Data

ASEAN-Canada Forum : regional economic integration : ASEAN and Canadian perspectives.
    (Report / ASEAN Studies Centre ; no. 9).
    1. ASEAN.
    2. NAFTA.
    3. Southeast Asia—Economic integration—Congresses.
    4. North America—Economic integration—Congresses.
    I.   Institute of Southeast Asian Studies. ASEAN Studies Centre.
    II. ASEAN-Canada Forum (2008 : Singapore)
    III. Series.
JZ5333.5 A9A85 no. 9   2010

ISBN 978-981-4279-14-7 (soft cover)
ISBN 978-981-4279-17-8 (E-book PDF)

Typeset by Superskill Graphics Pte Ltd
Printed in Singapore by Seng Lee Press Pte Ltd

This work was carried out with the aid of a grant from the International Development Research Centre (IDRC), Ottawa, Canada.

CONTENTS

Introduction   ix

I.   **Regional Economic Integration:**
     ASEAN and Canadian Perspectives   1
•   Summary of the Forum   3

II. **Background Papers**   11
1.   AFTA–NAFTA: Trade and Investment Issues   13
     John Whalley

2.   Trade and Investment Issues in ASEAN
     Economic Integration   27
     Myrna S. Austria

3.   Institutional Development in ASEAN   55
     Rodolfo C. Severino

4.   Governance Issues in NAFTA   63
     Paul J. Davidson

5.   Different Approaches to Dispute Resolution
     under ASEAN   87
     Locknie Hsu

6.   Dispute Resolution under NAFTA: Evolution and
     Stagnation   107
     J. Anthony VanDuzer

7.   Winners and Losers in ASEAN Economic Integration:
     A Perspective from Vietnam   142
     Vo Tri Thanh

8.   Winners and Losers in International Economic
     Integration: The Distributional Effects of NAFTA   158
     Dan Ciuriak

9.   Cross-border Labour Migration in ASEAN:
     Issues and Challenges   195
     Chia Siow Yue

10. Labour Market Integration within NAFTA   236
     Don J. DeVoretz

Annex I: Programme of the Forum   251

Annex II: List of Participants   256

Annex III: Rules-based Governance   265

INTRODUCTION

On 25–26 November 2008, the Regional Economic Studies Programme of the Institute of Southeast Asian Studies (ISEAS), and the International Development Research Centre (IDRC), Singapore organized a forum on "Regional Economic Integration: ASEAN and Canadian Perspectives". The forum gathered Southeast Asian and Canadian experts to focus on common issues related to regional economic integration. The broad objective of the forum was to promote research partnerships and build stronger economic, political and socioeconomic linkages between ASEAN and Canadian institutions.

The forum started with a keynote address by Professor Kishore Mahbubani, Dean of the Lee Kuan Yew School of Public Policy, National University of Singapore. Thereafter, the sessions examined the various aspects of regional integration — trade and investment issues, institutional development, governance and accountability, different approaches to dispute resolution, winners and losers in economic integration, labour mobility issues, etc.

The forum concluded that fundamentally the ASEAN Free Trade Area (AFTA) and the North American Free Trade Agreement (NAFTA) were two different kinds of agreements. First, while NAFTA focused entirely on trade, the scope of AFTA was much broader and went beyond issues of trade and investment alone. Secondly, NAFTA was a lightly institutionalized regional trade agreement. There was no formal institutional or policy development. For ASEAN, a secretariat was created in 1976, and expanded and strengthened in 1992, the year of AFTA's creation. Third, the dispute settlement mechanism system in ASEAN was different from that of NAFTA. The ASEAN provisions were scattered over a number of documents, and cover both trade/investment disputes and other (for example, political or territorial) disputes, while the NAFTA provisions were contained in a single document and could be applied only to trade and investment-related matters. Finally, although many studies have stated that trade liberalization is a win-win proposition, the distribution of costs and benefits is uneven. In the case of Canada, short-run gains in efficiency from expanded trade can be identified, but it is harder to determine longer-term dynamic gains. On the other hand, in the case of ASEAN, it is still grappling with the issue of the development divide, especially since the admission of Cambodia, Laos, Myanmar and Vietnam.

The forum's programme and a list of the names and contact data of the participants are at the end of this report.

The report begins with a brief summary of the important observations made during the discussions. This is followed by papers presented during the forum.

We hope that the summary and the papers will help policy-makers, the private sector and the interested public in understanding the regional integration process both in AFTA and in NAFTA.

I
ASEAN-CANADA FORUM 2008

REGIONAL ECONOMIC INTEGRATION: ASEAN AND CANADIAN PERSPECTIVES

ASEAN-CANADA FORUM 2008

REGIONAL ECONOMIC INTEGRATION: ASEAN AND CANADIAN PERSPECTIVES

Summary of the Forum

On 25–26 November 2008, the Regional Economic Studies Programme of the Institute of Southeast Asian Studies (ISEAS) and the International Development Research Centre (IDRC), Singapore, jointly organized a forum on "Regional Economic Integration: ASEAN and Canadian Perspectives". The programme and the full list of participants are presented in ANNEX I and ANNEX II.

The forum's broad objective was to promote research partnerships and build stronger economic, political and social linkages between institutions in the Association of Southeast Asian Nations (ASEAN) and Canada. In the process, it sought to shed light on various aspects of the ASEAN Free Trade Area (AFTA) and the North American Free Trade Agreement (NAFTA), to which Canada is a party.

Opened by Ambassador K. Kesavapany, ISEAS Director, Richard Fuchs, Director of IDRC Singapore, and Ambassador David Sevigny, Canadian High Commissioner in Singapore, the forum started with a keynote address by Professor Kishore Mahbubani, Dean of the Lee Kuan Yew School of Public Policy, National University of Singapore, who laid out the nature and emphasized the value of ASEAN-Canada relations.

The forum covered a comparison between the AFTA agreement and the NAFTA, institutional development in ASEAN and NAFTA, governance issues in the two regions, the different approaches to dispute settlement, the question of winners and losers in regional economic integration, and labour mobility and migration. The forum closed with a discussion of future research.

John Whalley, Professor of International Trade at the University of Western Ontario in London, Ontario, explained the broad differences between AFTA and NAFTA. AFTA, he pointed out, involved largely tariff-based integration among national economies initially linked through non-trade arrangements. He cited the fact that ASEAN members traded much more with countries outside the region than with one another. He also noted that, in the case of trade in manufactures, the reduction in trade barriers was seen as benefiting mainly one country. On the other hand, NAFTA was much wider in scope, increasing foreign direct investments into Mexico and intra-regional exports all around.

Myrna S. Austria, Economics Professor and Dean of the College of Business and Economics, De La Salle University, Manila, traced the evolution of ASEAN economic integration in terms of trade, investments and industrial production. She recalled that integration in ASEAN was largely market-driven by means of the global production networks of multinational companies, whose development was facilitated by the rapid decline of transportation and communications costs and the liberalization policies of the national governments. Dr Austria discussed what she saw as deterrents to trade and investments in ASEAN — the use of non-tariff barriers, including what she delicately referred to as "unofficial fees", the poor state of infrastructure and logistics, competition from China and India, and the proliferation of regional trading arrangements elsewhere in the world. She then put forward a number of recommendations, including the adoption of a single framework for regional trading arrangements in a way that strengthens market forces and the promotion of complementarities between ASEAN countries and China.

Rodolfo C. Severino, Head of the ASEAN Studies Centre at the Institute of Southeast Asian Studies (ISEAS), recalled the gradual process of strengthening and enlarging the ASEAN Secretariat, with a significant step taken in 1992 in conjunction with the conclusion of the AFTA agreement. He discussed other major steps in ASEAN's institutionalization, including the decision to create an ASEAN Economic Community, the establishment of a dispute settlement and other compliance mechanisms for ASEAN economic agreements, and the adoption and ratification of the ASEAN Charter.

Speaking about governance issues in NAFTA, Paul J. Davidson, Professor of Law and Chair of the Committee on Asian Studies at Carleton University, Ottawa, pointed out that NAFTA went beyond eliminating tariffs and other trade restrictions into other areas, including government procurement, services, investments, the entry of business persons, dispute settlement, and anti-dumping and countervailing duties. He also stressed that NAFTA provided for no supranational authority to work out, among other things, the harmonization of rules and standards or to amend the agreement. Neither did NAFTA have legal standing, unlike ASEAN, on which its Charter explicitly conferred a legal personality. Professor Davidson noted that the decisions of NAFTA's dispute settlement mechanism were not binding on the parties; rather, the panels played more of a conciliatory role. He pointed out that the agreement did not contain a common body of rules on dumping and subsidies. However, it allowed private parties not only to participate in the dispute settlement process but also to initiate a dispute settlement proceeding for a breach of state obligations. Finally, Professor Davidson invited attention to the dominance of the United States interests in the implementation of the agreement.

Hsu Locknie, Professor of Law at the Singapore Management University, discussed the evolution of dispute-settlement processes in ASEAN, specifically those provided for in the ASEAN Charter and in the earlier protocols for settling disputes on ASEAN's economic agreements. However, she noted the preference of the ASEAN member states to resort to international, rather than ASEAN, mechanisms to resolve their disputes.

Like Professor Davidson, J. Anthony VanDuzer, Professor of Law at the University of Ottawa, noted that NAFTA enabled private parties to resort to bi-national panels in disputes with states. However, he pointed out that, aside from private-government disputes, the parties to NAFTA had demonstrated a preference to have disputes settled in the World Trade Organization (WTO) rather than in the North American arrangements. Moreover, again like Professor Davidson, Professor VanDuzer noted that, under NAFTA, unlike in the WTO, the decisions of the panels were not binding; rather, greater reliance was placed on consultations and negotiations between parties. He explained in detail the dispute-settlement process under NAFTA, comparing it in places to the one under the WTO. Both Professors Davidson and VanDuzer cited the side agreements on labour rights and environmental protection as unique features of NAFTA.

Discussing the vexing question of "winners and losers" in economic integration, Vo Tri Thanh, Director of the Department for International Integration Studies at the Central Institute for Economic Management in Hanoi, declared that the benefits of international economic integration came with a number of challenges and costs, including widening development gaps between and within countries. While in theory international economic integration benefited all parties, in actuality it could harm individual sectors and social groups, which, if politically powerful, would wind up damaging the national economy. Dr Thanh cited numerous barriers to trade, like transportation costs and capital controls, that could make measuring the degree of integration difficult. He stressed the importance of domestic reforms in achieving economic integration and in ensuring the beneficial character of its effects. He warned of the risk of an integrated economy falling into what he called the "low-cost-labour trap" and of being vulnerable to financial crises elsewhere. East Asian economic integration, Dr Thanh pointed out, would not be possible without ASEAN integration, which, in turn, would not be achieved without narrowing the development gap within ASEAN. The quality of infrastructure, the strength of institutions and the effectiveness of internal reforms were all important for the success of economic integration.

Dan Ciuriak, Consulting Economist and Senior Associate at the Centre for Trade Policy and Law at the University of Ottawa and Carleton University, stressed that, while trade in theory and in aggregate was beneficial, the distribution of costs and benefits at the industry, firm and household levels was decidedly uneven — among consumers, among industries, among firms, between the environment and the economy, across genders, across generations, between labour and capital, and between skilled and unskilled workers. He recalled that NAFTA or the Canada-U.S. FTA on which it was based failed to result in income convergence between Canada and the U.S. NAFTA resulted both in the rise of illegal migration from Mexico to the United States and in the increase in Mexican migration from the southern rural areas to the northern industrial cities. Dr Ciuriak drew attention to the special sensitivity of agriculture and the importance of geographic factors in trans-boundary trade.

Chia Siow Yue, Senior Research Fellow at the Singapore Institute of International Affairs, examined the policies, practices and perceptions of the sending and recipient ASEAN countries on migrant labour, both the positive effects and the negative impact. She also looked into ASEAN cooperation pertaining to the conditions of migrant workers within ASEAN, including the conclusion of a few mutual recognition arrangements for certain professions and the commitments made for the protection of the rights of migrant workers. She put forward some recommendations in this regard.

Employing two analytical tools, the border and reservation income gain effects, Don J. DeVoretz, Professor of Economics at Simon Fraser University, British Columbia, concluded that the mobility patterns between NAFTA members would "depend more on the potential migrants' qualifications than on their country of origin". His other conclusion was that "the final degree of labour market integration of foreign workers will ultimately depend on the slope of the occupation curve in the sending country relative to the receiving country."

The forum ended with a discussion on future research and how to rekate it to policy and practice. Chaired by Denis Hew, Senior Fellow at ISEAS, the discussion featured Richard Barichello, Professor at the University of British Columbia in Vancouver, Professor Whalley, Deunden Nikomborirak, Research Director of Thailand Development Research Institute, and Mia Mikic of the trade policy section of the UN Economic and Social Commission for Asia and the Pacific (UNESCAP). Professor Barichello and Josef Yap, President of the Philippine Institute of Development Studies, are doing a study on this subject.

II
BACKGROUND
PAPERS

1
AFTA–NAFTA
Trade and Investment Issues

John Whalley

1. Introduction

This paper discusses and compares both the trade and investment dimensions of the ASEAN Free Trade Agreement (AFTA) and the North American Free Trade Agreement (NAFTA). The emphasis is on the difference in objectives, impacts and content.

The literature contrasting AFTA and NAFTA is relatively short, but there are a substantial number of works on each of the two free trade agreements. In the paper, I argue that the objectives underlying these agreements are quite different, as are both the impacts and their content. AFTA involves a largely tariff based integration attempt with some content in services between national economies which were initially linked through a non-trade agreement, ASEAN, rather than a trade agreement. It is also one in which, for these countries, the majority of trade volume (approximately 75 per cent) occurs with third parties outside of the agreement, mostly with countries in the Organization for Economic Cooperation and Development (OECD) and with China. As such, the integration achieved in AFTA is inevitably more limited than is the case with NAFTA. In addition, in terms of manufacturing trade, where the trade liberalization has been concentrated, most of the reductions in trade barriers have been seen as benefiting mainly one country, namely Singapore which, although small in population, is the largest in manufacturing activity in the region. This asymmetry of perceived benefits has made the achievement of deep liberalization much more difficult.

In the NAFTA case, the trade agreement was originally driven by a Canadian request in 1987 for a Canada-United States agreement, motivated by Canadian concerns of security of access to their largest market (the United States) rather than improved access *per se*. The subsequent Mexican entry to this arrangement in the form of NAFTA at the end of 1993 has generated large trade and investment impacts for Mexico, with large increases in Mexico's exports to the United States and also large impacts on foreign direct investment (FDI) inflows. The theme that the objectives and the impacts of these two trade agreements are sharply different thus comes through centrally in the discussion in the text.

It is also the case that the content of these agreements is widely different. AFTA remains largely a tariff-cutting agreement, with some content on services and cooperation agreements between ASEAN states. NAFTA is much wider ranging in content, with arrangements applying in energy, wine and spirits, agriculture, special rules in agriculture, environmental content, and special dispute settlement procedures. As a result, the point of comparison is between what is effectively a narrower-based tariff agreement and a much broader-ranging packaging of issues in the form of NAFTA.

2. Content of the Agreements

Prior to a discussion of the differences in objectives and impact of these agreements on trade and investment, it is useful to summarize their content.

NAFTA has its origins in the Canada-U.S. agreement of 1987 which was subsequently effectively trilateralized (with some modification) to include Mexico at the end of 1993. The Canada-U.S. agreement, in turn, has to be seen in its wider historical context of trade relations between Canada and the United States going back to Confederation.[1] Confederation in 1867 was in part a response to the termination of the Elgin Marcy Treaty in 1854 by the U.S. Congress, which used its rights under the treaty of notification of twelve months termination. This was terminated in 1866 and this started a search by, then Upper and Lower Canada, for secure market arrangements, and became one of the major factors behind Confederation in 1867.

After Confederation, the search in Canada was thus for secure markets, both in the United States and in Europe, principally in the United Kingdom. Much of this effort failed and by 1891, Canada adopted the National Policy under Sir John A. MacDonald which emphasized the development of the domestic market behind a large and secure national tariff, with subsidies to Western settlement. This policy of Canada's development has never been formally abandoned by any successive national government, although over the years it has been greatly modified. But the history of Canada's subsequent trade policy was a series of attempts to negotiate bilateral agreements with the United States, but when these failed, to resort to increased protections. This process reached its high point in 1911 with the so-called Free Trade Debate, after Laurier and Taft negotiated a trade agreement which was brought back to the House of Commons in Canada for debate, where the government of the day fell, and an election was fought over the issue of free trade. The free trade side failed in the election and Canada then moved towards a regime of high tariffs against the United States which, in the 1930s, was then modified with Commonwealth Preferences under the Ottawa Agreement in 1932.

Subsequently, when the United States began to move towards reciprocal negotiation after the New Deal Reciprocal Trade Agreements Act in 1933, there were reductions undertaken in tariffs in the United States. By the end of the war and with the creation of the GATT, Canada became committed to the multilateral process and trade negotiations under the framework of GATT rather than direct negotiations with the United States.

From 1947 to the early 1980s, Canada was committed to multilateral over bilateral arrangements on the argument that Canada needed the security of multilateral disciplines around any bilateral arrangements it might have with the United States. But this was to change in the 1980s with the Mulroney Government committed to the position that the United States was Canada's largest trading partner and most important market. Hence, there should be active bilateral negotiation with the United States because Canada could go further and faster down a bilateral rather than a multilateral route. This was to lead to the 1987 bilateral agreement with the United States which was driven principally from the Canadian side and by concerns over security of access to the U.S. markets, rather than improving said access *per se*. This reflected Canadian concerns over safeguard measures applicable to copper and other product areas which, under GATT rules, would have to be non-discriminatory and applied to Canada as well. The use of anti-dumping and countervailing measures against Canada by the United States was also a central concern.

The form of the Canada-U.S. agreement was only settled in the last few hours of negotiation, but effectively, it involved three distinct elements. One was tariff-cutting much as in the conventional GATT form, but tariffs by that stage were relatively low on most products with a few small tariff spikes. It also included a range of special sectoral agreements covering such matters as agriculture, autos, energy, financial services to address the concerns on the Canadian side over security of access, special agreements in the form of new dispute settlement arrangements applying to the use of anti-dumping and countervailing measures. These involved a set of new dispute settlement arrangements with panels which were to determine whether or not national measures were consistent with domestic law. These were in addition to conventional dispute settlement over the interpretation of the agreement.

The Canada-U.S. agreement generated high political drama and debate in Canada but little discussion in the United States. But after the Canada-U.S. agreement and Mexico's request to join in similar arrangements active debate on what was to become NAFTA was sparked in the United States, with much less debate on the Canadian side. The Canadians were initially opposed to NAFTA on the grounds that it would erode their margin of preference in U.S. markets but subsequently agreed to the NAFTA negotiation and largely participated as an observer.

The content of NAFTA is similar to that of the Canada-U.S. agreement but with some additions and differences in particular areas. One is in textiles where Mexico, as a member of the Multi-Fibre Arrangement as an exporter, was freed of MFA quotas in return for new and tightened rules of origin (ROO) involving yarn forward content rules. Another was in agriculture, with Mexican liberalization in corn and beans. In addition there were new areas added. One was land transportation arrangements, which proved to be important later in fuelling Mexican trade growth. Another was new intellectual property arrangements. In areas such as energy, there were changes relative to the Canada-U.S. agreement reflecting constitutional limitations on the Mexican Government's power to deal with what was viewed as "national heritage" in energy and oil, which deviated from the Canadian case. But in broad content, NAFTA emerged as similar to the Canada-U.S. agreement.

In the case of AFTA, it is a sub-agreement within ASEAN. The ASEAN Declaration states that the aims and purposes of the association are to accelerate economic growth, social progress and cultural development in the region and to promote regional peace and stability through abiding respect for justice and the rule of law in the relationship among countries in the region and adherence to the principles of the United Nations Charter.[2] AFTA is an outgrowth of the desire of ASEAN to further economic growth and, while ASEAN dates from 1967 and the days of the Vietnam War, AFTA was agreed to later in 1992. At the time that AFTA was first created, ASEAN only had six members, and accession to ASEAN has since required AFTA compliance. The stated goals of AFTA are to reduce inter-ASEAN tariff barriers and to attract foreign direct investment to the area.

AFTA has long been seen by the research community outside the ASEAN countries as a trade agreement which followed a defence agreement, and a trade agreement which largely reflected attempts to achieve political integration through tariff reductions, rather than through a large and significant wider economic agreement with major economic impact. Also, direct inter-ASEAN trade volumes are relatively small and asymmetric (see Table 1.1). ASEAN country trade is largely outside of ASEAN.

As a tariff-based negotiation, the AFTA commitments which were entered into in some areas were often less than with WTO commitments which followed multilaterally, which many of the individual AFTA countries individually entered into. And the content of the AFTA in such areas as services was relatively

TABLE 1.1
Intra- and Extra-ASEAN Trade, 2006

Values in US$ million; Shares in per cent

	Exports				Imports				Total Trade			
	Intra-ASEAN		Extra-ASEAN		Intra-ASEAN		Extra-ASEAN		Intra-ASEAN		Extra-ASEAN	
	Value	Share to country total	Value	Share to country total	Value	Share to country total	Value	Share to country total	Value	Share to country total	Value	Share to country total
Brunei Darussalam	1,887.3	24.8	5,732.0	75.2	745.8	50.1	743.1	49.9	2,633.2	28.9	6,475.1	7.1
Cambodia	235.4	6.7	3,279.1	93.3	991.2	33.9	1,931.8	66.1	1,226.5	19.1	5,210.9	80.9
Indonesia	18,483.1	18.3	82,315.5	81.7	19,379.2	31.7	41,686.3	68.3	37,862.3	23.4	124,001.8	76.6
Laos	289.8	72.0	112.8	28.0	500.7	85.2	86.8	14.8	790.5	79.8	199.7	20.2
Malaysia	40,979.6	26.1	116,247.3	73.9	32,290.7	25.2	96,025.5	74.8	73,270.2	25.7	212,272.7	74.3
Myanmar	2,149.7	61.2	1,365.0	38.8	1,174.7	55.5	940.8	44.5	3,324.4	59.0	2,305.9	41.0
Philippines	8,192.2	17.3	39,217.9	82.7	10,218.3	19.7	41,555.3	80.3	18,410.5	18.6	80,773.3	81.4
Singapore	83,801.6	30.9	187,806.3	69.1	62,300.4	26.1	176,181.6	73.9	146,102.0	28.6	363,987.9	71.4
Thailand	26,944.2	22.2	94,635.3	77.8	23,539.8	18.5	103,569.0	81.5	50,484.0	20.3	198,204.3	79.7
Vietnam	6,214.0	16.8	30,819.7	83.2	12,453.7	31.0	27,783.1	69.0	18,667.7	24.2	58,602.8	75.8
ASEAN	189,176.8	25.2	561,531.0	74.8	163,594.5	25.0	490,503.3	75.0	352,771.4	25.1	1,052,034.3	74.9

Source: ASEAN Trade Statistics <http://www.aseansec.org> (accessed 13 November 2008).

limited.[3] In addition, AFTA countries faced no political pressure
for regional negotiation comparable to NAFTA. It was not an
issue of a small country's access to a larger dominant country's
markets, seeking security of access. Prior to AFTA, the AFTA
countries generally traded largely outside of the AFTA region and
this pattern has remained after AFTA (see Table 1.2); the exception
was Singapore's exports to other ASEAN countries. Hence the
pressure for an AFTA negotiation was also reduced as it was seen
as yielding asymmetric benefits. It was seemingly to demonstrate
the solidarity and common political commitment of the ASEAN
member states that the negotiation was entered into.

Since AFTA has been formed however, AFTA has become
part of a deeper integration process in the ASEAN. This has
been market driven, but there have been further negotiations,

TABLE 1.2
Intra- and Extra-ASEAN Trade: 1990, 2006

Values in US$ million; Shares in per cent

Year	1990	2006
Intra-ASEAN exports	28,954.0	189,176.8
Share to Region total	20.1	25.2
Extra-ASEAN exports	115,195.0	561,531.0
Share to Region total	79.9	74.8
Intra-ASEAN imports	26,309.0	163,594.5
Share to Region total	16.2	25.0
Extra-ASEAN imports	136,019.0	490,503.3
Share to Region total	83.8	75.0

Sources: ASEAN trade statistics <www.aseansec.org> and WTO trade statistics
<www.WTO.org> (accessed 13 November 2008).

particularly in the services area, where commitments have been entered into which are "WTO+" in the sense that they are labelled and signalled as commitments that go beyond the WTO commitments of the ASEAN countries.

3. Trade and Investment Impacts

The impacts of the AFTA and NAFTA agreements on trade and investment differ sharply. In the case of NAFTA, the trade impacts involving Mexico in particular, have been both marked and dramatic (see Table 1.3). In the mid-1980s, Mexico's exports to the United States were around US$20 billion per year. By the time NAFTA was negotiated, they had already increased to the US$30 billion region by 1990. But following the implementation of NAFTA, Mexican exports to the United States surged further and have reached figures as high as US$210 billion. In recent years, Mexican exports have dipped as Chinese exports have entered the U.S. market. It is now a smaller exporter to the U.S. market than either Canada or China, but its exports have still increased sharply since pre-NAFTA days.

These surges have occurred in a number of sectorial areas and for differing reasons. One important area has been apparel where, with the termination of MFA quotas and the integration of much Mexican apparel activity into U.S. companies which bought out Mexican companies at the time of the negotiation, Mexico by early 2000 became the second largest shipper of textiles and apparel into the U.S. markets after China. In addition, much assembly activity, especially in autos, has occurred across the Mexican border and in the older Mequiladora Zone (the tariff-free part of the Mexican economy with a small geographical zone contiguous to the U.S. border), where imports were duty-free if they were then re-exported in the form of fabricated products. In

TABLE 1.3
U.S. Imports and Exports to Canada and Mexico, 1985–2007

Values in US$ billion

	Total Trade		Imports from		Exports to	
	Canada	Mexico	Canada	Mexico	Canada	Mexico
1985	116.3	32.8	69.0	19.1	47.3	13.6
1986	113.6	29.7	68.3	17.3	45.3	12.4
1987	130.9	34.9	71.1	20.3	59.8	14.6
1988	153.0	43.9	81.4	23.3	71.6	20.6
1989	166.8	52.1	88.0	27.2	78.8	25.0
1990	175.1	58.4	91.4	30.2	83.7	28.3
1991	176.2	64.4	91.1	31.1	85.1	33.3
1992	189.2	75.8	98.6	35.2	90.6	40.6
1993	211.7	81.5	111.2	39.9	100.4	41.6
1994	242.8	100.3	128.4	49.5	114.4	50.8
1995	271.6	108.4	144.4	62.1	127.2	46.3
1996	290.1	131.1	155.9	74.3	134.2	56.8
1997	319.0	157.3	167.2	85.9	151.8	71.4
1998	329.9	173.4	173.3	94.6	156.6	78.8
1999	365.3	196.6	198.7	109.7	166.6	86.9
2000	409.8	247.3	230.8	135.9	178.9	111.3
2001	379.7	232.6	216.3	131.3	163.4	101.3
2002	370.0	232.1	209.1	134.6	160.9	97.5
2003	391.5	235.5	221.6	138.1	169.9	97.4
2004	446.2	266.7	256.4	155.9	189.9	110.8
2005	502.3	290.5	290.4	170.1	211.9	120.4
2006	533.1	332.2	302.4	198.3	230.7	134.0
2007	565.9	346.8	317.1	210.7	248.9	136.1

Source: U.S. Census Bureau <www.census.gov/foreign-trade/www/> (accessed 13 November 2008).

northern Mexico there has been substantial activity which has combined imported components from the United States and low-wage labour from Mexico to fuel further fabrication.

In addition, trade between Mexico and the United States in particular has been enhanced by the liberalization of land transportation agreements on the Mexican side. These involved new express trains to Washington, changes in arrangements for the transportation of packages with the removal of Mexican state monopolies on shipment, and other arrangements. A sharp increase in U.S.-Mexico trade was a marked impact from NAFTA (see Table 1.3).

On the Canadian side, Canadian exports to the United States remained flat for some years after the Canada-U.S. agreement in 1987, but increased from the mid-1990s onwards. The Canadian share of exports going into the United States increased from 76 per cent at the time of the Canada-U.S. agreement to 85 per cent in 2005, but then fell back to 76 per cent by 2007.[4] As a result, the trade impact of NAFTA for Canada has been smaller and has changed integration less between the participating countries.

In the case of ASEAN, deeper integration between member countries due to AFTA does not seem to be evident from trade data (see Table 1.2). There has been some trade growth but nothing approaching the growth of trade which has occurred in the Mexican case.

But both agreements have also had impacts in other areas. On the FDI front, a major impact of NAFTA has been a sharp increase in FDI inflows into Mexico. This has been further fuelled by the policy stability associated with the trade agreement and the general change in policy direction in Mexico which accompanied NAFTA. These large FDI impacts have been a central feature of Mexican trade growth with the United States. As many

Mexicans have noted, however, comparable income growth in Mexico has not followed the large increases in trade, as has been the experience in the Asian cases. In turn, AFTA's impact on inter-ASEAN FDI has been only small and limited. Hence, the impact of AFTA would seem to be much smaller than NAFTA.

NAFTA has also had major impacts on the global trading system. An effect of NAFTA was the demonstration of the willingness of the world's largest trading partner to go bilateral with its largest trading partners. The result has been, following the negotiation of NAFTA, a series of countries expressing interest in joining a North American Free Trade Agreement. These range from Korea to New Zealand to Columbia and Costa Rica, which subsequently led to the United States-Central American Regional Trade Agreement. The NAFTA agreement has been a catalyst for wider changes in the trading system which, among other things, has involved a major acceleration in regional agreements. The latest estimates are that, by the end of this year, the WTO committee on regional agreements may have received 800 notifications of regional agreements of various kinds.[5]

On the other hand, ASEAN has seemingly not had similar effects. There has been no rush by other countries to join ASEAN agreements, even though ASEAN now negotiates regional agreements. ASEAN has become an entity itself involved in regional agreements, and these have been part of both ASEAN-wide regional agreements, such as with China and Japan, and individual ASEAN country agreements.[6] Singapore is particularly active in these areas through a whole series of Singapore-based initiatives.

4. The Future Evolution of NAFTA and AFTA and Concluding Remarks

Given their sharp differences in objectives, impact and content, the future evolution of these agreements is a matter of speculation.

The political pressures in North America are now for the renegotiation of NAFTA, given the commitments entered into in the presidential campaign on these matters. These, in turn, reflect the wider dissatisfaction in certain parts of the United States with all forms of trade agreements, including the WTO commitments. Hence, the pressures are now to find some mechanism for the renegotiation of parts of NAFTA. This, in turn, may focus on the dispute settlement procedures, which are reflective of the concerns of the U.S. Congress over a weakening of national sovereignty and national autonomy due to NAFTA. These two sets of trade agreements are also likely to be affected by the growth and evolution of issues which face the trading system, the interaction between regional and multilateral agreements, and how to treat such issues that reach outside the normal reach of trade agreements such as security in these things. The future evolution of AFTA in terms of potential renegotiation seems be less an issue and hence, while these agreements differ in objectives, impact and content, they will likely differ in their future evolution.

Notes

1. See the discussion in R.M. Hill and J. Whalley, "Canada-US Free Trade: An Introduction", *Canada-United States Free Trade*, Vol. 11 of the Research Studies, Royal Commission on the Economic Union and Development Prospects for Canada (Toronto, ON: University of Toronto Press, 1985), pp. 1–42.
2. ASEAN Website <http://www.aseansec.org/64.htm> (accessed 13 November 2008).
3. As of the time of writing, services agreements are limited to engineering, nursing, architecture and surveying only. (Refer to ASEAN Website <http://www.aseansec.org/6626.htm> for further information.)
4. Statistics Canada <http://www.statcan.ca/> (accessed 13 November 2008).

5.   J-A. Crawford and R.V. Fiorentino, "The Changing Landscape of
     Regional Trade Agreements", Discussion Paper no. 8, WTO
     Publications, 2005 <http://www.wto.int/english/res_e/booksp_e/
     discussion_papers8_e.pdf> (accessed 12 November 2008).
6.   See O.G. Dayaratna-Banda and J. Whalley, "Beyond Goods and
     Services: Competition Policy, Investment, Mutual Recognition,
     Movement of Persons, and Broader Cooperation Provisions of
     Recent FTAs involving ASEAN Countries", Working Paper no. 11232,
     NBER (Cambridge, Mass., 2005).

References

ASEAN Website. <http://www.aseansec.org> (accessed 13 November 2008).

Crawford, J-A. and R.V. Fiorentino. "The Changing Landscape of Regional
     Trade Agreements". Discussion Paper no. 8, WTO Publications,
     2005 <http://www.wto.int/english/res_e/booksp_e/discussion_
     papers8_e.pdf> (accessed 12 November 2008).

Dayaratna-Banda, O.G. and J. Whalley. "Beyond Goods and Services:
     Competition Policy, Investment, Mutual Recognition, Movement of
     Persons, and Broader Cooperation Provisions of Recent FTAs
     involving ASEAN Countries". Working Paper no. 11232, NBER,
     (Cambridge, Mass., 2005).

Hill, R.M. and J. Whalley. "Canada-US Free Trade: An Introduction".
     Canada-United States Free Trade, Vol. 11 of the Research Studies,
     Royal Commission on the Economic Union and Development
     Prospects for Canada (Toronto, ON: University of Toronto Press,
     1985), pp. 1–42.

Statistics Canada. <http://www.statcan.ca/> (accessed 13 November 2008).

WTO International Trade Statistics Database. <http://www.wto.org/
     english/res_e/statis_e/Statis_e.htm> (accessed 13 November 2008).

*Professor John Whalley is William G. Davis Chair in International
Trade, Department of Economics, University of Western Ontario,
London, Ontario.*

2
TRADE AND INVESTMENT ISSUES IN ASEAN ECONOMIC INTEGRATION

*Myrna S. Austria**

1. Introduction

The Association of Southeast Asian Nations (ASEAN) has gone a long way in opening up the region to greater trade and foreign direct investment (FDI) from the rest of the world. The competitive pressure arising from the process and the region's response to meet the challenge paved the way to the region's economic integration. Prior to the 1990s, this was considered by many as impossible, especially if one looks at the member economies' economic structures that are more competitive rather that complementary. With the exception of Singapore, the economies have similar resource endowments and levels of technological development; thus, resulting in the production and export of similar primary and labour-intensive products. They are also all heavily dependent on the developed countries, particularly the United States, Europe and Japan, for their export markets and sources of foreign direct investment and technology. These factors were perceived to make economic integration in the region difficult, if not impossible.

From the initial goal of establishing the ASEAN Free Trade Area in 1992,[1] ASEAN is now aiming to deepen economic integration through the ASEAN Economic Community (AEC) by 2015, a timeline which was initially set at 2020. The AEC is one of the three pillars of an ASEAN Community embodied in the Declaration of ASEAN Concord II (also known as Bali Concord) adopted during the 2003 ASEAN Summit.[2] The AEC is characterized as a single market and production base, with free flow of goods, services, investment, labour and capital. As an initial step towards the goal, the ASEAN leaders signed the Framework Agreement for the Integration of the Priority Sectors during the ASEAN Summit in 2004. The agreement outlined the steps to be taken to accelerate the integration of eight priority sectors and three services sectors.[3] Three years later, during the ASEAN Summit in November 2007, the ASEAN leaders signed the Declaration on the ASEAN Economic Community Blueprint, the master plan that guides ASEAN towards achieving AEC by 2015.

Deepening economic integration implies that markets of member economies are fully integrated as a result of the liberalized flow of goods, services and factors of production, producing unrestricted competition and convergence of prices across national borders (Austria 2004). While intra-ASEAN tariff rates have substantially gone down since 1992, a host of impediments to trade and investment remain. At the same time, individual ASEAN members are embarking on bilateral and regional linkages outside the region, a phenomenon that could hinder the realization of the vision of the AEC.

This paper will examine the main issues in facilitating greater trade and FDI in ASEAN, and analyse the challenges that lie ahead in achieving deeper economic integration. The paper is organized as follows. The second section discusses the major schemes that ASEAN has adopted to achieve economic integration. The third section examines the role of trade and FDI as drivers of economic integration in the region. Issues affecting trade and FDI in ASEAN are then discussed in the fourth section. The final section presents the summary and recommendations.

2. ASEAN Economic Integration Schemes

There are three major ASEAN schemes to achieve economic integration, namely: (i) ASEAN Free Trade Area (AFTA); (ii) ASEAN Investment Area; and (iii) ASEAN Industrial Cooperation Agreement (AICO). The highlights of each of these schemes are discussed below.

(i) ASEAN Free Trade Area

The initial steps to economic integration in the ASEAN region were achieved through the ASEAN Free Trade Area (FTA) established in 1992. The primary goal of AFTA is to increase ASEAN's competitive edge as the production base for the world market by lowering intra-regional tariff rates through the Common Effective Preferential Tariff (CEPT) scheme to 0–5 per cent within a fifteen-year period beginning 1993. Within ten years, AFTA succeeded in lowering the average tariff rates from 11.44 per cent in 1993 to 2.39 per cent in 2003 for the original AFTA signatories (that is, ASEAN-6)[4] (Austria 2003).

Over the years, however, AFTA took significant leaps toward the achievement of its goal. First, the deadline was twice accelerated. In 1995, it was moved from the original date of 2008 to 2003; and then in 1998, to 2002. Second, the coverage of AFTA was widened to include products that were originally excluded (like unprocessed agricultural products). Third, AFTA also widened its scope beyond the CEPT scheme by including other initiatives such as harmonization of standards, and reciprocal recognition tests and certification of products. Finally, AFTA's original goal of 0–5 per cent was deepened by targeting a zero-ending tariff rates on all products by 2010 for the original members and 2015 for Cambodia, Laos, Myanmar and Vietnam (CLMV).

(ii) ASEAN Investment Area

The promotion of investment in the region was guided initially by the Framework Agreement on ASEAN Investment Area (AIA) signed in October 1998. The AIA aims to establish a competitive investment area with a more liberal and transparent investment environment among the member economies. The scheme includes gradual elimination of impediments to investment, liberalization of investment rules and policies, granting of national treatment and most favoured nation (MFN) treatment to investors and investment of member economies, and opening up of industries to ASEAN investors by 2010 and to all investors by 2020.[5]

The AIA has significant implications for investment strategies and production activities in the region. By promoting the region as a single investment area, investors (both local and foreign) are encouraged to think in regional terms and adopt regional investment strategies. As will be discussed in greater detail in the next section, one such strategy is the operation of production networks of multinational companies across the region through the division of labour and industrial activities based on the cost competitiveness and comparative advantages of member economies.

The framework was amended in 2001, this time making more explicit the sectoral coverage of the agreement: manufacturing, agriculture, fishery, forestry, and mining and quarrying, and services incidental to these sectors. In February 2009, the AIA and the ASEAN Agreement for the Promotion and Protection of Investments (ASEAN IGA)[6] were revised and merged to form the ASEAN Comprehensive Investment Agreement (ACIA). The objective of ACIA is to create a free and open investment regime in ASEAN by 2015 through the following: (i) progressive liberalization of the investment regimes; (ii) provision of enhanced protection to investors of member economies and their investments; (iii) improvement of transparency and predictability of investment rules, regulations and procedures conducive to increased investment among the member economies; (iv) joint promotion of the region as an integrated investment area; and (v) cooperation to create favourable conditions for investment by investors of a member economy in the territory of the other member economies.

The ACIA is considered to be more comprehensive than AIA and IGA, covering four pillars namely liberalization, protection, facilitation and promotion. The comprehensive provisions will improve investor's confidence to invest in the region. The ACIA also includes additional provisions (like prohibition of performance requirements) and made improvements to existing provisions (like investment dispute), while reaffirming the non-discriminatory provisions on national treatment and MFN.

(iii) ASEAN Industrial Cooperation Agreement (AICO)

Introduced in 1996, AICO is an industrial cooperation scheme to promote ASEAN integration through joint manufacturing industrial activities between ASEAN-based companies.[7] Its primary objectives are increased industrial production in the region, increased investments from ASEAN and non-ASEAN sources, increased intra-ASEAN trade, enhanced technology base, and increased industrial complementation. It aims to exploit complementary locational advantages in the region through resource-pooling by granting the outputs of the participating companies the advanced final CEPT tariff rates. This means that prior to 2003, the application of the 0–5 per cent preferential tariff rate provided a head start to AICO products compared to non-AICO products. In 2004, AICO was amended to revise the applicable preferential tariff rate to 0 per cent.[8] The programme requires a minimum of two participating companies in two different ASEAN economies to form an AICO agreement.

Most companies that participated in the AICO scheme since its introduction are from the automotive industries. The companies consider the implementation of complementation scheme as critical to the expansion of their activity in the region (Flynn, Alkire, and Senter 1999).

3. Trade and FDI: The Drivers of ASEAN Economic Integration

There is a general consensus that economic integration in ASEAN is largely market-driven through the global production networks (GPNs) of multinational companies (MNCs) from developed economies. Under the production scheme, different stages of production are spread to locations that offer significant advantages in production costs and access to export markets. The labour-intensive segment of the production chain is usually located in developing countries (like ASEAN) where wages are low. International production sharing is commonly applied more intensively in trade in electronics and semiconductors, automotive, and textiles and garments. These are the same industries where integration is highest in the ASEAN region.

To a large extent, the integration of ASEAN into the production network was the result of the industrial restructuring of the newly industrializing economies (NIEs — South Korea, Hong Kong, Taiwan and Singapore), who were themselves the initial hosts of the offshore production of Japanese and American MNCs (Austria 2004). When wage rates in the NIEs began to rise in the 1990s, these economies lost their comparative advantage in the labour-intensive segment of the production chain, causing them to move their production offshore to ASEAN, China and other developing countries in South Asia. The outcome of this integration process was the significant improvement of economic performance in East Asia and the intensification of economic linkages among economies in the region.

The rapid decline in transportation and communication costs was a crucial factor that made the operations of the GPNs possible in the region. Equally crucial however, are the diminishing barriers to trade and investment due to the liberalization policies adopted by the ASEAN economies. On the one hand, their domestic policies play a crucial role in shaping their capacity to take part in the global production chain. In general, the unilateral trade and investment liberalization policies of the member economies fostered domestic efficiency, driving down costs and raised productivity and profitability. This increased the attractiveness of the individual ASEAN members and collectively as a region to MNCs, allowing the latter to exploit comparative advantages of each member country, leading to specialization and economies of scale in production.

On the other hand, the regional liberalization efforts through AFTA, AIA/ACIA and AICO are consistent with the domestic policies of opening up the economies to greater trade and investment, and thus reinforce market forces in the region. More importantly, as legal instruments, the integration schemes provide stability, certainty and transparency in the business environment in the region. The financial crisis of 1997–98 taught the painful lesson that integration of markets without formal agreements can create uncertainty for business.

The extent of economic integration in the region is shown by the pattern and structure of trade and FDI, discussed in the next sub-sections of the paper.

(i) Pattern and Structure of Trade

The increasing outward orientation of ASEAN is shown by the region's total trade which more than doubled during the period 2000–07 (see Figure 2.1). The region accounted for an average of 6 per cent per year of world trade during the period. In real terms, total trade in the region grew much faster during the period 2000–07 than in 1995–2000 (see Table 2.1). This is also true for all the member economies, except the Philippines. The expansion of trade is also shown by the degree of openness of the region, measured by the ratio of total trade to GDP (see Table 2.2).

TABLE 2.1

Average Annual Real Growth Rate of Total ASEAN Trade and Intra-ASEAN Trade, 1995–2007 (%)

Countries	Total trade		Intra-ASEAN trade	
	1995–2000	2000–07	1995–2000	2000–07
Brunei	–7.82	10.24	–8.56	12.62
Indonesia	0.46	7.38	5.02	12.06
Malaysia	1.88	5.92	4.52	5.76
Philippines	7.95	2.84	14.31	6.34
Thailand	–2.35	9.38	0.58	10.74
Singapore	0.69	8.07	0.59	9.52
ASEAN-6	0.86	7.30	2.55	8.85
Cambodia	3.97	19.34	–16.4	25.41
Laos	2.04	14.91	5.26	15.24
Myanmar	5.48	7.95	3.66	12.28
Vietnam	14.69	17.45	13.28	15.84
CLMV	11.90	16.52	6.69	15.98
Total ASEAN	1.26	7.87	2.76	9.34

Source: IMF Direction of Trade Statistics.

FIGURE 2.1
Total Trade and Percentage Share to World Trade, ASEAN, 1999–2007

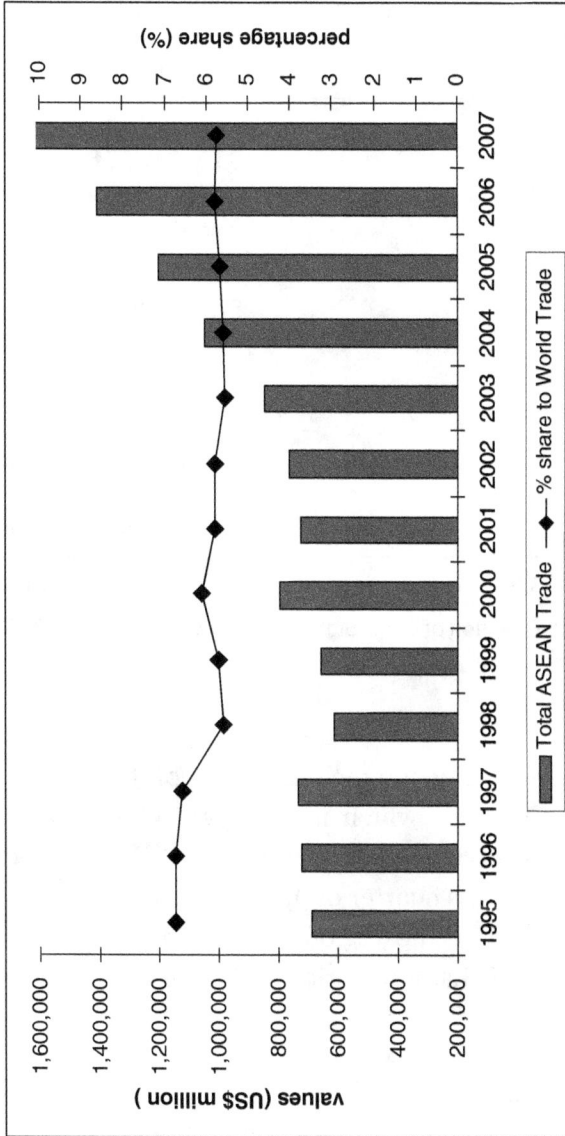

Source: IMF Direction of Trade Statistics.

TABLE 2.2

Degree of Openness, ASEAN, 1995–2007

Countries	1995	2000	2005	2007
Brunei	134.1	76.5	76.6	87.8
Indonesia	38.5	57.8	50.1	43.6
Malaysia	167.9	192.3	185.5	173.3
Philippines	60.5	95.8	89.8	73.5
Thailand	80.8	106.6	129.4	119.6
Singapore	287.8	294.1	331.5	348.6
ASEAN-6	103.4	136.0	135.2	125.5
Cambodia	56.5	69.7	42.0	122.3
Laos	50.3	62.3	68.3	85.1
Myanmar	64.5	56.4	59.4	75.9
Vietnam	67.4	96.5	129.9	158.9
CLMV	64.7	85.2	108.6	140.8
Total ASEAN	101.6	132.1	133.0	126.7

Sources: IMF Direction of Trade Statistics and World Economic Outlook Database, IMF.

The growing economic integration of the region is shown by intra-ASEAN trade, which in 2007 was almost three times the amount registered in 1995 (see Figure 2.2). Intra-regional trade represents about a quarter of the region's total trade; and just like the total trade of the region, it grew much higher during the period 2000–07 than the period 1995–2000 (see Table 2.1).

The region's pattern of trade reflects ASEAN's role in the global production networks (GPNs). First, the bulk of trade is accounted for by electrical machinery, equipment and parts (see Table 2.3). Second, the high growth of both total trade and intra-regional trade is consistent with the operations of GPNs which

FIGURE 2.2

Total Intra-ASEAN Trade and Percentage Share to Total ASEAN Trade, 1995–2007

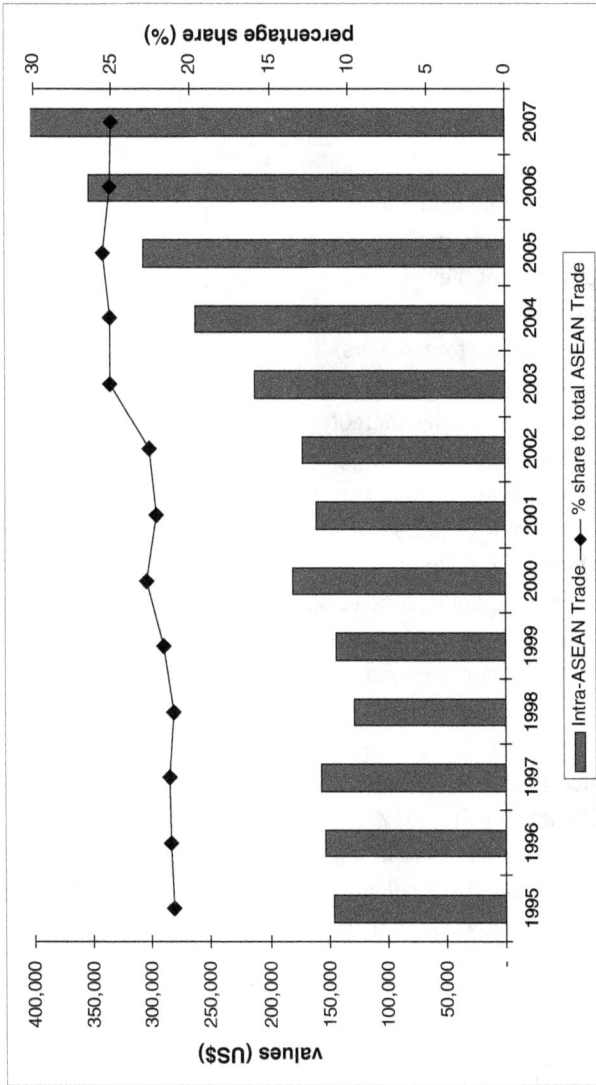

Source: IMF Direction of Trade Statistics.

TABLE 2.3

Top Ten ASEAN Trade Commodity Groups, 2006

2-digit HS Code	Description	% share to total ASEAN trade		
		Exports	Imports	Total trade
85	Electric machinery, equipment & parts; sound equipment; television	27.6	27.6	27.6
27	Mineral fuels, mineral oils & products of their distillation; mineral wax	14.3	17.9	16.0
84	Nuclear reactors, boilers, machinery & appliances	15.6	14.4	15.1
39	Plastics & articles thereof	2.7	2.7	2.7
29	Organic chemicals	2.8	2.3	2.6
87	Vehicles (not railway, tramway, rolling stock), parts & accessories	2.3	2.5	2.4
90	Optical, photographic, cinematographic, measuring, checking, precision, medical or surgical instruments/apparatus; parts & accessories	1.9	2.4	2.1
72	Iron & steel	0.8	3.1	1.9
40	Rubber & articles thereof	2.8	0.8	1.9
71	Natural & cultured pearls, precious & semi-precious stones, precious metals and metals clad therewith and articles thereof; imitation jewellery; coin	1.3	1.6	1.4
Top ten commodity groups		72.1	75.3	73.6
	Others	27.9	24.7	26.4
	Total	100.0	100.0	100.0

Source: ASEAN Secretariat.

are increasingly regionalized while the market for their final products is more globalized. Third, the bulk of intra-ASEAN trade occurs among the ASEAN-5, the host of GPNs in the region (see Table 2.4). Finally, the region's top trading partners (see Table 2.5), which accounts for almost 81 per cent of the region's trade, are also at the forefront of the production chain.

(ii) Pattern and Structure of FDI

Annual FDI flows increased during the period 1995–2006 (see Figure 2.3). Some setback was registered in 1998 because of the financial crisis but recovery started in 2003. The region accounted for an average share of 4.1 per cent of total FDI flows in the

TABLE 2.4

Percentage Distribution of Intra-ASEAN Trade by Member Economies, 1995–2007 (%)

Countries	1995	2000	2005	2007
Brunei	1.5	0.9	0.8	0.8
Indonesia	8.6	9.6	10.7	11.4
Malaysia	23.3	25.3	21.2	20.1
Philippines	3.7	6.3	5.2	5.2
Thailand	14.6	13.1	14.9	14.3
Singapore	43.7	39.3	40.5	39.7
ASEAN-6	95.3	94.4	93.5	91.5
Cambodia	1.0	0.3	0.1	0.9
Laos	0.3	0.4	0.4	0.6
Myanmar	1.0	1.0	1.2	1.2
Vietnam	2.4	3.9	4.8	5.9
CLMV	4.7	5.6	6.5	8.5
Total ASEAN	100.0	100.0	100.0	100.0

Source: IMF Direction of Trade Statistics.

TABLE 2.5

Top Ten Trading Partners of ASEAN, 2006

Trade partners	% share to total ASEAN trade		
	Exports	Imports	Total trade
ASEAN	25.2	25.0	25.1
Japan	10.8	12.3	11.5
USA	12.9	9.8	11.5
European Union – 25	12.6	10.1	11.4
China	8.7	11.5	10.0
South Korea	3.4	4.1	3.7
Australia	3.1	2.0	2.6
India	2.5	1.5	2.0
Taiwan	1.2	2.0	1.6
Hong Kong	1.8	1.0	1.4
Top ten	82.2	79.3	80.9
Others	17.8	20.7	19.1
Total	100.0	100.0	100.0

Source: ASEAN Secretariat.

world. This is small by international standards. Majority of FDI went to Singapore (see Figure 2.4). In terms of sectoral distribution, manufacturing received the bulk of FDI (see Figure 2.5).

There was also a shift in the major sources of FDI. Traditionally, the United States was the major source of FDI during the 1970s and 1980s. Since the late 1990s however, Japan and some European countries accounted for the bulk of FDI while South Korea, Taiwan, Hong Kong and China are increasingly investing in the region as well (see Table 2.6). Such pattern of FDI reflects the role of the region in the global production chain, as discussed earlier in this section of the paper.

FIGURE 2.3

FDI Flows to ASEAN, 1995–2006 (US$ million)

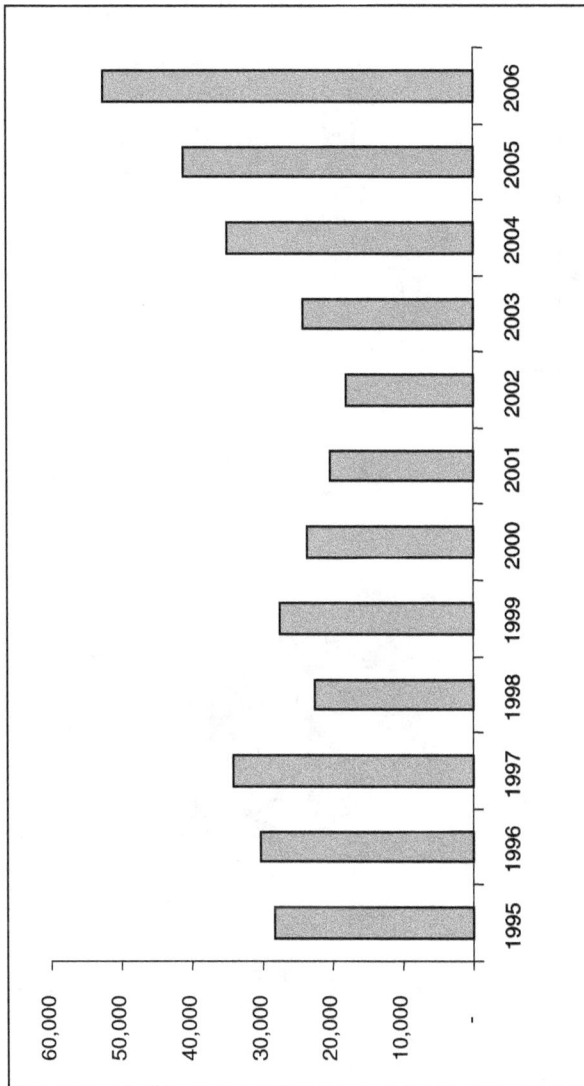

Source: ASEAN FDI Database 2007 (ASEAN Secretariat).

FIGURE 2.4

Total Cumulative FDI Flows, By Country, ASEAN, 1999–2006

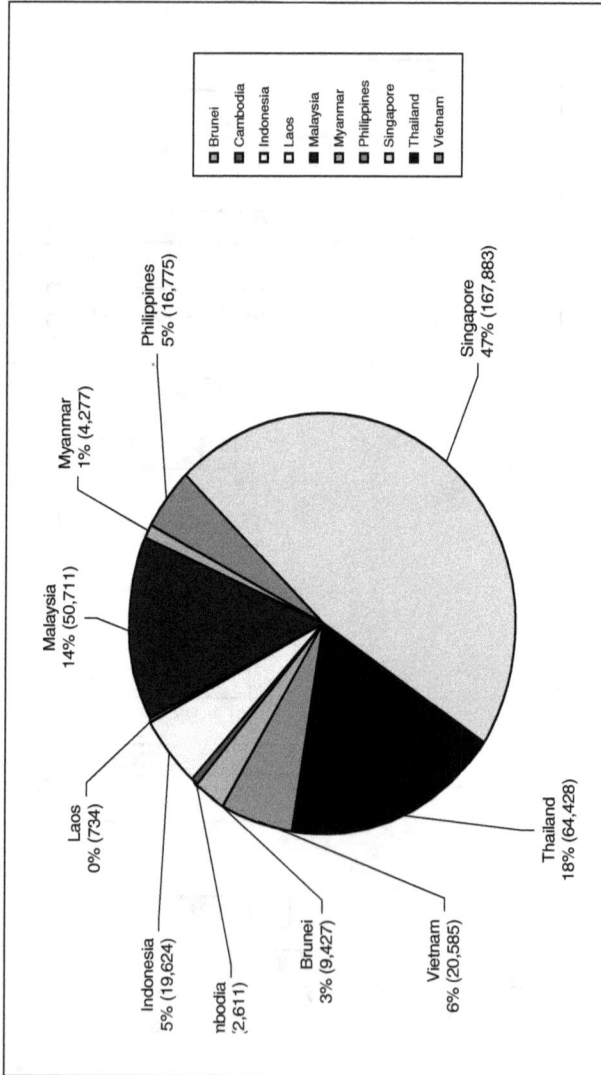

Brunei
Cambodia
Indonesia
Laos
Malaysia
Myanmar
Philippines
Singapore
Thailand
Vietnam

Philippines 5% (16,775)
Singapore 47% (167,883)
Myanmar 1% (4,277)
Malaysia 14% (50,711)
Laos 0% (734)
Indonesia 5% (19,624)
Cambodia (2,611)
Brunei 3% (9,427)
Vietnam 6% (20,585)
Thailand 18% (64,428)

Source: ASEAN Secretariat.

FIGURE 2.5

Total Cumulative FDI Flows, By Sector, 1999–2006

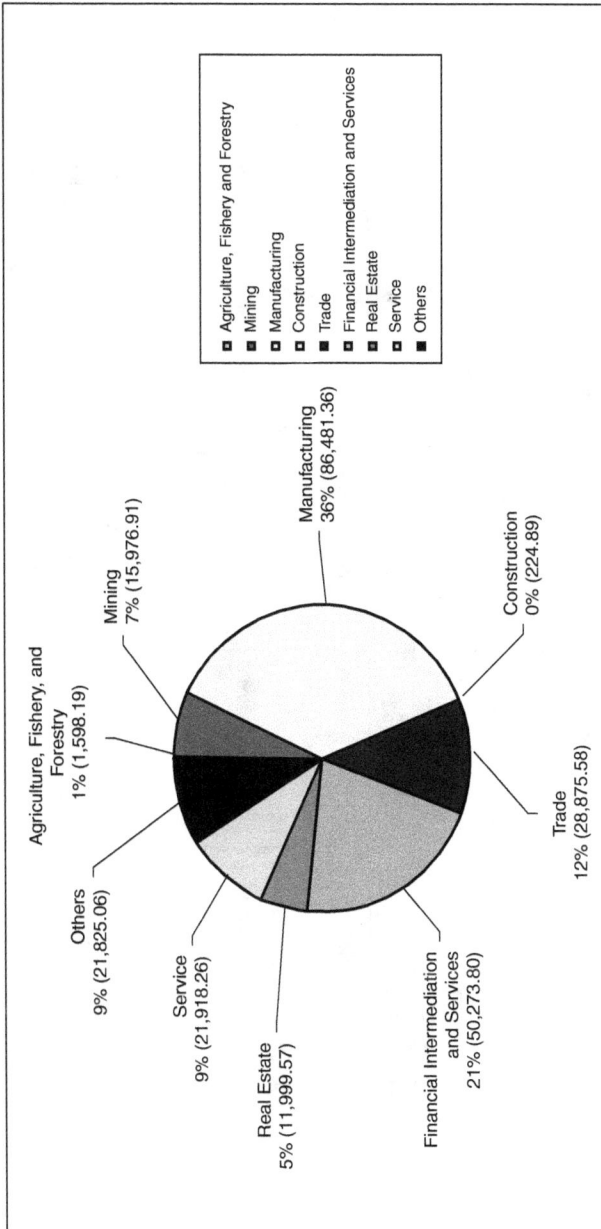

Legend:
- Agriculture, Fishery and Forestry
- Mining
- Manufacturing
- Construction
- Trade
- Financial Intermediation and Services
- Real Estate
- Service
- Others

Manufacturing 36% (86,481.36)
Mining 7% (15,976.91)
Agriculture, Fishery, and Forestry 1% (1,598.19)
Others 9% (21,825.06)
Service 9% (21,918.26)
Real Estate 5% (11,999.57)
Financial Intermediation and Services 21% (50,273.80)
Trade 12% (28,875.58)
Construction 0% (224.89)

Source: ASEAN Secretariat.

TABLE 2.6
Top Ten Major Sources of FDI, ASEAN, 2001–06

RANK	2001 Country	%	2002 Country	%	2003 Country	%	2004 Country	%	2005 Country	%	2006 Country	%
1	United States	23.6	ASEAN	21.2	United Kingdom	20.6	United Kingdom	15.3	Japan	17.6	Japan	20.6
2	Netherlands	14.2	Japan	16.8	Japan	16.6	Japan	16.3	United Kingdom	13.7	United Kingdom	12.8
3	Taiwan (ROC)	13.3	United Kingdom	14.0	ASEAN	11.4	United States	14.9	ASEAN	9.2	ASEAN	11.9
4	ASEAN	12.4	Netherlands	10.3	United States	7.6	ASEAN	8.0	United States	7.3	United States	7.4
5	Japan	10.8	Denmark	3.0	Netherlands	6.3	Netherlands	6.5	Netherlands	5.1	Netherlands	5.5
6	United Kingdom	7.0	Hong Kong	2.7	Taiwan (ROC)	4.1	Cayman Islands	5.8	France	2.4	Germany	3.0
7	Bermuda	3.8	Taiwan (ROC)	2.5	Rep of Korea	2.8	Germany	2.7	Hong Kong	1.9	Hong Kong	2.6
8	Germany	5.3	Canada	2.1	Luxemburg	2.5	Rep of Korea	2.3	Rep of Korea	1.4	Rep of Korea	2.1
9	Cayman Islands	4.0	France	1.4	Cayman Islands	2.4	China	2.1	China	1.2	China	1.8
10	Belgium	2.5	Finland	1.1	France	1.4	Bermuda	1.4	Germany	1.2	Taiwan (ROC)	1.3

4. Issues Affecting Trade and Investment in ASEAN

There are a number of major issues currently affecting trade and FDI in the ASEAN namely, (i) prevalence and extensive use of NTBs, particularly in the priority sectors for integration; (ii) the state of infrastructure and logistics in the region; (iii) the emergence of China and India as a priority investment target for GPNs; (iv) proliferation of bilateral and regional trading arrangements (BTAs/RTAs); and (v) ASEAN becoming a hub for bilateral and regional FTAs in East Asia. Each of these are discussed briefly below.

(i) Prevalence and Extensive Use of NTBs

As discussed in Section 2, ASEAN has achieved significant progress in tariff liberalization, with the average tariff rate now at less than 5 per cent. However, this achievement has been countered by non-tariff barriers (NTBs) that are persistent and on the rise, and for some, in even more complex forms (Austria 2009).

The more recent studies on NTBs in ASEAN show that these measures still abound in the region and are preventing the free movement of the priority goods sectors for integration across the national borders. These studies include de Dios (2006), Eddy and Owen (2007), Parsons (2007) and James, Minor and Dourng (2007). While there are variations in the main findings because of differences in data sources and approaches, certain categories of NTBs have consistently been identified as a source of concern.

De Dios (2006) found twenty-four types of NTBs affecting the priority sectors for integration using the ASEAN NTM Database; and ninety types using UNCTAD TRAINS. Please refer to Appendix A for details. Using the ASEAN Database, she found that prevalent and extensive NTMs pervade the priority sectors for integration (see Table 2.7). She defined prevalent as being geographically

TABLE 2.7
Summary of Incidence of NTBs in the
Priority Goods Sectors for Integration

Sectors	Incidence	NTBs
Fisheries, agro-based, automotive, automotive, ICT	Prevalent & extensive	Non-automatic licensing Technical regulations
Electronics	Prevalent & extensive	Non-automatic licensing Prohibitions Technical regulations
Healthcare	Prevalent & extensive	Non-automatic licensing Prohibitions Technical regulations Labelling Testing & inspection
Rubber-based	Prevalent but not extensive	Technical regulations
Wood-based, textiles & apparel	Extensive but not prevalent	Additional taxes & charges Non-automatic licensing Quota linked with export performance Single channel for exports

Source: de Dios (2006).

widespread or applied by several members; and extensive as being affecting the majority of the tariff lines in the priority sectors.

The incidence of NTBs has not changed as shown by a comparison of de Dios (2004) using the 2004 ASEAN Database.

This was expected as no updates or revisions to their notifications have been made by the ASEAN members since the establishment of the database in 2004. Using the UNCTAD TRAINS database, the same study of de Dios (2006) found that in general, NTBs of all types are pervasive in all the sectors, especially in the fisheries and agro-based sectors.

The findings of de Dios (2006) are confirmed by Eddy and Owen (2007) based on the ASEAN Region-wide Business Survey. The survey shows that the customs clearance process is the primary concern of the business sector. In particular, the complexity of the refund process is perceived as having a serious impact on trade compared to other measures; and the declaration of goods is considered lengthy. In addition, para-tariff and price control measures are considered to restrict trade, particularly in the Philippines and Cambodia. Of the priority sectors, the automotive sector is the most severely affected by these measures. Unofficial fees hinder trade as these are requested at least occasionally to facilitate customs clearance and licence application and renewal, and to expedite testing and inspection process in customs. The unofficial fees not only increase the costs of doing business in the region but also lengthens the import process itself.

(ii) Infrastructure and Logistics

As discussed in Section 3, economic integration is driven primarily by FDI-driven GPNs who are constantly on the lookout for new markets, low-cost assembly points, as well as parts and component suppliers that would strengthen their competitive position in the world market. MNCs are particularly concerned about systemic efficiencies in their entire global production chain, where a given location is judged by how cost-efficiently it performs a given function in coordination with other functions located elsewhere (UNCTAD 2002).

However, the state of the region's infrastructure and logistics left much to be desired, particularly in the CLMV. The poor infrastructure and logistics increase production costs and hence, lowers the competitiveness of industries in the world market. Given the regional and global orientation of the operations of GPNs, a good infrastructure and logistics oriented to the world-wide management of the value chain is crucial. This means reducing power and communication costs, providing adequate port systems, cutting travel time, and offering travel and shipment options. Crucial also is the role of the logistics service industry, like freight forwarders who specialize in arranging transportation, storage and handling of goods within and between countries in the region.

(iii) The China and India Challenge

Investors around the globe pay attention to Asia but they are focusing their attention on China and India. There is no doubt that China has emerged as the priority investment site of GPNs. Since the late 1990s, there has been a shift in network location away from the traditional export platform in Southeast Asia and toward China. For example, because the electronics industry is highly sensitive to assembly costs, China with its cheap labour, has emerged to be the principal gainer in the export market for electronic products, particularly in telecommunication equipment, computers and disk drives (Wilson 2003), while ASEAN is slowly losing its comparative advantage in this segment of the production chain.

It is also argued that the increase of investment in China is a consolidation of production in response to the increasing popularity of global suppliers (Sturgeon and Lester 2004). This development poses a serious challenge to ASEAN and other developing economies wanting to participate in GPNs as part of their development strategy. The less developed members of the ASEAN — Cambodia, Laos, Myanmar and Vietnam (CLMV) appear to be at greatest risk in the immediate future since they are in danger of being "leapfrogged" in the value chain (Wilson 2003).

(iv) The Rise of Bilateralism and Regionalism around the Globe

The proliferation of RTAs/FTAs in North America and Europe, and recently, also in East Asia, has created many new competitors for ASEAN, both for export markets and sources of FDI. ASEAN members know that they face discriminatory deals from such arrangements in which they are not members. This is particularly relevant for the ASEAN-5 who are hosts to a critical mass of global electronics players from the United States, Europe, Japan, South Korea and Taiwan (Austria 2005). Since RTAs/FTAs are characterized by lower barriers to trade and investment, reduced transaction costs, harmonized standards and legal norms, GPNs would prefer to locate their subsidiaries or outsource their production in economies in which their own economies are linked through FTAs. Also, the rules of origin (ROO) in FTAs and RTAs encourage MNCs to locate in economies that belong to the same RTA/FTA as their source economies in order to overcome ROO. In short, RTAs/FTAs in which an economy is not a member may displace that economy's exports. Thus, a stronger and more competitive ASEAN is necessary to overcome this differential treatment, and to strengthen ASEAN's negotiation leverage against RTAs.

(v) ASEAN becoming a Hub for Bilateral and Regional FTAs

ASEAN as a group as well as ASEAN's individual members (although mostly the more developed members) are currently enjoying the privilege of being "courted" or pursued by their trading partners to establish FTAs or comprehensive economic partnerships (see Table 2.8). Also, the ASEAN-based processes (ASEAN+1, ASEAN+3, East Asia Summit (ASEAN+6), ASEAN Regional Forum) are defining the evolving architecture of regional cooperation in East Asia. However, these occurred without the guidance of a common framework. The absence of common framework in all these efforts could be potentially dangerous for ASEAN as it could lead to a series of agreements that are very different from each other. This could give rise to the "spaghetti bowl" effects, where each agreement differs in scope and tariff reduction schedules, rules of origin, etc. This could make the cost of doing business in the region more expensive.

TABLE 2.8
Status of ASEAN's Free Trade Agreements,
as of December 2007

Economies	Concluded	Under negotiation	Proposed	Total
ASEAN	2	4	0	6
Brunei	3	0	4	7
Cambodia	1	0	2	3
Indonesia	3	1	6	10
Laos	3	0	2	5
Malaysia	4	5	4	13
Myanmar	1	1	2	4
Philippines	2	0	4	6
Singapore	11	10	5	26
Thailand	6	6	6	18
Vietnam	1	1	2	4

Source: ADB (2008), Table 3.

Likewise, new rules of origin arising from different FTA agreements can divert sourcing of inputs away from existing partnerships, which is currently driven by market forces and without the benefit of RTAs.

5. Summary and Challenges Ahead

There is no doubt that trade and investments in the region are influenced largely by the operations of GPNs. GPNs in turn played a crucial role in the region's economic integration. The challenge facing the region now is how to strengthen its position and remain competitive in the international production chain. Since MNCs are particularly concerned about systemic efficiencies in their entire global production chain, the challenge is how to make the entire set of ASEAN membership cost efficient and more attractive as investment destinations and export markets (Austria 2004). In other words, there must be no weak link in the entire chain if the region were to function as a production base for the GPNs. Cambodia, Laos, Myanmar, Vietnam (CLMV) and Brunei are the weakest link in the chain and this lessens the attractiveness of the region to the FDI-driven production networks.

ASEAN should adopt a single common framework in their BTAs/FTAs. The framework should be designed in such a way that it does not destroy the market forces prevailing in the region but rather, strengthen them.

Also, there must be a complementarity in the production chain among the ASEAN-10, the NIEs and China. For the ASEAN-10, the role of the region in the production network is highly concentrated to the labour-intensive assembly and testing segment of the production chain. This has given rise to exports that are highly import-dependent and hence, domestic value added is minimal. There are risks with continuing the existing pattern of production and trade. It involves the type of FDI that is highly mobile, that is, footloose. Hence, cost advantages can be easily eroded and lost due to wage increases and the emergence of more attractive locations. Thus, unless ASEAN member countries undergo industrial upgrading, their prospects of staying in the value chain become weak (Austria 2004). The key strategy for the ASEAN-5 is not to compete with China but to find niches which are complementary to China in the value chain. With industrial upgrading, MNCs can locate their labour-intensive activities in China, CLMV and Brunei while maintaining their high-value production segment in the NIEs and the ASEAN-5.

Notes

*   Full Professor, Economics Department and Dean, College of Business and Economics, De La Salle University, Manila. The author would like to thank Ms Angelica Torres for the excellent research assistance.

1.   Prior to AFTA, there was the ASEAN Preferential Trading Area (PTA) in 1977 where margin of preferences were granted to imports among the ASEAN members. However, PTA did not succeed as the margin of preferences was too small to provide ASEAN importers a strong competitive edge over non-ASEAN importers.

2.   The other pillars are ASEAN Security Community and ASEAN Socio-Cultural Community.

3.   The goods sectors include agro-based products, fisheries, healthcare products, rubber-based products, wood-based products, textile and garments, electronics and ITC, and automotive. The services sectors include e-ASEAN, healthcare, air travel and tourism.

4.   The original AFTA signatories include Brunei, Indonesia, Malaysia, the Philippines, Thailand and Singapore.

5.   National treatment means that investors from each member economy will be granted similar treatment as domestic (host

country) investors. On the other hand, most favoured nation (MFN) means that investors from a member economy will be accorded similar treatment *vis-à-vis* other ASEAN-based investors.

6. The ASEAN IGA was signed in December 1987.
7. AICO replaced the ASEAN Industrial Joint Venture (AIJV) and the Brand-to-Brand Complementation (BBC) scheme.
8. The preferential tariff rate shall cease when tariff rate of the product reaches the final CEPT rate.

References

Austria, Myrna. "ASEAN Free Trade Area: Lessons Learned and the Challenges Ahead". In *Regional Cooperation and Identity Building in East Asia in the Age of Post-Cold War Globalization*, edited by Park Sa-Myung and Supachai Yavaprabhas (Seoul: Korea Association of Southeast Asian Studies, 2003).

———. "The Pattern of Intra-ASEAN Trade in the Priority Goods Sector, 2004". <http://www.aadcp-repsf.org>.

———. "Enhancement and Deepening of the Competitiveness of the Philippine Electronics Industry Under a Bilateral Setting". Paper presented during the PASCN Annual Conference, with the theme "Prospects for a Philippine-U.S. Free Trade Area", Philippine Institute for Development Studies, Makati, 26 January 2005.

———. "Tackling Non-Tariff Barriers in ASEAN". In ASEAN Studies Centre Report No. 4, *ASEAN Economic Community Blueprint*. Singapore: Institute of Southeast Asian Studies, 2009.

De Dios, Loreli. "Non-tariff Barriers to Trade in the ASEAN Priority Goods Sectors". In *Brick by Brick, The Building of an ASEAN Economic Community*, edited by Denis Hew (Singapore: Institute of Southeast Asian Studies, 2007).

Eddy, Catherine and Rowena Owen. "An Investigation into the Measures Affecting the Integration of ASEAN's Priority Sectors (Phase 2): Region-wide Business Survey". REPSF Project No. 06/001e, May 2007.

Flynn, M., K. Alkire, and R. Senter. *Shifting Strategies: The Big Three in ASEAN*. University of Michigan Transportation Research Institute, 1999.

James, William, Peter Minor, and Kakada Dourng. "An Investigation into the Measures Affecting the Integration of ASEAN's Priority Sectors (Phase 2): The Case of Textiles and Apparel". REPSF Project No. 06/001c, April 2007.

Parsons, David. "An Investigation into the Measures Affecting the Integration of ASEAN's Priority Sectors (Phase 2): The Case of Electronics". REPSF Project No. 06/001b, June 2007.

United Nations Conference on Trade and Development (UNCTAD). *Trade and Development Report, 2002*. UNCTAD/TDR, Geneva, 2002.

Wilson, P. "The Export Competitiveness of Dynamic Asian Economies: 1983–1995". *Journal of Economic Studies* 27, no. 6 (2000): 541–65.

Myrna S. Austria is the Dean of College of Business and Economics at De La Salle University, Manila. She is also a Full Professor of the Economics Department at the same college.

3
INSTITUTIONAL DEVELOPMENT IN ASEAN

Rodolfo C. Severino

For nine years after its founding on 8 August 1967, the Association of Southeast Asian Nations (ASEAN) did not have a central secretariat, although there were occasional suggestions for the establishment of one. To ASEAN at that time, the important thing was for leaders, ministers and officials to get to know one another, to form friendships with one another, and to build confidence among themselves. Working informally and pragmatically was the only way to ensure that they would regard one another with less suspicion and greater comfort.

It was not until 24 February 1976, on the occasion of ASEAN's first summit meeting, in Bali, that the ASEAN foreign ministers signed an agreement establishing the ASEAN Secretariat. (It was also the occasion when ASEAN concluded its first binding agreement, the Treaty of Amity and Cooperation in Southeast Asia.) The Secretariat was to be in Jakarta, with the Indonesian Government, in 1981, turning over to the association the land and building where it is now located.

The Secretariat at that time was rudimentary at best. Its officers were seconded from their respective governments. The secretary-general was nominated by members in the alphabetical order of the countries' English names and for a term of two years. In order to make clear that the secretary-general would not perform any supranational functions, he was called the "Secretary-General of the ASEAN Secretariat". The quip went around at that time that he was more secretary than general.

The 1976 agreement went into great detail, specifying that the Secretariat would have three bureau directors — one each for economic, science and technology, and social and cultural affairs. The agreement also stipulated that there would be a foreign trade and economic relations officer, an administrative officer, an information officer, and an assistant to the secretary-general. The ASEAN Standing Committee, the association's governing body of national officials, would appoint these officers for terms of three years, renewable once for another three years. The Secretariat was allowed to hire locally recruited personnel.

A 1983 agreement empowered the ASEAN Standing Committee to expand the Secretariat's professional staff beyond the officers listed in the original agreement. In 1985, the term of office of the secretary-general was lengthened to three years. Another agreement, in 1989, added the office of deputy secretary-general, who would be appointed in alphabetical order for a three-year term. That agreement retained the three bureau directors but refrained from specifying the tasks to be assigned to each of them. It provided for nine assistant directors and additional officers as the ASEAN Standing Committee deemed necessary. The agreement specified three-year terms for these officers of the Secretariat, renewable for another three years, and laid down in some detail the duties of the deputy secretary-general and those of the bureau directors, all of whom had to be officials of their governments during their tenure.

It was only in July 1992, almost twenty-five years after ASEAN's founding, that the ASEAN Secretariat took on more or less its present form. ASEAN decided to strengthen the Secretariat, mainly in ways outlined by the heads of government at their fourth summit in January. The secretary-general would now be the secretary-general of ASEAN and not just of its Secretariat. He — so far, the secretary-general has always been a he — was accorded the rank of minister and would be selected by the foreign ministers and appointed by the heads of government. His term of office was lengthened to five years, subject to extension. More importantly, the secretary-general's mandate was expanded to include initiating, advising, coordinating and implementing ASEAN activities. He was also to

> serve as spokesman and representative of ASEAN on all matters, ... conduct consultations with the Contracting Parties, the private sector, the Non-Governmental Organizations and other constituencies of ASEAN, [and] coordinate ASEAN dialogues with international and regional organizations and with any dialogue country that may be assigned to him.

The Secretariat was also enlarged. Now, its officials would consist of a deputy secretary-general, who would remain on a three-year term with one extension of up to three years, and four bureau directors, eleven assistant directors, eight senior officers, and others decided upon by the ASEAN foreign ministers, all on three-year terms renewable once. The July 1992 protocol was silent on the alphabetical rotation of either the secretary-general or the deputy secretary-general, stipulating that the secretary-general would be appointed "on the basis of merit" and that the deputy secretary-general would be openly recruited. The Secretariat's other officers were to be openly recruited on the basis of merit but also on the principle of "equitable distribution" among ASEAN nationals.

The decision to expand and strengthen the Secretariat was apparently motivated by two impulses — to demonstrate a stronger commitment to regional purposes and to manage the ASEAN Free Trade Area, which was also agreed upon at the 1992 summit. It is significant that among the new functions prescribed for the secretary-general were to "monitor the implementation of the Agreement on the Common Effective Preferential Tariff (CEPT) Scheme for the ASEAN Free Trade Area (AFTA), serve as a member of and provide support to the ministerial-level Council set up to supervise, coordinate and review the implementation of the ASEAN Free Trade Area".

A 1997 agreement sought to strengthen the Secretariat further. A second deputy secretary-general was added, with both deputy secretaries-general to be appointed in alphabetical order for terms of three years, this time without extension. While the number of bureau directors would remain at four, there would now be fifteen assistant directors and fifteen senior officers, as well as additional openly recruited staff that the ASEAN Standing Committee would deem "necessary".

Despite these measures to strengthen the Secretariat, ASEAN's regional institutions remain weak in comparison to those of the European Union. ASEAN has no court of justice. It has no central bureaucracy similar to the European Commission. Except, in some cases, for the economic area, ASEAN agreements provide for no penalties for non-compliance with their provisions. Until very recently, the ASEAN Secretariat did not participate in the ASEAN Regional Forum on political and security issues except in the forum's annual ministerial meetings. Not least, the ASEAN Secretariat is relatively small and has an operating budget of less than US$10 million, to which each of the ten ASEAN countries contribute exactly equal shares.

In spite of the relative weakness and small size and budget of ASEAN's regional institutions, however, ASEAN has succeeded in removing tariffs on almost all intra-ASEAN trade, the secretary-general is recognized as ASEAN's face before the international community, and ASEAN is taken seriously by the rest of the world.

Even before the effectivity of its new Charter, ASEAN has in place a number of dispute settlement mechanisms. Contrary to the belief in some quarters, the ministerial-level High Council of the Treaty of Amity and Cooperation in Southeast Asia is *not* a dispute settlement mechanism. It only "takes cognizance" of disputes and recommends modes of settlement. What the treaty has done is lay down norms for interstate relations: the rejection of the use or threat of force, the peaceful settlement of disputes, and non-interference in internal affairs. These norms are enshrined in the charters of many associations of nations and underpin the entire interstate system. In practice, ASEAN countries have brought their bilateral disputes to international adjudicating bodies like the International Court of Justice and the International Tribunal for the Law of the Sea and abided by their judgments.

ASEAN does have a dispute-settlement mechanism for its economic agreements. As first adopted in 1996, the mechanism called for consultations and the exercise of good offices, conciliation and mediation. In case consultations failed, the Senior Economic Officials Meeting (SEOM), a long-established ASEAN body, was to form a panel to recommend how a dispute was to be resolved. SEOM would then rule on the panel's report. The ASEAN Economic Ministers (AEM), a forum formed in 1976, would serve as an appeals body in such cases. In case of a failure to comply with a ruling, compensation would be exacted or related concessions were to be suspended.

The 2003 ASEAN Summit in Bali adopted the recommendations of the High Level Task Force on the ASEAN

Economic Community on strengthening regional economic institutions. Decision-making by economic bodies was opened to modalities other than consensus. A legal unit was established in the ASEAN Secretariat. On the basis of the task force recommendations, the summit decided to set up the ASEAN Consultation to Solve Trade and Investment Issues, a mechanism to resolve operational problems expeditiously, and the ASEAN Compliance Body, an adjudicating body that would be patterned after the World Trade Organization's Textiles Monitoring Body. It also decided to "enhance" ASEAN's dispute settlement mechanism. The summit agreed to improve "the capability of the ASEAN Secretariat to conduct research and analytical studies related to trade, investment and finance".

A year later, ASEAN improved the dispute settlement mechanism for economic agreements. In a protocol issued in November 2004, the AEM enabled the secretary-general to offer his good offices and conciliation and mediation services. They adopted the terms of reference for panels set up by SEOM to resolve economic disputes. They spelled out the conditions for SEOM to establish such a panel. The ministers also set up an Appellate Body of seven independent personages, three of whom would be involved in any one case. However, the body's report would still be subject to SEOM's decision to adopt it or not. The protocol stressed that a panel's and the Appellate Body's findings and recommendations must be complied with. A status report on compliance had to be submitted to SEOM, which would decide whether to impose compensation and/or the suspension of concessions. Principles for the suspension of concessions were laid down. In case of objections to the level of suspensions, the protocol called for a system of arbitration. A dispute settlement fund would also be established. Not least, the protocol specified time-frames for each of the steps involved in the dispute-settlement process, which should not exceed a total of 445 days.

The new ASEAN Charter, signed by the ASEAN leaders on 20 November 2007, not only codifies ASEAN symbols and practices. It seeks to strengthen the Secretariat and streamline and expedite decision-making. It places squarely on the leaders' shoulders the responsibility to make decisions should consensus fail at lower levels. Although, as in other international associations, consensus is the preferred mode of decision-making, the Charter does not rule out voting at the summit. The Charter mandates the secretary-general to report to the leaders the state of compliance or non-compliance with ASEAN agreements. A Committee of Permanent Representatives is the new governing body charged with making decisions on operational matters. Based in Jakarta for closer contact with the ASEAN Secretariat, the committee takes the place of the ASEAN directors-general, who are now to coordinate national implementation of ASEAN decisions, take a leading role in the national preparations for ASEAN meetings, serve as the national repositories of ASEAN information, and enhance public awareness of ASEAN. To strengthen the Secretariat's administration, there will be four deputy secretaries-general. The Charter directs that dispute settlement mechanisms be established in all areas of ASEAN cooperation. Not least, the Charter calls for the organization of an ASEAN human rights body.

The Charter explicitly provides that the five-year term of the secretary-general is non-renewable and codifies the ASEAN practice, previously implicit, of rotating the position among nationals of the member states in alphabetical order.

With respect to ASEAN's agreements on regional economic integration and cooperation, the Charter makes clear that the aim is to create in Southeast Asia as "a single market and production base". At the same ASEAN summit that approved the ASEAN Charter, the ASEAN leaders adopted the "blueprint" for the creation of the ASEAN Economic Community, which specified in detail the steps to be taken, including timelines. The leaders called for the development of a "scorecard" to keep track of the blueprint's implementation.

The Charter, of course, is only a tool for the greater institutionalization of ASEAN. ASEAN, after all, has no court of justice, no central commission, and no regional parliament. Everything depends on the seriousness with which the member states approach the integration of the regional economy, on the depth with which each member state identifies its national interest with the regional welfare.

It is also important to keep in mind that economic integration is but one part, albeit a supremely important part, of the broader sense and process of regionalism in Southeast Asia.

Rodolfo C. Severino is the Head of ASEAN Studies Centre at the Institute of Southeast Asian Studies (ISEAS), Singapore.

4
GOVERNANCE ISSUES IN NAFTA[1]

Paul J. Davidson

The first priority for a ... country seeking to achieve sustainable economic development in the twenty-first century is to practice good economic governance.[2]

1. Introduction

Governance structures are necessary to manage the increasing economic interdependence of economies across the North America region, and to reduce its negative effects. As a mid-size economy, the existence of a rules-based, rather than a power-based trading system is important to Canada's ability to effectively engage in the international economic system. Canada's trading relationship with the United States and Mexico is largely governed by the North American Free Trade Agreement (NAFTA), which governs the economic relations among these three countries. This paper explores some of the governance issues raised by NAFTA. It commences by looking at some of the governance issues which had an impact on the enactment and implementation of the agreement, namely the constitutional issue, and issues regarding the form and extent of the cooperation. It then discusses some of the governance issues raised by NAFTA — the delegation deficit, the question of legal personality, issues raised by the dispute settlement mechanisms within NAFTA, and "social" governance within the NAFTA framework. The paper concludes with a note on the over-riding role of government, and "softer" governance outside the agreement itself.

2. The Constitutional Issue

As a treaty, NAFTA has no legal force in Canadian law unless implemented by appropriate legislation — a treaty does not have direct application in Canada. Canada is a federal state: under the British North America Act, which established Canada, the jurisdiction to legislate is divided between the federal government and the provinces/territories. Domestically it is governed by the common law in nine provinces and three territories, and the civil law in Québec. Although it is clear that the federal government may enter into treaties regardless of the subject matter, it has been held that the federal parliament may only enact legislation to implement treaty obligations that fall squarely within an enumerated federal head of power, and that the subject matter of many international agreements aimed at regulating trade and investment may be outside the legislative competence of the federal parliament and within the legislative competence of the provincial legislatures.[3] This is increasingly a concern as international economic activity intrudes into the "domestic policy space" of provinces. As such, an initial governance issue is to ensure that a procedure is in place to have appropriate federal-provincial cooperation to implement the provisions agreed to by the NAFTA parties. A detailed discussion of this issue is beyond the scope of this paper, but competence to enter into and implement this type of agreement is a matter which should be considered by any parties considering such an agreement, or amendments to an existing agreement.

Constitutional issues are not unique to the Canadian situation. They are important for any system of governance, as they determine who can do what.

3. The Form of Cooperation

Members of the World Trade Organization (WTO) are constrained in entering into agreements affecting economic activity that is covered by one of the agreements administered by the WTO. Of particular note in regard to agreements for economic cooperation, are the provisions of Article XXIV of the General Agreement on Tariffs and Trade (GATT) and Article V of the General Agreement on Trade in Services (GATS). As Canada, the United States, and Mexico, were all signatories to GATT at the time they negotiated NAFTA, they were bound by the framework established by GATT to govern trade relations among the contracting parties to GATT (now administered by the WTO). The main aim of GATT is to do away with discrimination in international trade through the imposition of a general most favoured nation (MFN) obligation. GATT does allow preferential trade to take place in certain circumstances; Article XXIV provides an exception for customs unions, free trade areas, and interim agreements leading to them.

A Customs Union (CU) is defined in Article XXIV, para. 8(a):

(a) A customs union shall be understood to mean the substitution of a single customs territory for two or more customs territories, so that
  (i) duties and other restrictive regulations of commerce … are eliminated with respect to substantially all the trade between the constituent territories of the union or at least with respect to substantially all the trade in products originating in such territories; and
  (ii) … substantially the same duties and other regulations of commerce are applied by each of the members of the union to the trade of territories not included in the union.

A Free Trade Area (FTA) is defined in Article XXIV, para. 8(b):

(b)   A free-trade area shall be understood to mean a group of two or more customs territories in which the duties and other restrictive regulations of commerce ... are eliminated on substantially all the trade between the constituent territories in products originating in such territories.

One of the main differences between a CU and a FTA is that in a CU, the members of the CU must ensure that, "substantially the same duties and other regulations of commerce are applied by each of the members of the union to the trade of territories not included in the union", whereas in an FTA, the members of the FTA can maintain their own trade policy *vis-à-vis* trade of territories not included in the union. Thus in a CU, it is necessary to negotiate these common "duties and other regulations of commerce". One concern, in an asymmetrical relationship, where the members of the proposed union have different trade policies, is that the more powerful member(s) may dictate the terms. This was a concern in deciding the form of agreement to govern the economic cooperation between Canada and the United States, in the original Canada-U.S. FTA, which was the precursor of NAFTA. An FTA was chosen as this enabled Canada to retain control over its trade policy *vis-à-vis* third parties. Under this type of an agreement, Canada was free to apply its own tariff schedule and other trade regulations to its trade with third parties. For example, Canada was able to maintain its own MFN tariffs for WTO members, its British Preferential Tariff for Commonwealth trading partners and its General Preferential Tariff system for qualifying developing countries.

The NAFTA model may be the more politically viable option for establishing an agreement for economic cooperation in parts of the world where "sovereignty" concerns continue to be of concern to national political decision-makers.

4. GATT+

An initial question is the extent of the economic cooperation. Modern economic relations have become increasing complex. "… [T]rade policy is no longer [just] about trade measures at the border."[4] However, the current GATT/WTO framework is limited in its scope of regulation. Until the Uruguay Round, the framework was confined to regulating trade in goods (GATT), and it was only after initial reluctance, that the framework was expanded to the regulation of trade in services (GATS). A number of agreements go beyond the requirements of GATT/GATS in providing for economic cooperation. A distinction is commonly made between shallow and deep integration: "shallow" integration referring to the elimination of the traditional border measures, tariffs and non-tariff measures; "deep" integration referring to policies that are beyond the border. "[A]lmost all of the deep integration features of recent RTAs are outside the WTO rules."[5] These are sometimes referred to as "GATT +" ("WTO +") agreements. As these agreements are frequently regional in nature, the term Regional Trading Arrangement (RTA) is often used to apply to these relationships. NAFTA is a GATT+ RTA.

The NAFTA creates a classic free trade area consistent with Article XXIV, para. 8(b) of GATT. However, NAFTA goes beyond the requirement of eliminating tariffs and other restrictive trade regulations and deals with the governance of other areas, such as government procurement; services, investment and temporary entry for business persons; financial services; and dispute settlement procedures and special arrangements for dealing with anti-dumping and countervailing duties. Thus, this agreement is much broader in scope than other free trade agreements which have been negotiated under GATT. The basic principle underlying the agreement as a whole is "Canada and the United States will treat each other's goods, services, investment, suppliers and investors as they treat their own insofar as the matters covered by [the] Agreement are concerned."

5. "Delegation Deficit"[6]

One problem of governance with regard to NAFTA is that it is difficult to amend. Trade governance has evolved considerably since the agreement was ratified. However, NAFTA lacks any institutions to alter or expand on the framework for governance. Common forms of regulation in order to facilitate integration within the domestic economies of parties to an economic cooperation agreement, are most easily undertaken within a supranational structure, such as that of the European Community (EC). Without a common supranational legislative structure, it is difficult to achieve harmonized rules and standards, since each step toward hamonization must be negotiated and agreed upon, and must take the form of an amendment to the treaty or its annexes. "NAFTA's rigidity is largely a result of its design: the negotiators eschewed any mechanisms within the treaty to consider changes or opportunities for reconsidering certain clauses. ... the treaty excludes any form of political delegation to change the agreement, whether 'constitutional delegation' (that is, built-in mechanisms for review), or 'political and administrative delegation' for the day-to-day implementation, enforcement, and managing of the treaty (that is, political institutions to 'fill the gaps' of the treaty with secondary rules and regulations as necessary)."[7]

As a result of this "delegation deficit", Bioette and Selee have argued that, "there is a limit on the scope and depth of the NAFTA; more importantly, the NAFTA may not be sustainable in the long run, its relevance slowly 'eroding'."[8]

6. Legal Personality

NAFTA does not have a legal personality separate from the member states, with juridical personality and legal standing. That is, NAFTA as an entity separate from the member states does not have the capacity to enter into legal relations and to have rights and duties under the international legal system. One result of this is that "NAFTA" is unable to engage in discussion with trading partners regarding the governance of trading relations with them, for example, formation of RTAs with other regions.

NAFTA is not a member of the WTO, as compared with the European Community, which has international legal personality and is a member of the WTO. "This mixed situation of the EC in the WTO creates a complex internal governance situation for the EC, and a complex legal situation for WTO members outside the EC which seek to determine responsibility for EC and Member State compliance with WTO Agreements."[9]

This situation can be compared to ASEAN. One of the primary objectives of the ASEAN Charter is to provide ASEAN, as separate from the member states, with juridical personality and legal standing. The ASEAN Charter formally accords ASEAN legal personality as a full-fledged intergovernmental organization, moving it from its current state as a loosely-organized regional entity (and therefore making ASEAN a subject of international law in its own right). In Chapter II of the charter, ASEAN member states confer on ASEAN, as an intergovernmental organization, a legal personality, which is separate from theirs.[10]

7. Dispute Settlement within NAFTA[11]

The dispute settlement mechanisms provided in NAFTA form an important component of the governance of economic relations among the partners of NAFTA. NAFTA provides three dispute settlement mechanisms depending on the nature of the dispute. As dispute resolution is discussed elsewhere, the following discussion does not examine the mechanisms in detail, but only gives a brief review of the objectives of the different mechanisms before considering some of the governance issues which are raised by each.

8. Chapter 20 Disputes

Article 2003 of NAFTA provides:

> The Parties shall at all times endeavor to agree on the interpretation and application of this Agreement, and shall make every attempt through cooperation and consultations to arrive at a mutually satisfactory resolution of any matter that might affect its operation.

If the parties are unable to arrive at a mutually satisfactory resolution, then, the dispute settlement system of Chapter 20 provides for establishing panels to examine complaints by one party against another in fulfilling NAFTA's commitments.

Chapter 20 raises a number of issues. The panels do not make decisions which are binding on the parties. Rather, they play more of a conciliatory role. A panel produces a report which sets out the panel's findings of facts, its conclusions regarding whether the measure in dispute is inconsistent with NAFTA or causes nullification and impairment, as well as any recommendations[12] for resolving the dispute. This report is forwarded to the parties who "shall agree on the resolution of the dispute, which normally shall conform with the determinations and recommendations of the panel" (Article 2018).

Under NAFTA, a party is not obliged to bring its regime into compliance with the agreement, and the parties are free to agree on something else, including compensation. This can be compared to the WTO dispute settlement system, where a member of the WTO is bound to bring its domestic regime into conformity with the recommendations of the WTO panel or Appellate Body, and compensation is only for the limited and temporary purpose of promoting compliance. That is, under NAFTA the final decision is a political one, rather than a juridical one.[13]

Further, Chapter 20 provides that most disputes may be settled either under the coverage of the trilateral trade regime of NAFTA or under the dispute settlement mechanism (DSM) of GATT at the discretion of the complaining party. Prior to the creation of the World Trade Organization with its DSM, Chapter 20 of NAFTA was more efficient and attractive than the dispute settlement mechanism that prevailed under GATT. However, "[t]he gap in terms of rapidness and effectiveness between the two mechanisms has been narrowed considerably mainly due to the conversion of the positive consensus formula of the GATT system to a negative consensus mechanism now dominating the WTO Understanding."[14] This may result in resolution of the NAFTA disputes coming more within the governance system of the WTO.

> In the end, the three governments may feel that the submission of serious issues to continental dispute settlement is largely futile. If a case is going to end up in political bargaining, it runs the risk of inflaming, not depoliticizing Canadian-American conflicts. If continental dispute settlement

degenerates into a shoving contest where might prevails over right, the concerned governments may choose instead the global dispute settlement system embodied in the WTO. With numerous members, a substantial subsidy code, and a more authoritative process for resolving conflicts, the WTO is better able to offset the asymmetric power relationship with the United States that CUFTA and NAFTA failed to mitigate.[15]

9. Chapter 19 Disputes

Chapter 19 of the NAFTA deals with the review of, and dispute settlement in, anti-dumping and countervailing duty matters. NAFTA does not institute any common body of rules concerning dumping and subsidies to be observed by the three countries. Rather, Article 1902 provides that "Each Party reserves the right to apply its anti-dumping law and countervailing duty law to goods imported from the territory of any other Party" and "Each Party reserves the right to change or modify its antidumping law or countervailing duty law". Chapter 19 was a "second best" option for Canada, which had wanted an exclusion from the application of U.S. anti-dumping (AD) and countervailing duty (CVD) law. Chapter 19 was originally a temporary compromise in the Canada-U.S. FTA, which became permanent in NAFTA. This can be compared to the Australia-New Zealand Closer Economic Relations Trade Agreement (ANZCERTA). Under ANZCERTA anti-dumping actions can no longer be taken in respect of trade in goods to which ANZCERTA applies.

In order to deter the use of AD and CVD for protectionist purposes, Chapter 19 provides a mechanism for the review of final decisions of administrative agencies, or of statutory amendments of another party's anti-dumping or countervailing duty statute.

The first mechanism is governed by Article 1904 of the NAFTA. The review mechanism replaces domestic judicial review of administrative agencies' decisions by an international panel review. Under this mechanism, private parties affected by an anti-dumping or countervailing proceeding are entitled to request a panel, but they have to do it through the representation of their own governments — they have no jurisdiction to call for a panel by themselves. A further limitation on the process is that the panel is not entitled to judge or change the domestic legislation of the non-complying country, but only to review whether AD or CVD final determinations were enacted in compliance with the relevant domestic legislation and procedures. In other words, their goal is only to countercheck whether trade remedy laws were applied according to domestic legislation. The panel may only confirm final decisions of the domestic administrative agency or remand part or the totality of those decisions to the agency in order that the agency adopts a final decision consistent with the arbitral award.

Although Chapter 19 offers exporters a direct route for making their case and appealing the results of trade-remedy investigations before an independent and objective panel, and has worked reasonably well, it has not always been effective. The United States has not always shown itself willing to comply, and particularly not when the U.S. International Trade Commission's determinations have been remanded. The Canada-U.S. softwood lumber dispute has dragged on interminably, undermining the credibility and legitimacy of the mechanism. "[M]any in the United States have come to see the treaty dispute settlement mechanism as a 'political and administrative body', as opposed to a strictly judicial one and 'the importance of having a dispute settlement mechanism that was exclusively judicial, not political' has been argued."[16]

Secondly, Chapter 19 establishes a panel mechanism in case any modification to an existing law impairs a prior panel decision (that is, has the function and effect of overturning a prior decision of a panel made pursuant to Article 1904), or is not consistent with Article 1902.[17] If the panel's award determines that the legal reform is not consistent with the agreement, parties "shall immediately begin consultations and shall seek to achieve a mutually satisfactory solution to the matter within 90 days of the issuance of the panel's final declaratory opinion" (Article 1903(3)(a)). If this is not possible, the complaining party has two options: either to take comparable legislative or equivalent executive action; or to terminate the agreement with regard to the amending party on sixty-day written notice to that party.

10. Chapter 11 Disputes

As discussed above, NAFTA goes beyond the requirements of GATT in the governance of the international economic relations among its parties. One of the most contentious areas has been that of the regulation of investment. Chapter 11 of the NAFTA requires Canada, the United States, and Mexico to each meet certain standards in relation to foreign investment.

Most controversial in regard to the governance of investment, has been the dispute settlement provisions of Chapter 11. Chapter 11 provides for the resolution of disputes between any of the states party to the NAFTA (Canada, Mexico and the United States) and investors from another NAFTA party. The investment chapter sets forth the consent of the NAFTA parties that such disputes may be submitted to arbitration under the ICSID Convention, under the ICSID Additional Facility Rules or under the Arbitration Rules of the United Nations Commission on International Trade Law (UNCITRAL). Of particular note is that the procedure not only allows participation of private parties in the dispute settlement process, but that it allows private parties to initiate a dispute proceeding for the breach of state obligations under the agreement, without having to involve their own state's intervention in the dispute. In effect, private parties have rights under international law (NAFTA) which can be the subject of a dispute between a private party and state. In that sense, Chapter 11 contributes to a form of international economic governance in which private parties have a role as well as the nation state. However, although NAFTA does extend the scope of participation in the governance process, "[t]he only 'citizens' whose rights in Canada were extended by continental governance are corporations[18] based in the United States or Mexico, which received a powerful new defence against governments whose regulations might reduce their earnings."[19]

An initial issue is the appropriate arbitration process. Arbitration under the ICSID Convention is available for the resolution of investment disputes between member countries of ICSID and nationals of other member countries. Arbitration under the ICSID Additional Facility Rules is available for cases where one, but not both, of the countries concerned is an ICSID member. Two of the NAFTA parties, Canada and Mexico, are not yet ICSID members. Until Canada and Mexico have ratified the convention, ICSID Additional Facility Rules for arbitration and UNCITRAL Rules for arbitration are available for disputes between the U.S. investors and either Canada or Mexico or between the United States and investors from either of the two other countries. In respect of disputes between Canadian investors and Mexico, or between Mexican investors and Canada, only UNCITRAL Rules for arbitration are available (since, as indicated above, ICSID Additional Facility Rules for arbitration are not available when neither the home nor the host country of the investor is an ICSID member). In cases under the Additional Facility Rules or the UNCITRAL Rules, the award is subject to national laws on the recognition of foreign arbitral awards, and the arbitration proceeding is subject to the domestic law of the place where the arbitration takes place. For investors, the major advantage of the ICSID system is that it is self-contained. ICSID tribunals have the power to make interim measures and are exempt from the scrutiny or control of domestic courts in contracting states. As well, the ICSID Convention provides that "Each Contracting State shall recognize an award rendered pursuant to this Convention as binding and enforce the pecuniary obligations imposed by that award."[20]

Canada has signed but not yet ratified the ICSID Convention. Federal implementing legislation has been passed and received Royal Assent on 13 March 2008.[21] However, ratification awaits passage of implementing legislation by some provinces. The delay with ratification relates to the constitutional issue discussed above. Under Canada's Constitution, its provincial governments are responsible for the regulation of property and civil rights and the administration of justice in the province, so that provincial/territorial legislation is required as well as federal legislation to implement the convention.

Chapter 11 has attracted considerable criticism on several bases:

> The process has been criticized for its lack of legitimacy, accountability and transparency. It allows only a very limited form of review; there is no opportunity for appeal; and there is little legal precedent for these cases.

> It has also been argued that the selection process for the three-person jury is flawed: the panellists are not drawn from a permanent list of arbitrators, meaning that there is no

consistency; the choosing of jurors by each party can lead to bias; and it is difficult to avoid conflict of interest in jurors.[22]

As well, it has been argued that the process imposes severe constraints on national sovereignty. Particular concern has been expressed regarding Chapter 11's "regulatory chill" impact on the ability of NAFTA states to regulate, *inter alia*, in the interests of environmental protection. For example, critics worry that because of the broad interpretation that has been given to the expression "tantamount to expropriation", companies can use the investor protection provisions not as protection but as an aggressive mechanism, either to prevent governments from introducing legislation, or to seek compensation for losses.

> Many of the Chapter 11 actions have been based on complaints that pollution regulations harm business, raising concerns that companies are trying to use the trade treaty to stop governments from taking actions to protect public health or the environment.[23]

There are also examples of proposed regulations having been dropped after threats of Chapter 11 suits.

> In December 2001, the Government of Canada proposed a regulation to "prohibit the display of 'light' and 'mild' descriptors on tobacco packaging." Phillip Morris International Inc. (representing several tobacco companies) submitted a document to the Government of Canada protesting the ban and citing Chapter 11. If Canada had been required to compensate Phillip Morris under Chapter 11, the legislation might have been too expensive to apply. The proposed regulation was never fully developed. Plain packaging

regulations for tobacco products were also sidelined, which
some have attributed in part to the threat of a Chapter 11
suit.[24]

NAFTA-style investor-rights provisions were incorporated in
Chapter 15 of the Singapore–U.S. Free Trade Agreement of May
2003, however, the Australia–U.S. Free Trade Agreement (AUSFTA)
of 2004 contains no such investor-state dispute mechanisms.
Capling and Nossal have argued that the reason lies in the
"blowback", the unintended and negative consequences created
by NAFTA's Chapter 11, and conclude that the abandonment of
NAFTA-style protections in the AUSFTA sets important precedents
for the future of international free trade agreements.[25]

11. "Social" Governance within the NAFTA Framework

The North American Agreements on Labour and Environmental
Cooperation were negotiated and implemented in parallel to the
NAFTA. These "side agreements" established commissions, which
were set up to mitigate the adverse effects that economic
liberalization was expected to have on environmental and labour
conditions. "It was clear that these agreements were designed to
deter an anti-NAFTA movement stressing the relocation of highly
polluting or low-technology industries from the United States to
Mexico."[26] In the fall of 1992, the prospects for the United States
Congress' approval of the proposed North American Free Trade
Agreement (NAFTA) were uncertain because of opposition from
environmental groups and labour unions. In order to garner support
for the agreement, President Clinton declared that he would not
support NAFTA unless and until there were meaningful side
agreements on the environment and labour, and proposed a
"NAFTA-Plus" agenda. The NAFTA-Plus agenda initiated by Clinton

led to the negotiation of two new agreements — the North American Agreement on Labour Cooperation (NAALC) and the North American Agreement of Environmental Cooperation (NAAEC). They "are examples, however modest, of a form of governance that emerges from what we refer to as continentalism from below. We regard this as a form of continental governance, given the fact that some of their staffing is supra-national, and their recommendations are considered by the NAFTA states."[27]

12. North American Agreement on Labour Cooperation

The North American Agreement on Labour Cooperation (NAALC) was designed to facilitate greater cooperation between Canada, the United States and Mexico in the area of labour, as well as to promote the effective enforcement of each country's labour laws and regulations. The Commission for Labour Cooperation was created in 1994 by the NAALC to promote cooperation on labour matters between NAFTA members and the effective enforcement of domestic labour law.

In Canada, the provinces participate in this governance through the Canadian Intergovernmental Agreement regarding the NAALC. This agreement gives the provinces a means to participate in developing and managing Canada's involvement in the NAALC. However, not all provinces are signatories to this agreement.

The commission has not had a great impact on the governance of labour cooperation. However, it has had an inadvertent effect on the participation of labour unions from the three countries in the governance process.

For its part, NAFTA's Commission for Labour Cooperation (NACLC) has proven so disappointing in enforcing labour

rights that its main achievements appear negative: the
frustration that labour unions from the three countries have
experienced in trying to use NACLC's processes to defend
their rights has generated some genuine trinational solidarity
among them when they have organized industrial action against
certain TNCs with operations in the three countries.[28]

13. North American Agreement on Environmental Cooperation (NAAEC)

The NAAEC requires that each party ensures its laws provide for
high levels of environmental protection without lowering standards
to attract investment. The Commission for Environmental
Cooperation (CEC) was created in 1994 by the NAAEC to enhance
regional environmental cooperation, reduce potential trade and
environmental conflicts and promote the effective enforcement
of environmental law. It also facilitates cooperation and public
participation in efforts to foster conservation, protection and
enhancement of the North American environment. The CEC thus
provides a mechanism for public participation in this area of
governance. However, although the commission "has generated
some innovative collaboration between scientific, business, and
citizens' groups and issued some news-making reports, ... its
achievements seem mainly to lie in stimulating civil-society
environmentalism in Mexico".[29]

Clarkson and Torres-Ruiz conclude that although the CEC
and NACLC have fostered minor trilateral interconnections
among environmentalists and labour unions, which have
generated governance when they are expressed in concerted
action to launch a complaint against a NAFTA Government for
not enforcing an environmental or labour law, "the phenomenon
can only be allotted minor importance, given the two institutions'
tightly circumscribed authority".[30]

14. Government Trumps Governance

Although governance is a broader notion than government, and a "government" is not essential to governance, governments can play an important role in governance.

> The paradigm shift in Washington provoked by the terrorist disaster of 2001 instantly redrew the boundary between governance and government in North America.[31]

The growth in cross-border trade created by NAFTA had generated increased attention to border governance issues by the private sector, as business coalitions lobbied their governments to invest in the transportation infrastructure and security technology needed to create a near-borderless trading environment among NAFTA partners. However, with the terrorist disaster of 2001, the United States shifted to immediately restrict crossings at its two land borders.

> This unilateral action demonstrated that once Washington declared its national security at stake, the U.S. government would simply reassert its control over the policy space it had previously vacated. The subsequent demands that Canada and Mexico do what Washington felt was necessary to make their exports safe for the United States showed how much governance in North America was driven by the government of the United States.[32]

15. Conclusion

This paper has discussed some of the issues involved in the governance of the international economic relations among Canada, the United States, and Mexico. In particular, it has looked at some of the issues raised by NAFTA, which is central to the "hard law" aspect of the rules-based regime of governance. However, much of the "governance" of trans-border trade and investment within the North American market takes place at a "less formalized" level, for example, within corporate networks or through business associations — a "soft law" form of governance[33] **(Annex III)**. "Decisions about what products to make and how to sell them are no longer made in Canada for the Canadian market, but in Cleveland for the North American market. ... the same shifts in organization and governance can be seen in the consumer goods industry, in automobiles and automobile parts, in telecommunications and many other sectors."[34]

Notes

1. I would like to thank Professor Anthony VanDuzer for his valuable comments on an earlier draft of this paper.
2. Kym Anderson, "Globalization, WTO, and ASEAN", *ASEAN Economic Bulletin* 18, no. 12 (2001): 19.
3. For further discussion of this issue see, *inter alia*, Paul J. Davidson, "Uniformity in International Trade Law: The Constitutional Obstacle", *Dal. L.J.* 11 (1988): 677–97.
4. M.R. Mendoza, P. Low, B. Kotschwar, eds., "An Overview", in *Trade Rules in the Making: Challenges in Regional and Multilateral Negotiations* (Washington, D.C.: Organization of American States, Brookings Institution Press, 1999), p. 1.
5. P.J. Lloyd, "Implications for the Multilateral Trading System of the New Preferential Trading Arrangements in the Asia-Pacific Region", PECC Seminar on Developing Patterns of Regional Trading Arrangements in the Asia-Pacific Region: Issues and Implications, Vancouver, BC, Canada, 11–12 November 2002 <http://www.pecc.org/publications/papers/trade-papers/1_SII/9-lloyd.pdf>.
6. David N. Biette and Andrew Selee, "NAFTA in the Context of Modern Trade Governance: A Sustainable Institution?" <http://

www.wilsoncenter.org/index.cfm?fuseaction=events.event_summary&event_id=168254> (accessed 4 November 2008).

7. Ibid.

8. Ibid.

9. Frederick M. Abbott, "The North American Integration Regime and its Implications for the World Trading System", in *The EU, the WTO, and the NAFTA: Towards a Common Law of International Trade?*, edited by J.H.H. Weiler (New York: Oxford University Press, 2000), pp. 176–77.

10. Charter of the Association of Southeast Asian Nations, Article 3, reproduced in Paul J. Davidson, *Trading Arrangements in the Pacific Rim* (New York: Oxford University Press, 1995), Document I.B.5.t.2.

    Details as to the extent of this legal personality have yet to be established. "Details of what ASEAN can or cannot do with its legal personality will be discussed and stated in a supplementary protocol after the signing of the Charter." — ASEAN Secretariat, Media Release, "ASEAN Leaders Sign ASEAN Charter", Singapore, 20 November 2007 <http://www.aseansec.org/21086.htm> (accessed 25 March 2008).

11. The following discussion of dispute settlement in NAFTA is not intended to give a comprehensive treatment of this topic. Dispute settlement in NAFTA is dealt with in more detail in paper 6 by Professor Anthony VanDuzer in this report. The following discussion examines some of the governance issues raised by the NAFTA dispute settlement mechanisms.

12. It is not necessary for panels to make recommendations, though they may.

13. This can be compared to the dispute settlement provisions in the ASEAN Charter.

14. Isidro Morales, "NAFTA: The Governance of Economic Openness", *Annals of the American Academy of Political and Social Science*

565: *Civil Society and Democratization* (September 1999): 44 <http://www.jstor.org/stable/1049536> (accessed 9 March 2008).

15. Stephen Clarkson, "Canada's Secret Constitution: NAFTA, WTO and the End of Sovereignty?", Canadian Centre for Policy Alternatives, October 2002 <http://www.policyalternatives.ca/documents/National_Office_Pubs/clarkson_constitution.pdf> (accessed 4 November 2008).

16. Biette and Selee, *supra*, note 6, p. 1. See also, "Dispute Settlement in the NAFTA: Fixing an Agreement Under Siege", Report of the Standing Committee on Foreign Affairs and International Trade, May 2005 <http://www2.parl.gc.ca/HousePublicationsPublication.aspx?DocId=1856888&Language=E&Mode=1&Parl=38&Ses=1> (accessed 11 January 2009).

17. Article 1902 provides that "Each Party reserves the right to change or modify its antidumping law or countervailing duty law ..." However, the article goes on to provide that such an amendment must satisfy certain criteria.

18. In principle, there is no reason why individuals cannot be complainants, and they have been in some cases. However, the primary "beneficiaries" of the Chapter 11 procedures have been corporations.

19. Clarkson, "Canada's Secret Constitution", *supra*, note 15, p. 10.

20. ICSID Convention, Article 54(1).

21. <http://www.parl.gc.ca/LEGISINFO/index.asp?Language=E&Chamber=N&StartList=A&EndList=Z&Session=15&Type=0&Scope=I&query=5295&List=stat>.

22. Bronwyn Pavey and Tim Williams, "The North American Free Trade Agreement: Chapter 11", 26 February 2003 <http://dsp-psd.tpsgc.gc.ca/Collection-R/LoPBdP/inbrief/prb0254-e.htm#Regulatory> (accessed 7 November 2008) (footnotes omitted). There has been movement toward open hearings. In October 2003 Canada and the United States publicly stated their intent to consent to open hearings in every case. Mexico joined this

consensus in July 2004. As a result, virtually all Chapter 11 hearings are now open to the public.

23. Martin Mittelstaedt and Luke Eric Peterson, "Ban on Pesticides May Face NAFTA Test", *Globe and Mail*, 22 October 2008, p. A6.

24. Pavey and Williams, *supra*, note 22.

25. Ann Capling and Kim Richard Nossal, "Blowback: Investor–State Dispute Mechanisms in International Trade Agreements", *Governance: An International Journal of Policy, Administration, and Institutions* 19 (2006): 151–72.

26. Morales, *supra*, note 14, p. 46.

27. Stephen Clarkson and Antonio Torres-Ruiz, "An Elusive Problem: Distinguishing Government from Governance to Analyze North America", paper presented at the Annual Meeting, Canadian Political Science Association, University of Western Ontario, London, Ontario, 2 June 2005 <http://www.chass.utoronto.ca/~clarkson/publications/An%20Elusive%20Problem%20-%20Distinguishing%20Government%20from%20Governance%20to%20Analyze%20North%20America%20-%20v05.pdf> (accessed 5 November 2008), p. 13.

28. Ibid.

29. Ibid. For a more in-depth treatment of the NACEC, see Roberto A. Sanchez, "Governance, Trade, and the Environment in the Context of NAFTA", *American Behavioral Scientist* 45 (2002): 1369 <http://abs.sagepub.com/cgi/content/abstract/45/9/1369> (accessed 7 November 2008).

30. Ibid.

31. Ibid., p. 16. See also, Morales, *supra*, note 14, p. 47.

32. Ibid.

33. See Annex III for discussion of "hard law" and "soft law".

34. David Zussman, President, Public Policy Forum, "The Impact of North American Integration on Canadian Governance", notes for an address at the Canadian Comprehensive Auditing Foundation

Conference, "Building Excellence: Governance, Management and Accountability in the Public Sector", 20 March 2001 — Session on "Tomorrow's Issues Today" <http://www.ppforum.ca/common/assets/speeches/en/ow_s_03_20_2001.pdf> (accessed 7 November 2008).

Paul J. Davidson is a Professor in Department of Law and Chair of the Committee on Asian Studies at the Carleton University, Ottawa, Canada.

5
DIFFERENT APPROACHES TO DISPUTE RESOLUTION UNDER ASEAN

Locknie Hsu

1. Introduction

On 21 October 2008, Indonesia ratified the ASEAN Charter, becoming the tenth and final member of ASEAN to do so.[1] Under Article 47 of the Charter, all members must sign and ratify it.[2] Upon the coming into force of the Charter, a new formal legal framework comes into being for the organization. Within this framework are elements of a dispute settlement mini-charter as well. This mini-framework can be found primarily in Chapter VIII of the Charter. While some of its elements are not new, in that they reaffirm the use of existing dispute settlement mechanisms within ASEAN agreements, it does provide an "umbrella" framework that sets out general directions and principles for disputes arising out of ASEAN.

Apart from provisions in this new Charter, ASEAN's dispute settlement provisions are found in a number of sources. The major ones are the:

– Protocol on Enhanced Dispute Settlement Mechanism;
– Framework Agreement on Enhancing ASEAN Economic Cooperation;
– ASEAN Framework Agreement on Services;
– Framework Agreement on ASEAN Investment Area;

–   ASEAN Agreement for the Promotion and Protection of Investments; and
–   Treaty of Amity and Cooperation in Southeast Asia.

Therefore, unlike the North America Free Trade Agreement (NAFTA), whose dispute settlement provisions are primarily in a single document and apply to trade- and investment-related matters, ASEAN provisions are scattered over a number of documents, and cover both trade/investment disputes and other (for example, political, or territorial) disputes.

For the purpose of this article and in the context of this forum, focus will be placed on the dispute settlement mechanisms for economic agreement disputes.

2. ASEAN Legal Framework for Dispute Resolution

As has been pointed out by Singapore's Attorney-General, Professor Walter Woon, the ASEAN Charter adopts a "common sense approach" to dispute settlement.[3] The main guiding principles are found in Article 22:

> 1. Member States shall endeavour to resolve peacefully all disputes in a timely manner through dialogue, consultation and negotiation.

> 2. ASEAN shall maintain and establish dispute settlement mechanisms in all fields of ASEAN cooperation.

The Charter provides generally for the use of good offices, mediation and conciliation in any dispute.[4] It envisages new mechanisms in Article 25, which states:

> Where not otherwise specifically provided, appropriate dispute settlement mechanisms, including arbitration, shall be established for disputes which concern the interpretation or application of this Charter and other ASEAN instruments.

Article 28 also permits members to have recourse to modes of peaceful dispute settlement under Article 33(1) of the UN Charter, unless otherwise provided for by the Charter.

Beyond this, Article 24 provides a trifurcated plan for disputes:

– where disputes relate to specific instruments its dispute settlement mechanisms should apply;
– where disputes do not concern interpretation of any particular ASEAN instrument, the mechanisms in the Treaty of Amity and Cooperation among Southeast Asia should apply; and finally
– "where not otherwise specifically provided, disputes which concern the interpretation or application of ASEAN economic agreements shall be settled in accordance with the ASEAN Protocol on Enhanced Dispute Settlement Mechanism."

For a "serious breach" of the Charter itself, or "non-compliance", the matter is to be referred to the ASEAN Summit (Article 20.4).[5]
Article 26 provides:

> When a dispute remains unresolved, after the application of the preceding provisions of this Chapter, this dispute shall be referred to the ASEAN Summit, for its decision.

This appears to be somewhat cryptic, as it does not make clear what are considered "unresolved disputes" according to the mechanisms established in previous provisions.

Article 27 of the Charter deals with compliance and assigns primary responsibility for monitoring compliance to the secretary-general of ASEAN.

Non-economic Disputes

The Treaty of Amity and Cooperation in Southeast Asia[6] has, as one of its basic principles, "settlement of differences or disputes by peaceful means" (Article 2(d)) and may apply to non-economic disputes between signatory states.[7]

ASEAN members have had their share of non-economic disputes, ranging from refugee movement, to title and border issues.[8] The most recent conflict relates to the Thai-Cambodian dispute over land at the Preah Vihear grounds.[9]

3. Disputes Relating to ASEAN Economic Agreements

(i) General – Protocol for Enhanced Dispute Settlement Mechanism 2004

The Framework Agreement on Enhancing ASEAN Economic Cooperation 1992 establishes the basis for the ASEAN Free Trade Area (AFTA). Article 9 of this agreement contains a very general provision on dispute settlement:

> Any differences between the Member States concerning the interpretation or application of this Agreement or any arrangements arising therefrom shall, as far as possible, be settled amicably between the parties. Whenever necessary, an appropriate body shall be designated for the settlement of disputes.

The companion agreement, Agreement on the Common Effective Preferential Tariff Scheme for the ASEAN Free Trade Area, signed in 1992, also contains a rather basic dispute settlement provision, in Article 8.[10]

In 1996, ASEAN leaders decided to establish a more elaborate dispute settlement process specifically for economic disputes, through the Protocol on Dispute Settlement Mechanism.[11] Many of the protocol's provisions mirrored those of the WTO's Dispute Settlement Understanding (DSU), which establishes the WTO's dispute settlement system in detail. The 1996 Protocol reserved some important decision-making powers in dispute settlement to the Senior Economic Officials Meeting, a political organ rather than an adjudicatory organ that would base its decisions on legal principles and rules. In 2004, ASEAN leaders decided to refine the process, expanding the rules-based element, bringing the mechanism into closer alignment with the DSU system. The result of the 2004 decision, the Protocol on Enhanced Dispute Mechanism 2004,[12] is now the primary instrument for ASEAN's dispute settlement process applicable to economic disputes. It applies specifically to all ASEAN "economic agreements".[13] This phrase is not defined in the protocol but it states that it includes disputes brought pursuant to:

–   the Framework Agreement on Enhancing ASEAN Economic Cooperation (1992);
–   agreements listed in Appendix I of the 2004 Protocol; and
–   future ASEAN economic agreements.[14]

The Protocol of 2004 seeks to ensure that binding decisions can be made based solely on legal considerations and all expeditiously enforced.[15]

The 2004 Protocol process has been supported by a number of accompanying infrastructural changes. These include the establishment of:

(i)   a legal unit being established at the ASEAN Secretariat, to
       provide legal advice on trade disputes (that is, an advisory
       mechanism);
(ii)   a mechanism known as the ASEAN Consultation to Solve
       Trade and Investment Issues (ACT), which is a non-binding
       Internet-based problem-solving network to resolve
       complaints within thirty days is ready to provide speedy
       resolution to operational problems in ASEAN economic
       agreements (that is, a consultative mechanism); and
(iii) an ASEAN Compliance Body (ACB) wherein ASEAN
       member countries can make use of mediation and peer
       pressure in dispute resolution. The ACB could ensure that
       cases lodged before the ACB should be resolved within
       ninety days. (This was inspired by the Textiles Monitoring
       Body in the WTO.[16])[17]

The purpose of these was to achieve "improvement of the existing
ASEAN Dispute Settlement Mechanism to ensure expeditious and
legally binding resolution of any economic disputes".[18]

        Although the protocol mechanism (and its predecessor) has
existed for some years, it has yet to be used by ASEAN members.
In fact, it is noteworthy that some members have chosen to deal
with a dispute relating to an ASEAN economic agreement without
resorting to the mechanism.[19]

        In addition, ASEAN has a companion, relatively little-known
notification procedure for

        any action or measure that [member states] intend to take:
        a.   which may nullify or impair any benefit to other Member
              States, directly or indirectly under any ASEAN economic
              agreement; or

b.   when the action or measure may impede the attainment of any objective of an ASEAN economic agreement.[20]

Under Article 4 of the Notification Procedure, a member state is required to provide

sufficient information regarding the proposed action or measure to be taken, which shall include:

a.   a description of the action or measure to be taken;
b.   the reasons for undertaking the action or measure; and
c.   the intended date of implementation and the duration of the action or measure.

As this is a notification procedure, it is not intended to resolve a dispute arising from the action or measure.

A member state is required under Article 2 to make a notification *before* taking such an action or measure. Furthermore, subject to any other notification period provided for in an ASEAN economic agreement, notification is to be made "at least 60 days before such an action or measure is to take effect". Notification is also to be made to the SEOM and the ASEAN Secretariat under Article 3.

Under Article 6, a member state is required, "without discrimination" to "allow adequate opportunities for other Member States to present their comments in writing and discuss these comments upon request". The provision states that discussions entered into with other member states are to be for the purpose of "seeking further clarification about the action or measure". Comments are to be presented within fifteen days of the notification. Under Article 5, it is noteworthy that the contents of the notification and all information relating to it are to be treated with confidentiality.

a. The 2004 Protocol Process in General

The dispute settlement system established by the 2004 Protocol mirrors many aspects of the WTO's DSU system. Three important aspects resemble the DSU system: the panel and Appellate Body structure and many of the procedural rules governing their operations, the implementation phase (which includes the use of countermeasures, where permitted) and the existence of a supervening authority like the WTO's Dispute Settlement Body, in the form of the SEOM. There are also some salient differences — including time-frames and other matters — some of which are highlighted below.

b. Choice of Forum and Applicability of Customary International Law

The protocol permits member states to resort to other fora "for settlement of disputes involving other member states", and a member state may do so at any stage before a party has made a request to the SEOM to establish a panel under the protocol.

By contrast to the WTO's DSU, the Protocol does not explicitly state that the principles of customary rules of interpretation of public international law apply to interpretation of its provisions.[21] However, this silence does not mean that such rules — which the WTO dispute settlement machinery has repeatedly confirmed as including principles in the Vienna Convention on the Law of Treaties — would not apply to the Protocol if it is viewed as a treaty.

c. Consultations

Unsurprisingly, the 2004 Protocol provides for consultations — like the DSU — on any representations that member states may make "with respect to any matter affecting the implementation, interpretation or application" of the covered economic agreements.[22]

A response to a request for consultations must be made within ten days after receipt of the request. Consultations are to take place within thirty days of such receipt.

Article 4 also provides for use of the good offices of the ASEAN secretary-general, and of conciliation and mediation of disputes.

d. Panels

A member state may request the SEOM to establish a panel, where:

– the member state in question does not respond to the request for consultations;
– does not enter into consultations in the requisite time period; or
– consultations fail to settle a dispute within sixty days after receipt of the request for consultations.[23]

The SEOM is to operate under the "reverse consensus" rule — as in the DSU — and shall establish a panel unless it decides not to by consensus.

The request for establishment of a panel is, as is the case under the DSU, to be in writing:

– indicating whether consultations were held;
– identifying the specific measures at issue; and
– providing a brief summary of the legal basis of the complaint, "sufficient to present the problem clearly".

Terms of reference are to be drawn up and these are to be circulated to all member states.[24]

As is with the case under the DSU, the function of a panel is to "make an objective assessment of the dispute before it (including an examination of the facts of the case and the applicability of and conformity with the sections of the Agreement or any covered agreements), and its findings and recommendations in relation to the case."

Panel procedures are set out in Appendix II of the protocol. Unlike the period under the DSU, a panel under the protocol has sixty days to submit its findings and recommendations to the SEOM.[25] This is a very short period, considering that matters may vary in complexity, amount of evidence to be presented and examined, and that ASEAN countries function with a variety of languages (thereby likely giving rise to the need for translations of documents and laws in some cases, and hence, delays).

Panel reports are to be adopted by the SEOM on, again, the reverse consensus rule.[26]

e. Other Features

The protocol provides for cases where there are multiple complainants (Article 10), as well as for the participation of third parties (Article 11). As is the case with the DSU, third parties are parties with a "substantial interest" in the matter before the panel, and are given an opportunity to be heard by the panel and to make written submissions to it. They may also receive written submissions of the disputing parties, up to the first substantive panel meeting. Third parties' rights are therefore limited in that they will not be able to receive disputing parties' written submissions beyond that, or to attend any panel meeting beyond the first one. This mirrors the DSU (Article 10). However, WTO practice has shown that "enhanced" or additional third party rights may be given or declined on a case-by-case basis. The 2004 Protocol does not address this possibility, and it remains to be seen if a panel under the protocol will similarly provide such enhanced third party rights in any case.

Like panels under the DSU, protocol panels have the right to seek "information and technical advice from any individual or body which it deems appropriate" under Article 8.4.[27]

As is the case with DSU panels,[28] panel deliberations are confidential under the protocol (Article 8.5).

f. Appeals

The protocol provides for an appellate process, resembling that in the DSU. The period for completion of appeal proceedings is generally sixty days (Article 11.5).[29] As with DSU appeals, appeals under the protocol are to be limited to issues of law covered in the panel report and legal interpretations developed by the panel (Article 11.6).[30] Proceedings are to be confidential (Article 11.9).

Under Article 18 of the protocol, the total period for disposal of disputes under it until the stage in Article 16.7 (which relates mainly to objections to levels of suspension in a case of countermeasures) is 445 days.

g. Panel and AB Recommendations

As with panels and the Appellate Body under the DSU, where a measure is found to be inconsistent with an agreement, the panel/Appellate Body under the protocol is to "recommend" that the member state bring the measure into conformity.[31]

Article 14 of the protocol mirrors Article 19 of the DSU, except that Article 14 also requires the panel and Appellate Body to deal with the issue of expenses to be borne by the disputing parties, including third parties, to replenish the ASEAN DSM Fund established in Article 17 of the protocol. The initial sum for this fund is to be contributed to equally by ASEAN member states, is a revolving fund, separate from the Secretariat's regular budget, and to be administered by the Secretariat. Article 17 states: "Any drawdown from the fund shall be replenished by the parties to the dispute" in line with Article 14.3 of the protocol. The fund is to be used to meet expenses of the panels, the Appellate Body and "any related administration costs of the ASEAN Secretariat". It is not meant for legal expenses including those for legal representation incurred by a disputing party.

h. Implementation

The 2004 Protocol contains a surveillance process for implementation of panel/Appellate Body findings and recommendations (Article 15), and for implementation by a member state within a given period. The latter differs somewhat from the DSU system in that under the protocol, parties to the dispute who are required to comply shall comply within sixty days from the SEOM's adoption of the panel findings and recommendations, or in the event of an appeal, sixty days from the SEOM's adoption of the findings and recommendations of the Appellate Body report, unless the parties to the dispute agree on a longer time period.[32]

Countermeasures are permitted under the protocol (Article 16). Compensation is also possible but similar to the DSU philosophy, it is to be a temporary and voluntary measure.[33] The protocol also contains a set of principles and procedures for the imposition of countermeasures (Article 16.3).[34]

One of the issues that have arisen in the implementation phase under the DSU is that of "sequencing". This arose because of a discrepancy in the period that elapses before a party may seek to impose countermeasures, and the period for determining whether there has been effective compliance by the party whose measure has been challenged successfully.[35] This discrepancy can also be found in Articles 16.2 and 16.7 of the protocol, which does not deal with resolution of this issue. In practice, WTO members have held back on the request for authorization of countermeasures pending arbitration on compliance. It remains to be seen if ASEAN member states will do likewise, if the same situation arose.

Apart from the legalistic dispute resolution system in the 2004 Protocol, an ASEAN Economic Community (AEC) "scorecard" system has also been set up to aid ASEAN members in monitoring compliance with their obligations.[36] The first scorecard was to be presented during the December 2008 ASEAN Summit.[37] This compliance-monitoring mechanism is closely linked to dispute settlement as it is intended to shed light on members' implementation of obligations.

i. Role of Secretariat

Article 19 of the protocol sets out the responsibilities of the Secretariat in dispute settlement proceedings. Apart from assisting panels and the Appellate Body, it is also to assist the SEOM in monitoring and maintaining surveillance of implementation.

(ii) ASEAN Investment Disputes

The primary sources of dispute settlement provisions for ASEAN investment disputes are the Framework Agreement on ASEAN Investment Area and the ASEAN Agreement for the Promotion and Protection of Investments of 1987 (sometimes called the ASEAN Investment Guarantee Agreement, for short).[38]

To date, it appears that only one dispute has proceeded on to arbitration pursuant to these two instruments, namely, in the case of *Yaung Chi Oo v Union of Myanmar*.[39]

In November 2007, in a continuing push towards greater economic integration, ASEAN leaders adopted the ASEAN Economic Community Blueprint.[40] This plan aims not only to set out firmer deadlines and targets to move towards a single ASEAN market, but includes objectives of providing "enhanced protection to all investors and their investments to be covered" under a comprehensive agreement that will be arrived at, upon review of the above two existing investment agreements.

The targeted actions toward this end are

> to strengthen among others the following provisions:
> - investor-state dispute settlement mechanism;
> - transfer and repatriation of capital, profits, dividends, etc.;
> - transparent coverage on the expropriation and compensation;
> - full protection and security; and
> - treatment of compensation for losses resulting from strife.

As part of the ongoing reform of the investment protection and promotion regime in ASEAN, ASEAN leaders decided in August 2007 to "revise, combine and enhance" the two agreements.[41] This will culminate in a new ASEAN Comprehensive Investment Agreement (ACIA), expected to be completed during the December 2008 ASEAN Summit. While details of this agreement are not available at time of writing, some "guiding principles" have been announced.[42] Among the new features expected under the ACIA are: inclusion of portfolio investments (with the possibility of reservations), clear and transparent procedures for obtaining approvals in writing for investments (to be covered),[43] more comprehensive and detailed investor-state dispute settlement provisions, and a new article on consultation among ACIA member states on ACIA matters and its implementation. The ACIA will also include a compensatory adjustment for modification of commitments. It is also expected to contain both state-to-state and investor-state dispute settlement mechanisms.

In the area of e-commerce, the blueprint also seeks to harmonize the legal infrastructure for electronic contracting and dispute resolution, and to develop and implement better practice guidelines for electronic contracting, guiding principles for online dispute resolution services, and mutual recognition framework for digital signatures in ASEAN.[44]

4. Conclusion

The ASEAN system of dispute settlement is found in a number of instruments and covers both economic and non-economic disputes. The system has been evolving since the formation of ASEAN, with priority first being given to the peaceful settlement of mainly political disputes, as can be seen from early instruments such as the Treaty of Amity and Cooperation in Southeast Asia. As the economic integration of ASEAN began to take shape and gather momentum, particularly with the establishment of an ASEAN Free Trade Area in 1992, a separate dispute settlement system covering economic disputes was deemed to be necessary, and led first to a protocol in 1996, which was replaced subsequently by the Protocol on Enhanced Dispute Settlement Mechanism of 2004. This is presently the key dispute settlement mechanism that covers all disputes arising from ASEAN economic agreements. At the same time, the development of the ASEAN investment regime has led to two main documents containing dispute settlement provisions, which are currently under review, with a view to the new ACIA being adopted by end 2008. At the same time, the new Charter provides an "umbrella" framework for dispute settlement structures within ASEAN.

ASEAN member states have so far remained distant from the above systems, preferring to resolve their disputes in other ways.

While ASEAN leaders have pushed in recent years towards a more rules-based system for resolving economic disputes[45] — possibly following the relative success of the WTO rules-based dispute settlement system that has been functioning for more than ten years now — member states have yet to make use of the mechanisms that have been set up. It remains to be seen what circumstances might eventually lead member states to begin to avail themselves of these mechanisms, and whether initial cases build confidence in the system as to encourage further use.

Notes

1. See press release of the ASEAN Secretariat, 21 October 2008 <http://www.aseansec.org/22022.htm>.
2. The Charter comes into force on the thirtieth day following the date of deposit of the tenth instrument of ratification with the ASEAN secretary-general.
3. Woon, "The ASEAN Charter Dispute Settlement Mechanisms", paper presented at the Third Annual Meeting of the Attorney-General's Chambers, 23–27 April 2008 <http://www.agc.gov.my/agc/agc/rev/agcjc/3rd/pdf/Singapore-The_ASEAN_Charter_Dispute_Settlement_Mechanisms.pdf>; see also the related papers from the offices of the Attorney-General's Chambers of Malaysia and Brunei at <http://www.agc.gov.my/agc/agc/rev/agcjc/3rd/3rdevents.html>. See also generally, UNCTAD, Dispute Settlement, Regional Approaches, ASEAN, 2003 <http://www.unctad.org/en/docs/edmmisc232add29_en.pdf>.
4. Article 23.
5. The Charter does not elaborate on what amounts to a "serious breach". See also Article 51 of the Charter.
6. Text available at <http://www.aseansec.org/1217.htm>.
7. Interestingly, a dispute between Indonesia and Malaysia which could have come before the High Council established under Article

14 of the treaty, was instead settled by the International Court of Justice. See generally, R. Severino, *Southeast Asia in Search of an ASEAN Community* (Singapore: Institute of Southeast Asia Studies, 2006), p. 168.

8. For a summary of disputes, see Amitav Acharya, *Constructing A Security Community in Southeast Asia* (Routledge, 2001), pp. 129–31.

9. See account in *Time*, 15 October 2008 <http://www.time.com/time/world/article/0,8599,1850442,00.html>.

10. Article 8 provides:

> 1. Member States shall accord adequate opportunity for consultations regarding any representations made by other Member States with respect to any matter affecting the implementation of this Agreement. The Council referred to in Article 7 of this Agreement, may seek guidance from the AEM in respect of any matter for which it has not been possible to find a satisfactory solution during previous consultations.
>
> 2. Member States, which consider that any other Member State has not carried out its obligations under this Agreement, resulting in the nullifications or impairment of any benefit accruing to them, may, with a view to achieving satisfactory adjustment of the matter, make representations or proposal to the other Member States concerned, which shall give due consideration to the representations or proposal made to it.
>
> 3. Any differences between the Member States concerning the interpretation or application of this Agreement shall, as far as possible, be settled amicably between the parties. If such differences cannot be settled amicably, it shall be submitted to the Council referred to in Article 7 of this Agreement, and if necessary, to the AEM.

See full text at <http://www.aseansec.org/12375.htm>.

11. The text of the original protocol, signed in 1996, is at <http://www.aseansec.org/4924.htm>.

12. In 2004, the enhanced protocol was signed, in order to render the dispute settlement process more rules-based and to reduce

politicization in the resolution of disputes under it. The text is at <http://www.aseansec.org/4924.htm>.

13. Article 1:1 of the protocol.

14. Ibid. Together, these are called the "covered agreements". Under Article VII of the ASEAN Framework Agreement on Services, the protocol also applies disputes arising from the services agreement (although the reference was to the 1996 Protocol at the time, as the agreement was signed on 15 December 1995); see text at <http://www.aseansec.org/6628.htm>. Article VII also envisages the possibility of establishing a special dispute settlement mechanism for this agreement.

15. See para. 11 of the 36th ASEAN Economic Ministers Meeting Joint Media Statement <http://www.aseansec.org/16377.htm>.

16. For an explanation on the TMB, see <http://www.wto.org/english/tratop_e/texti_e/texintro_e.htm>.

17. Ibid., paras. 9 and 11. The new features arose from the Declaration of ASEAN Concord II (the "Bali Concord", text at <http://www.aseansec.org/19096.htm>) of 2003. This included implementation of the new features, which had been recommended by a specially-appointed High Level Task Force (their recommendations may be viewed at <http://www.aseansec.org/hltf.htm>).

18. Bali Concord, ibid. For a comparative table of the dispute settlement mechanisms of the Australia-New Zealand Closer Economic Relations Trade Agreement (ANCERTA), ASEAN Free Trade Area (AFTA), NAFTA and the EU, see N. Akrasanee and J. Arunanondchai, "Institutional Reforms to Achieve ASEAN Economic Integration", in *Roadmap to an ASEAN Economic Community*, edited by Denis Hew (Singapore: Institute of Southeast Asia Studies, 2005), pp. 73–77.

19. The Philippines suspended its tariff reductions under ASEAN's Common Effective Preferential Tariff (CEPT) scheme in January 2003 for some petrochemical resins via Executive Order No. 161 of 2003, to which Singapore requested compensation — successfully.

See ibid., p. 65. See also <http://www.icis.com/Articles/2003/07/25/506586/philippines-names-petchems-in-sing-dispute.html>. For a follow-up on this suspension, see Presidential Executive Order No. 316 in relation to the compensation, at <http://www.ops.gov.ph/records/eo_no316.htm>, and Presidential Executive Order No. 486 of 2006, lifting the suspension of the tariffs.

20. ASEAN Protocol on Notification Procedures, 8 October 1998 <http://www.aseansec.org/12367.htm>.

21. See Article 3.2 of the DSU.

22. Article 3.

23. Article 5.1.

24. Article 6.3.

25. Article 8.2. In "exceptional" cases, it may take an additional ten days. Under Article 12.8 of the DSU, the period from composition of the panel to issue of the final panel report to parties is generally set at six months.

26. Article 9.

27. See Article 13 of the DSU.

28. See Article 14 of the DSU.

29. This mirrors the period in Article 17.5 of the DSU.

30. See Article 17.6 of the DSU for an equivalent provision.

31. Article 14 of the Protocol; compare this with Article 19 of the DSU.

32. Contrast this with the three options in Article 21.3 of the DSU. See also Articles 15.2–15.3 of the protocol for extensions.

33. See Article 22.1 of the DSU.

34. Compare with Article 22.3 of the DSU.

35. See time-frames in Article 21.5 (compliance panel proceeding) and Article 22 (authorization of countermeasures) of the DSU.

36. See Joint Media Statement of the Fortieth ASEAN Economic Ministers' (AEM) Meeting, Singapore, 25–26 August 2008 <http://www.aseansec.org/21886.htm>. "The Ministers underscored the importance of compliance to timely implementation of the AEC Blueprint's measures, and emphasised that the *AEC Scorecard and*

the Enhanced Dispute Settlement Mechanism (DSM) are the most appropriate monitoring and compliance tools for ASEAN." (Italic emphasis added.) The scorecard mechanism was raised by ASEAN economic ministers in 2007, as a tool that "would enable review and assessment of the progress of ASEAN economic integration as well as the community building, see <http://www.aseansec.org/21887.htm>, para. 8.

37. At the time of writing, the December ASEAN Summit has just been postponed to March 2009 due to the tense situation in Bangkok, the summit venue.

38. Text available at <http://www.aseansec.org/6462.htm>.

39. ASEAN I.D. Case No. ARB/01/1 (2003), 42 ILM 540 (2003). The matter did not proceed to full hearing as the respondents' jurisdictional challenges succeeded.

40. Text available at <http://www.aseansec.org/21083.pdf>.

41. See Joint Media Statement of the Fortieth ASEAN Economic Ministers' (AEM) Meeting, Singapore, 25–26 August 2008 <http://www.aseansec.org/21886.htm>, paras. 37–39.

42. See <http://www.aseansec.org/20834.htm> at para. 9 and <http://www.aseansec.org/21886.htm> at para. 38.

43. This was one of the points of contention in the *Yaung Chi Oo* case; *supra*, note 39.

44. Para. 59, ibid.

45. See also the preamble, Articles 1.7 and 2.2(h) of the charter, which refer to adherence to the rule of law.

Locknie Hsu is an Associate Professor at the School of Law, Singapore Management University.

6
DISPUTE RESOLUTION UNDER NAFTA
Evolution and Stagnation

J. Anthony VanDuzer

1. Introduction

Canada is highly integrated into the global economy. Its most important trade and investment relationship, by far, is with the United States. Canada's economic relationship with Mexico is much smaller but is growing rapidly in importance such that Mexico is now a significant location for Canadian investment and was Canada's fifth largest trading partner in 2007. Most trade and investment activity involving Canada and its North American partners takes place without disputes arising. Inevitably, however, in such a broad and deep relationship, sometimes government actions by one of the parties to the North American Free Trade Agreement (NAFTA) cause concerns for one or both of the others regarding whether the actions comply with NAFTA.

NAFTA provides a variety of mechanisms to address disputes that may arise. Like most trade agreements, NAFTA provides a process by which a party state may seek resolution of disputes regarding the interpretation of the agreement or whether a given measure of another NAFTA party state is consistent with its obligations. This general state-to-state dispute settlement procedure in Chapter 20 shares many characteristics with dispute settlement under the World Trade Organization's (WTO) Dispute Settlement Understanding (DSU),[1] but also has a number of distinctive features.[2]

NAFTA Chapter 19 creates a unique process whereby a private party from one NAFTA state that is involved in a trade remedies case[3] in another NAFTA state can elect to have a decision in the case reviewed by a bi-national panel instead of a domestic court. Amendments to trade remedies laws may also be reviewed by bi-national panels.

NAFTA Chapter 11 imposes substantive obligations on each party regarding how it will treat investors of the other parties. Where an investor of one NAFTA party experiences losses as a result of actions of another NAFTA party that are contrary to that state's obligations in Chapter 11, the investor may seek compensation in binding arbitration.

The North American Agreement on Labour Cooperation (NAALC) and the North American Agreement on Environmental Cooperation (NAAEC) (the so-called NAFTA side agreements) are intended to facilitate cooperation between the NAFTA parties on labour rights and environmental protection and to encourage the effective enforcement of each country's laws in these areas. Each contains procedures for consultation and dispute resolution that can be initiated in limited circumstances where a NAFTA party has failed to enforce its own labour or environmental laws.

Other papers in this volume address the NAALC, the NAAEC and Chapter 19. This paper describes and analyses the effectiveness of dispute resolution under Chapters 20 and 11. Experience with both Chapter 20 and Chapter 11 since NAFTA came into force on 1 January 1994 has disclosed problems which could be most directly addressed by amending NAFTA. Since the NAFTA states have been unwilling to engage in negotiations to formally amend the agreement, however, this has not occurred. In the absence of amendment, the evolution of these two procedures presents stark contrasts.

Perhaps the defining characteristic of Chapter 20 is that it is rarely resorted to by any of the three NAFTA parties. It has not evolved to meet their needs. The WTO dispute settlement process has proven much more attractive to the NAFTA countries as a result of procedural differences and, in some cases, strategic considerations. Through an examination of the nature of the Chapter 20 process and a comparison with the WTO's DSU,[4] some of the reasons for NAFTA states' reluctance to use Chapter 20 are identified.

Unlike Chapter 20, the initiation of investor-state arbitration under Chapter 11 is in the hands of investors from the three states. Increasingly, NAFTA investors have resorted to this process. The experience of Canada, the United States and Mexico with Chapter 11 in the more than fifty cases that have been initiated to date has demonstrated a need to make some adjustments to certain aspects of the process. Although a reluctance to engage in discussions regarding the amendment of NAFTA has precluded direct changes to the agreement, the parties have adopted interpretations of the agreement and other actions short of amendment. Such tinkering has resulted in some significant changes to how investor-state arbitration under NAFTA operates in practice, but it has not resulted in a binding regime that comprehensively addresses the problems that have arisen.

2. State-to-State Dispute Settlement under NAFTA Chapter 20

(i) Overview of the Process

Under Chapter 20, unlike the WTO, panel decisions do not have a binding character and compliance with the treaty is not the only goal of the process. Much greater reliance is placed on the parties reaching a mutually satisfactory solution. This softer, less legalistic character of the Chapter 20 process is discussed in detail below.

The dispute settlement section of Chapter 20 begins with the commitment of the parties to seek agreement on issues regarding the interpretation or application of the agreement and to cooperate and consult to achieve a mutually satisfactory resolution of any matter that might affect NAFTA's operation.[5] In terms of its scope, the dispute settlement process in Chapter 20 is available to deal with disputes among the parties "regarding the interpretation and application of"[6] NAFTA or whenever a party believes that an actual or proposed measure of another party is or would be inconsistent with that state's obligations under the agreement. It is also available where a party is concerned that a measure of another party nullifies or impairs the benefits that the first party reasonably expected to receive under the agreement, even if the measure is not a violation of NAFTA.[7]

Like the WTO process, the Chapter 20 process begins with consultations. The parties are obliged to make every attempt to resolve the matter in a mutually satisfactory way.[8] The third NAFTA party state that is not directly involved in the dispute may nevertheless participate in consultations if it considers that it has a "substantial interest" in the dispute.[9]

If consultations fail to resolve the dispute within thirty days of the delivery of the request for consultations, any of the consulting states may request a meeting of the NAFTA Free Trade Commission (FTC), a body established under the agreement composed of cabinet level representatives from each party.[10] Usually the FTC members are the trade ministers of Canada, the United States and Mexico. The FTC must meet within ten days and "endeavour to resolve the matter promptly".[11] The FTC may seek to assist the parties to reach a mutually satisfactory solution by calling on technical advisers, establishing working groups or expert groups, using good offices, conciliation, mediation or other dispute resolution procedures, or making recommendations. Involvement by the FTC is a feature of the Chapter 20 process that distinguishes it from the WTO process, where a panel may be immediately requested if consultations fail.[12] Although the parties to WTO disputes may agree on good offices, conciliation, or mediation and the director-general may offer such assistance, these mechanisms are seldom used in practice.

Where the FTC has failed to resolve the dispute within thirty days from the date that it first met (or any other period agreed by the parties), any NAFTA party involved in the consultations may request the establishment of a panel to hear the dispute. The third NAFTA state can join as a complaining party if it considers that it has a substantial trade interest in the dispute.[13]

Once a panel has been requested, the FTC is obliged to establish one. Panels consist of five members that are to be appointed from a roster that the three countries establish by consensus. The roster is to contain the names of up to thirty individuals who possess specified expertise, are independent of all NAFTA countries and who comply with the code of conduct established by the FTC.[14] The FTC finally agreed to a roster for the first time in late 2006 with a three-year term ending in December 2009.

In the usual case, where there are only two disputing parties, the parties must first try to agree on a panel chair. In the three cases under Chapter 20 to date, the chair has not been a national of a party. If there is no agreement within fifteen days of delivery of the request for a panel, one of the disputing parties, chosen by lot, can choose the chair, who may not be a national of that party.[15]

The process for appointing the other panel members is distinctive to NAFTA.[16] Each disputing party selects two panelists from the roster who are nationals of the other party. If no selection is made within fifteen days, the panelists not appointed are to be selected by lot from the roster. Where all three NAFTA countries are involved in the dispute, the process operates somewhat differently.

One notable distinction between the WTO DSU and Chapter 20 is that under the DSU, is the appointing process that operates where the parties fail to agree on the panelists. Panels are normally composed of three panelists.[17] Panelists are proposed by the WTO Secretariat and agreed on by the parties.[18] If there is no agreement within twenty days after the date for the establishment of a panel, at the request of either party, the director-general in consultation with the chairman of the dispute settlement body (DSB) and the chairman of the relevant WTO Council or Committee, must determine the composition of the panel.[19]

Once a NAFTA panel is in place, the proceedings are conducted in accordance with the Model Rules of Procedure for Chapter 20 Panels established by the FTC.[20] Each party has an opportunity to make initial written submissions, make rebuttal submissions, and to make their case at an oral hearing. A NAFTA party that is not a disputing party may, on notice to the others, attend all hearings and make written and oral submissions.[21] The parties' submissions, any communications with the panel, the hearings, the panel's deliberations and the panel's initial report are all confidential.[22] Nevertheless, each party is permitted, but not obliged, to disclose their own pleadings and the submissions of other parties subject to the redaction of confidential information. Hearing transcripts may also be made public by a party fifteen days after the final panel report has been made public.[23]

A panel may seek the advice of an expert, either on its own initiative or at the request of a party. Similarly, a panel may request a written report of a scientific review board on any factual issue raised by a disputing party. The NAFTA parties must be given notice of and have an opportunity to comment on the factual issues referred to the board, and be given an opportunity to comment on the eventual report.[24]

A panel must provide its initial report within ninety days of the appointment of the last panelist.[25] The initial report must set out the panel's findings of fact, conclusions regarding any inconsistency with NAFTA or nullification and impairment, and any recommendations for resolving the dispute.[26] It is not necessary for panels to make recommendations.[27] Under the DSU, by contrast, where non-compliance is found, panels and the Appellate Body must recommend that the member bring its regime into compliance with its obligations.[28]

Within fourteen days after receipt of the report, the NAFTA parties may submit their written comments. The panel's final report must be submitted within thirty days after delivery of the initial report. Separate opinions may be included in the report, though the author is not to be identified.[29] It is the responsibility of the disputing parties to deliver the report to the FTC. The final report must be published within fifteen days unless the FTC decides otherwise.[30] All reports to date have been published.

Once a final report has been delivered to the parties, the next step is for the disputing parties to agree on a resolution. The resolution "normally" should conform to the panel's conclusions and recommendations, including, "wherever possible", not implementing or removing any measure that is not in compliance with NAFTA or causing nullification and impairment.[31] While compliance is the preferred remedy, as an alternative, the parties may resolve the dispute through the payment of compensation or in some other way.

If a panel concludes that a measure does not comply with NAFTA or is causing nullification and impairment, and there has been no mutual agreement on a resolution within thirty days, the complaining NAFTA countries may suspend trade concessions of equivalent effect under NAFTA.[32] A disputing party can ask the FTC to establish a panel to review any suspension of concessions that it thinks is "manifestly excessive".[33]

This requirement to agree on a resolution is an important difference between the Chapter 20 process and the process under the WTO DSU. Under the WTO, panel and Appellate Body reports are automatically adopted by the DSB (in the absence of a consensus of WTO members not to adopt) and a WTO member is bound to bring its domestic regime into conformity with the recommendations of the panel or the Appellate Body. In the WTO process, compensation is only for the limited and temporary purpose of promoting compliance.

Finally, NAFTA establishes a scheme to govern disputes that arise under both the WTO and NAFTA. Such situations arise frequently because there are substantial overlaps in the substantive coverage of the two agreements. Indeed some WTO obligations are incorporated into NAFTA.[34] In general, if a dispute settlement proceeding has been initiated under either NAFTA or the WTO, proceedings cannot be initiated in the other forum.[35] It is up to the complaining state to decide which forum to use, subject to some limitations, which require NAFTA dispute resolution in particular cases.[36]

(ii) Analysis of the Effectiveness of Chapter 20

There have only been three cases that have been the subject of panel decisions under Chapter 20, though consultations under

Chapter 20 have been initiated in a dozen or so other cases.[37] In the first case (*Agricultural Products from the United States*), the United States challenged Canada's conversion of certain quantitative restrictions on a few agricultural products into new tariffs.[38] Canada's action, which was taken to implement its WTO commitments, was found to be consistent with its NAFTA obligations. In the second (*Brooms from Mexico*), Mexico challenged a U.S. safeguard action against imports of Mexican brooms.[39] The United States was found to be acting in a manner inconsistent with its NAFTA obligations. It removed the safeguard within nine months of the date of the panel decision. In the last case, decided in 2001 (*Mexican Cross-border Trucking*), Mexico challenged U.S. restrictions on trucking from Mexico.[40] Even though the panel found that the U.S. restrictions were contrary to NAFTA, to date, the United States has not provided access to the U.S. market for Mexican trucks.

The small number of cases under Chapter 20 contrasts sharply with the number of cases brought by NAFTA parties in the WTO. Since the WTO came into force, NAFTA parties have initiated thirty-three claims against other NAFTA parties leading to eighteen panel decisions and eleven Appellate Body decisions. One of the reasons for the attractiveness of the WTO to the NAFTA parties is that the WTO covers some matters that are not addressed in NAFTA, including the critically important areas of anti-dumping, subsidies and countervailing measures. More than two-thirds of the WTO cases involving the NAFTA parties in complaints against each other have related to trade remedies issues that could only have been litigated at the WTO.[41] Nevertheless, several features of the NAFTA state-to-state dispute settlement likely account for the apparent reluctance of parties to use the formal Chapter 20 process.

Ultimately, NAFTA relies on the agreement of the parties to resolve disputes. Even where a violation of NAFTA is found, there is no unequivocal obligation on the party in violation to bring their regime into compliance. While the other party may suspend concessions if no mutually agreed solution to the problem is found, solutions other than compliance, including compensation, are possible. Where disputes are particularly sensitive politically, the prospect of resolving them in the non-binding NAFTA process, which may be entirely confidential if the FTC decides not to issue the panel report, may make it an attractive forum. Nevertheless, the inherent inequality in any negotiation between Canada and Mexico, on the one hand, and the United States, on the other, means that having to negotiate for a mutually agreed solution may be especially difficult if the dispute involves the United States. In many cases, a process that provides a binding result will be preferable.

The timelines of achieving results through Chapter 20 dispute settlement may also be discouraging Canada, the United States and Mexico from using the process. The timelines set out in Chapter 20, if complied with, would result in a final panel decision within approximately eight months (240 days) of a request for consultations, with retaliation permitted in a further thirty days where no agreed resolution has been reached. In practice, however, these timelines have not been met due to delays at each stage in the process. The consultation period has been extended beyond the stipulated thirty days. Also, often it has been difficult to set up panels. In part, this is because of the NAFTA parties' failure to agree on a roster of panelists. States have tried to agree on the selection of panelists on an *ad hoc* basis for each dispute. This has caused substantial delays. Panel selection took six months in two of the cases under Chapter 20 and sixteen-and-a-half months in the other.[42] In a few cases, it has proven impossible to establish a panel at all.[43] The other time periods set in Chapter 20 have been described as unreasonably short and have been routinely exceeded. No panel has completed its work within the minimum time specified.[44] The time from a request for consultations to a panel decision has been highly variable, ranging from seventeen months[45] to more than five years.[46]

Some have suggested that delays in the process are partly attributable to a lack of institutional support for Chapter 20 dispute settlement.[47] The NAFTA parties did not create much in the way of infrastructure to support the operation of the agreement. The Free Trade Commission is charged with setting up a secretariat with offices in each state to provide assistance to it, as well as administrative assistance to the dispute settlement panels established under Chapters 19 and 20.[48] The NAFTA Secretariat has been established but is hampered by a lack of independence from the parties. It is formally accountable to the FTC, and each national section of the Secretariat is more or less integrated into the governments of the three party states. In the case of the United States, for example, the U.S. section is housed in the Department of Commerce.

As well, the professional capacity of the NAFTA Secretariat is limited and has been eroded over time. While they were headed by lawyers initially, neither the U.S. nor the Canadian sections have lawyers on staff.

As a result of these weaknesses, the national sections of the Secretariat play only a minor supporting role in the Chapter 20 process. Their role is limited largely to administrative assistance, such as booking rooms and providing for the transmission and storage of. A better resourced and professional secretariat could play a much more effective role in supporting the process such as by assisting with the drafting of orders and decisions and providing institutional memory for the benefit of the *ad hoc* Chapter 20 panels.[49] With the benefit of such support for the Chapter 20 process states might be more inclined to use it.

(iii) Comparison with WTO DSU

Compared to Chapter 20, the DSU provides a more predictable and consistent process for state-to-state dispute settlement leading to binding decisions backed up by a robust though imperfect compliance process. The dispute settlement process under NAFTA is neither as automatic as the process under the DSU nor will it lead to compliance with the same degree of certainty and predictability. As noted, WTO panel and Appellate Body reports are automatically adopted by the DSB, and upon adoption a WTO member is bound to bring its domestic regime into conformity with the recommendations in the report. The DSB engages in continuing surveillance of a member's efforts to bring its regime into compliance and a complaining state may require a dispute settlement panel to determine whether a member's measures do bring its regime into compliance. While the WTO compliance process can be time consuming and is not always effective, it is not subject to the kinds of unpredictable delays and uncertainty that characterizes the Chapter 20 process.

Delays are not as significant in the WTO process as under Chapter 20. In contrast to the very long delays in the appointment of panelists under Chapter 20, in cases under the DSU, the director-general has the power to appoint panelists if parties do not act with dispatch. This is not to suggest that delays do not occur at the WTO. Delays occur at the consultation, panel selection, and panel decision stages. Nevertheless, despite the presence of delays, the timelines in a WTO case typically are more reliable than those in NAFTA. Assuming that the specified timelines in the DSU are met, the process takes approximately seventeen months from the request for consultations to the adoption of the report (including an appeal). One study in 2005 found that the average time for a WTO case from the request for consultations to the adoption of the panel report in practice was between twenty and twenty-one months, though many cases take substantially longer.[50]

There are several other aspects of the process under the DSU that are not found in Chapter 20 and that may be attractive to NAFTA parties. The possibility of appeals on questions of law to the WTO Appellate Body is an important safeguard against poor and inconsistent decision-making by *ad hoc* panels that does not exist under NAFTA.[51] As well, the possibility of multiple states participating as third parties or joining in a complaint under the WTO means, at least in some cases, that the WTO process may provide a way to exert more pressure on a state whose measures do not conform to its obligations. This may be particularly important for Canadian and Mexican complaints against the United States.

Finally, the WTO may be attractive because it gives much more profile to a dispute than one brought under Chapter 20. Requests for consultation must be notified to the WTO and are made public. WTO dispute settlement decisions attract substantial attention. A NAFTA party interested in demonstrating its commitment to a particular view, or achieving a result in one case that may assist it in challenging similar measures in other WTO members, would be interested in proceeding at the WTO rather than under NAFTA.

(iv) Conclusion

The Chapter 20 process is more flexible and less legalistic than the WTO as well as more deferential to the parties' concerns about sovereignty. One commentator has characterized NAFTA panel reports as akin to a guideline.[52] Nevertheless, while Chapter 20 dispute settlement may be attractive in some politically sensitive cases, unpredictable and lengthy delays as well as a lack of institutional support reduce its effectiveness relative to the WTO. As well, in the frequent cases where a binding result, the support of like-minded states, or increased publicity is desirable, the WTO will be preferred.

3. Investor-state Dispute Settlement under NAFTA Chapter 11

(i) Introduction

NAFTA Chapter 11 imposes substantive obligations on each NAFTA party with a view to protecting foreign investors from the other NAFTA states against discriminatory or unfair treatment by host governments. By helping to guarantee a stable, consistent, and fair legal regime in host states, the expectation is that foreign direct investment will be encouraged. In this context, investor-state dispute settlement represents both a strong signal that the NAFTA states are committed to the investor protection provided in the treaty and a mechanism to ensure that compensation is available where government action infringes on these protections.

The Chapter 11 process has been used extensively. To 31 October 2008, fifty-four notices of intent to submit a claim have been filed with a NAFTA state and made public.[53] In 2008, seven new notices of intent were filed, all relating to claims against Canada. Experience with investor-state arbitration under Chapter 11 over the past fifteen years has resulted in a much better understanding of the implications of the kinds of obligations Chapter 11 imposes. Experience has also demonstrated that certain adjustments to Chapter 11 would be desirable. When they have negotiated new investment agreements with other states, Canada and the United States have deviated from the NAFTA model in terms of both the substantive obligations and some aspects of the investor-state procedures. It has not been possible, however, for the parties to revise their obligations to each other in the same way through amendments to NAFTA. Nevertheless, through interpretations of the agreement, statements regarding their commitment to certain kinds of procedures, and their practices in investor-state arbitration, the NAFTA states have been able to achieve some adjustments to the way the process works in practice in most circumstances.

The first part of this section sets out an overview of the procedure in a Chapter 11 investor-state arbitration. The second part identifies three procedural issues that have arisen in the context of cases decided under Chapter 11 and describes how the NAFTA states have addressed them.

(ii) Overview of the NAFTA Chapter 11 Procedure

Investor-state arbitration under NAFTA gives an investor of one NAFTA party state the right to initiate binding arbitration against another NAFTA party when the investor has suffered an injury as a consequence of a measure of that other party that is inconsistent with its substantive obligations under Chapter 11. A successful claim results in an award of financial compensation in favour of the investor against the state. Some of the general categories of obligations imposed on NAFTA parties by Chapter 11 are the following:

1.   NAFTA investors must be accorded the better of national treatment and most favoured nation (MFN) treatment (Articles 1101, 1102 and 1103);

2.   Investments of NAFTA investors must be given at least the
        minimum treatment required by international law including
        "fair and equitable treatment and full protection and security"
        (Article 1105); and

3.   NAFTA states must observe certain standards in connection
        with the expropriation of investments of NAFTA investors
        relating to the purpose of the expropriation, the process to
        be followed, and the compensation to be paid (Article 1110).

Proceedings take place under a set of international arbitration
rules chosen by the investor from several permitted under NAFTA,
as modified by the provisions of the treaty itself. An investor may
choose one of the following sets of arbitral rules:

1.   The arbitration rules under the International Convention on
        the Settlement of Investment Disputes (ICSID Arbitration
        Rules);[54]

2.   The arbitration rules under the International Centre for the
        Settlement of Investment Disputes Additional Facility (ICSID
        Additional Facility Rules);[55] or

3.   United Nations Commission on International Trade Law
        Arbitration Rules (UNCITRAL Rules).[56]

The International Center for the Settlement of Investment Disputes
(ICSID) provides facilities as well as the ICSID Arbitration Rules
for the resolution of disputes between investors from states that
are parties to the ICSID Convention and other states that are
parties to the convention. Since Canada and Mexico are not parties,
arbitration of cases under the ICSID Arbitration Rules is not an
option. Canada has signed the ICSID Convention and, in March
2008, passed legislation permitting ratification. Canada expects to

ratify the ICSID Convention as soon as implementing legislation is passed by the few provinces that have yet to do so.

In 1978, the Administrative Council of ICSID created the "Additional Facility" which permitted ICSID to provide its facilities and rules for disputes that were outside its jurisdiction because either the investor's state or the state complained against were not parties to the ICSID Convention.[57] Arbitration under the ICSID Additional Facility Rules is generally similar to the process under the ICSID Convention. Currently, ICSID Additional Facility arbitration is only available where the Unites States is either the state complained against or the investor's state.

The initial steps in an investor-state arbitration are set out in NAFTA. After the commencement of arbitration, the arbitral rules chosen by the investor govern most aspects of the process, subject, in some areas, to the provisions in the treaty. The typical steps in a investor-state arbitration are set out below.

1.   An investor of one NAFTA state delivers a "notice of intent to submit a claim to arbitration" to another party that the investor claims has breached its treaty obligations causing a loss to the investor at least ninety days in advance of filing the arbitration claim itself (Article 1119).

2.   The investor and the NAFTA state complained against engage in consultations. This step is not mandatory and may occur before or after a notice of intent is delivered (Article 1118).

3.   The investor delivers a claim to arbitration to the NAFTA state complained against at least ninety days after filing the notice of intent to submit a claim to arbitration. The claim must contain the investor's choice of arbitration rules. The date the claim is delivered is the date that the arbitration commences and the arbitral rules selected by the investor

begin to apply. The claim must include a consent to arbitration and a waiver of claims to other relief based on the same measure in other fora except for claims for injunctive, declaratory, and other relief that do not involve the payment of damages. At least six months must have passed since the events giving rise to the claim (Article 1120).

4. An arbitral tribunal composed of three members is constituted. Each disputing party chooses an arbitrator and the parties seek to agree on the third. If an arbitral tribunal has not been constituted within ninety days, the secretary-general of ICSID must appoint any arbitrator not appointed (Articles 1123–1125).

5. Typically, the arbitral tribunal deals with a number of preliminary motions at this stage, often including a challenge to the jurisdiction of the tribunal, setting rules for the disclosure of information, scheduling the exchange of submissions and hearings, and other procedural issues. Where two or more investor claims raise common questions of law or fact there is a process by which the claims may be consolidated into a single proceeding (Article 1126).

6. The investor and the NAFTA state complained against make written submissions in accordance with an order of the arbitral tribunal regarding the procedures to be followed.

7. An oral hearing on the merits of the claim is held.

8. An award on the merits is issued. If the investor is successful, the NAFTA state complained against may seek to have the award set aside in court. Set aside proceedings have been initiated by states in at least three cases. This cannot occur where the award is under the ICSID Arbitration Rules which preclude domestic judicial review of arbitration awards. There is an internal annulment process instead.[58]

9.   If the investor is successful and the award is not set aside, the investor may commence enforcement proceedings in national courts after the expiry of between 90 and 120 days following the award depending on the rules. State-to-state dispute settlement under Chapter 20 may be initiated by an investor's state if a state against which an award has been made does not comply with the award.[59]

One important feature of Chapter 11 is that the FTC has the power to issue binding interpretations of the agreement.[60]

4. Three Issues Regarding the Operation of NAFTA Chapter 11

The significant number of cases under Chapter 11 have meant that it is now one of the leading sources of international investment law.[61] A number of issues have arisen in the cases to date. As noted, political reluctance to engage in negotiations on actual amendments to the agreement have prevented the parties from implementing changes to the process that would address these issues in a thoroughgoing and legally binding way. In relation to the three issues being discussed, a combination of interpretations of the agreement, statements regarding how the process is to operate, and decisions by arbitral tribunals have helped to ensure that some of these issues have been addressed in practice.

(i) Transparency

The arbitral rules selected by the investor largely determine the procedures followed in a Chapter 11 investor-state arbitration. These rules are based on a model of international commercial arbitration that contemplates little public disclosure of information about the process. Under the three sets of arbitral rules contemplated in Chapter 11, as under most arbitral rules, detailed procedural requirements, including those related to disclosure, are left to the tribunal and, in practice, are usually established by the tribunal with the consent of the parties. NAFTA itself only requires that there be a public record of investors' claims filed[62] and permits Canada and the United States to decide whether they will disclose arbitral awards, once made.[63] For Mexico, disclosure of awards may only be made with the consent of the investor.[64] In the absence of guarantees in NAFTA regarding the transparency of the Chapter 11 process, there have been widespread concerns about the prospect that sometimes very large claims for compensation based on government measures that may have been adopted to achieve legitimate and important public policy goals will be adjudicated in a process to which the public has no access.

In July 2001, the FTC adopted the FTC Interpretive Note on Transparency to address these concerns. It provides, in part, as follows:

> Nothing in the NAFTA imposes a general duty of confidentiality on the disputing parties to a Chapter Eleven arbitration, and ... nothing in the NAFTA precludes the Parties from providing public access to documents submitted to, or issued by, a Chapter Eleven tribunal ... *apart from the limited specific exceptions set forth expressly in those rules.*

> Each party agrees to make available to the public in a timely manner all documents submitted to, or issued by, a Chapter 11 tribunal, subject to redaction of:

> i.   confidential business information;
> ii. information which is privileged or otherwise protected from disclosure under the Party's domestic law; and
> iii. *information which the Party must withhold pursuant to the relevant arbitral rules, as applied.*[65] [emphasis added]

Following the issuance of the FTC Interpretive Note on Transparency, disclosure in Chapter 11 cases has tended to include the investor's notice of intent to file a claim to arbitration, the investor's claim, the respondent state's statement of defence, any orders of the tribunal, the parties' written submissions, transcripts of oral submissions, correspondence from the tribunal, evidence, formal responses of the parties to tribunal questions, and all submissions from non-disputing state parties.[66] In practice, states provide direct and easy access to most documents related to Chapter 11 arbitrations on their websites, including documents that are produced before the arbitral process has formally commenced. Often, however, there are lags between the time documents are filed in the arbitration and when they appear on government websites and some documents are not available at all. More prompt but still not complete disclosure is provided by some private sites, including, in particular <naftaclaims.com>.

While the commitment expressed in the FTC Interpretive Note on Transparency and the practice in recent cases may be encouraging from the point of view of transparency, there are few legal guarantees regarding public access to information about Chapter 11 proceedings. The FTC Interpretive Note on Transparency does not purport to guarantee disclosure before an arbitral tribunal has been established. Notices of intent are not routinely disclosed by the United States. Mexico appears never to have disclosed some notices of intent that it has received. Once the arbitration has commenced, in particular cases, transparency is a matter of procedure determined by the tribunal. Tribunal decisions are made taking into account the views of the parties and are often based on their consent. A state or an investor may seek an order limiting disclosure and it may be successful.

The FTC Interpretive Note on Transparency is limited in one other important way. It only addresses disclosure of documents not the openness of oral hearings. This may be because, in relation to oral hearings, Article 25(4) of the UNCITRAL Rules provides that all hearings must be in camera unless the parties consent to a more open process. Article 39 of the ICSID Additional Facility Rules is similar in effect. The tribunal must decide, with the consent of the parties, who, in addition to the parties, may attend oral hearings. These rules give either party a veto over the attendance of the public, the press, or public interest representatives at oral hearings.[67] The most that a NAFTA party state can do is seek agreement from the investor to open hearings.[68] In 2003, Canada affirmed that it will consent, and will request the consent of disputing investors and, as applicable, tribunals to having hearings open to the public, subject to the protection of confidential information. Both Mexico and the United States made identical public commitments in 2004.[69] In practice, hearings have been open via closed circuit television in at least three cases,[70] and, in other cases, transcripts of hearings have been made public.[71]

The transparency practices that have evolved in NAFTA cases supported by FTC Interpretive Note on Transparency provide significant transparency in practice, but lack the more robust character of the rules governing judicial procedures. Investors, states, and the public cannot be sure about what procedures will be followed in a particular case or what documents will be made public.

(ii) Participation in NAFTA Chapter 11 Cases by Amicus Curiae or Friends of the Court

Neither the three sets of arbitral rules contemplated in Chapter 11 nor the chapter itself creates a right for parties other than the investor, the state complained against and the other NAFTA parties[72] to participate in arbitrations. Participation by non-disputing third parties is unheard of in private commercial arbitration proceedings.[73] There is, however, some precedent for non-disputing parties to participate in international fora in which the international responsibility of states is adjudicated, such as the WTO.[74] Chapter 11 tribunals held that they have the power to permit participation by non-disputing third parties as *amicus curiae*[75] beginning in 2001 with rulings in *Methanex*[76] and *UPS*.[77] Subsequently, in 2003, the FTC issued a Statement on Non-disputing Party Participation, which recommended a process for Chapter 11 tribunals to follow when considering applications for *amicus* participation and setting out criteria to be considered in deciding whether to permit such participation and the form of application for leave to file *amicus* submissions.[78] The consistent practice of tribunals to date suggests that applications for leave to participate as *amicus curiae* will be dealt with in a manner consistent with the FTC's statement.

Neither NAFTA practice nor rules in the FTC Statement on Non-disputing Party Participation are binding on future tribunals, however.[79] In 2006, ICSID amended the ICSID Arbitration Rules and the Additional Facility Rules to expressly provide that tribunals have the power to permit participation by *amicus curiae*, setting out criteria that are similar to those in the FTC Statement on Non-disputing Party Participation. These amendments, on which Canada and Mexico had no say as non-parties to the ICSID Convention, changed the rules applicable to all new cases under the ICSID Additional Facility Rules, including cases under NAFTA where the investor chooses these rules.[80] The amendments are limited in their scope, however. Unlike the FTC Statement on Non-disputing Party Participation, they do not address the form or procedural requirements for *amicus* submissions.

While the FTC's statement is more comprehensive, it fails to address a number of important issues. Nothing in the FTC's statement contemplates any more than that tribunals consider whether there is any basis to allow *amicus curiae* submissions to be made. It remains unclear when an *amicus* submission will be accepted. Also, many second level issues remain. Some relate to what process should be followed by tribunals. When should *amicus* applications be filed? Is there a right to respond to responses from other parties to an *amicus* application? In addition, transparency and *amicus* participation are closely linked. More comprehensive binding rules regarding both transparency and *amicus curiae* are needed if *amicus* participation is to be informed and effective.

(iii) Issues of Jurisdiction

In most NAFTA investor-state cases, jurisdictional issues have been raised. This is due to the fact that the NAFTA states consent to arbitrate only in relation to claims falling under the treaty. NAFTA has detailed provisions defining what claims may be made, including

1.   procedural requirements that must be met by an investor as a condition of the tribunal having jurisdiction;
2.   categories of investors that may initiate investor-state arbitration;
3.   categories of investments in relation to which investors may seek relief;
4.   kinds of government actions that may be complained about; and
5.   obligations that those government actions must have breached.

In almost every case, there has been some objection raised by the state complained against that the investor, its investment, the nature of the government action challenged, or the investor's claim did not fit into the categories defined in the treaty.

Several problems have arisen in connection with jurisdictional challenges. One concern has been the way in which tribunals have dealt with such challenges. Investor-state tribunals under NAFTA are competent to rule on their own jurisdiction.[81] In some cases, jurisdictional claims have been decided as a preliminary matter while in others the decision has been joined to the final award on the merits of the case. In regard to the latter practice, concerns have been expressed that NAFTA states have had to defend frivolous claims that should have been dismissed at an early stage on the basis of a preliminary decision of the tribunal.[82]

Another problem has been that frequent jurisdictional disputes have caused substantial delays in Chapter 11 cases. While state challenges to jurisdiction must inevitably cause some delay, an additional source of delay has been uncertainty regarding what are jurisdictional issues. Tribunals have struggled with two distinct categories of issues in this regard. The first category includes the failure by the investor to follow precisely the procedures contemplated in NAFTA. In the first case against Canada, the tribunal determined that procedural requirements were jurisdictional only if the state's consent to arbitrate was "conditioned absolutely on the fulfilment of the specified procedural requirements at a given time".[83] The defects in that case, including the failure by the investor to deliver its consent to arbitrate on time, had been substantially remedied at the time the tribunal was considering the jurisdictional challenge. The tribunal held that the procedural irregularities did not prejudice Canada and, thus, did not impair Canada's consent to arbitrate.[84] A more rigid approach was taken in *Waste Management No. 1*.[85] An investor's failure to deliver a proper consent to arbitrate on time resulted in the tribunal dismissing the claim for lack of jurisdiction, even though a proper consent had been delivered at the time of its decision.

The second category of cases in which jurisdictional challenges have been raised includes objections that the investor's allegations, if true, would not amount to breaches of NAFTA and would therefore be outside the tribunal's jurisdiction. Here, too, the approach of tribunals has been inconsistent. In one case, the tribunal struck out certain portions of the investor's claim on the basis that the facts pleaded could not be a breach of NAFTA.[86] In another case, however, the tribunal dismissed similar objections on the basis that it could not enquire into the scope of the substantive provisions alleged to be breached as a preliminary matter.[87] In the tribunal's view, such objections did not go to jurisdiction but to the merits of the claim.

In relation to jurisdictional challenges, it will be difficult for the NAFTA parties to ensure that objections to jurisdiction are dealt with as a preliminary matter without an amendment to the agreement. What constitutes a jurisdictional question could be addressed through amendment too but, in the absence of an amendment to the agreement, will be clarified progressively and slowly though successive investor-state cases.

(iv) Conclusions

The experience of the NAFTA parties in the cases to date has disclosed several weaknesses in the investor-state procedure in Chapter 11. The transparency of NAFTA investor-state arbitration will continue to depend on the initiative being taken by the state complained against and the cooperation of the investor, as well as the attitude of the tribunal. Recently, the fragility of transparency in Chapter 11 proceedings was demonstrated in *Chemtura*, in which, at the investor's request, the tribunal ordered that the hearings be closed.[88] Similarly, rules regarding participation by *amicus curiae* in Chapter 11 cases are not binding or sufficiently comprehensive. Uncertainty regarding what kinds of issues go to the tribunal's jurisdiction continue to cause delays and the absence of requirements for jurisdictional issues to be addressed early on in the arbitration may, in some cases, result in time being wasted by having a full arbitration on frivolous claims.

Amending NAFTA to incorporate rules regarding transparency, *amicus curiae* participation, and procedures regarding jurisdictional challenges is not in the cards. The recent amendments to the ICSID Arbitration and Additional Facility Rules provide a few more developed rules on *amicus curiae* without treaty amendment by changing the arbitration rules applicable to some NAFTA investor-state arbitrations. Also, the FTC's Interpretive Note on Transparency and its non-binding statement on *amicus* participation appear to have had a significant impact on practice, such that changes to NAFTA in these areas may be considered less urgent.

5. Final Comments

With respect to state-to-state dispute settlement under Chapter 20, little evolution has occurred since NAFTA came into force on 1 January 1994 to address its various weaknesses, some of which have been clearly demonstrated in the three cases to date. In part, this stagnation may be due to the availability of a more robust and certain process at the WTO that produces binding results and, at least in some cases, offers advantages to the NAFTA parties that cannot be obtained through Chapter 20. Unless the NAFTA states are willing to amend NAFTA, or at least invest more resources and support for the process, the current stagnation of Chapter 20 seems likely to continue.

Investor-state dispute settlement under NAFTA is governed by arbitral rules that give tribunals substantial control over the procedures adopted. In such a system, truly durable reforms to how the investor-state process works can only be achieved by amending the NAFTA or the applicable arbitral rules. Nevertheless, since amending NAFTA appears to be off the table, and reforms to the applicable arbitral rules are likely to be incremental and slow, the NAFTA parties have tried to adjust the process through the positions they take before tribunals and though interpretations and statements of the FTC. The result, at least in terms of transparency and the engagement of *amicus curiae*, has been that Chapter 11 has evolved in limited ways to respond to the needs of the state parties in practice. Nevertheless, without legal guarantees through amendments to NAFTA, the nature of this evolution will not be certain, binding, or uniform.

Notes

1. Understanding on Rules and Procedures Governing the Settlement of Disputes, 15 April 1994, 33 I.L.M. 81 (Annex 2 to the Marrakesh Agreement establishing the WTO [Dispute Settlement Understanding]).
2. A similar process applies in NAFTA Chapter 14 to the resolution of disputes relating to the NAFTA obligations regarding financial services (including insurance).
3. That is, a case in which a national administrative agency decides whether anti-dumping or countervailing duties should be applied to imports of certain products.
4. Dispute Settlement Understanding.
5. North American Free Trade Agreement Between the Government

of Canada, the Government of Mexico, and the Government of the United States, 17 December 1992, Can. T.S. 1994 No. 2, 32 I.L.M. 289, Article 2003 [NAFTA].

6. Ibid., Article 2004.

7. These so-called "non-violation" complaints can be made only in relation to the NAFTA provisions dealing with trade-in goods. Ibid., Article 2004, referring to Chapters 3–8 with some exclusions.

8. Ibid., Article 2003.

9. Ibid., Article 2006.

10 . The FTC is established under Article 2001 of NAFTA. The time period that must elapse before a panel may be requested may vary from forty-five days if a third NAFTA party has participated in the consultations to fifteen days if the dispute relates to perishable goods. The parties may also agree to a longer period of time. Ibid., Article 2007(1).

11. Ibid., Article 2007(4).

12. Dispute Settlement Understanding, Article 6.

13. Ibid., Article 2008(3).

14. Panelists are to have "expertise or experience in law, international trade or other matters covered by this agreement, or the resolution of disputes arising under international trade agreements". Ibid., Article 2009(2)(a).

15. If a panelist chosen by a party is not on a national roster, a disputing party can challenge the appointment and the party has to choose someone else. Panelists can be removed where the parties determine that the person has violated the code of conduct. Ibid., Articles 2011(3), (4).

16. Ibid., Article 2011.

17. Dispute Settlement Understanding, Article 8.5.

18. Ibid., Article 8.6.

19. Ibid., Article 8.7.

20. NAFTA, Article 2012.

21. Ibid., Article 2013.

22. Ibid., Article 2012(1); Model Rules of Procedure for Chapter 20 of the North American Free Trade Agreement, Rule 35 [Model Rules of Procedure].

23. Supplementary Procedures to Rule 35 on the Availability of Information.

24. NAFTA, Articles 2014–2015.

25. Ibid., Article 2016(2).

26. Ibid., Article 2016(2)(b).

27. Dispute Settlement Understanding, Articles 16–17, 19.

28. Ibid., Article 19.

29. NAFTA, Articles 2016(3), 2017(2).

30. Ibid., Article 2017(4).

31. Ibid., Article 2018(1).

32. Ibid., Article 2019(1). As under the WTO, the sectors chosen for the suspension of benefits should be the same as those that have been affected by the measure that is inconsistent with the agreement or causing nullification and impairment. There are special rules applicable to the suspension of benefits in the financial services sector.

33. Ibid., Article 2018.

34. For a summary, see Jon Johnson, *The North American Free Trade Agreement: A Comprehensive Guide* (Toronto: Canada Law Book, 1994), p. 488.

35. NAFTA, Article 2005(6).

36. For a summary of these exceptions in ibid., Articles 2005(3) and (4), see Johnson, *The North American Free Trade Agreement*, p. 488.

37. There is no comprehensive record, official or unofficial, of consultations.

38. *Tariffs Applied by Canada to Certain U.S.-Origin Agricultural Products (United States v. Canada)* (1996), CDA-95-2008-01 (Ch. 20 Panel), available at NAFTA Secretariat Website <http://www.nafta-sec-alena.org/DefaultSite/index_e.aspx?DetailID=393>.

39. *U.S. Safeguard Action Taken on Broomcorn Brooms from Mexico (Mexico v. United States)* (1998), USA-97-2008-01 (Ch. 20 Panel)

[*Brooms from Mexico*], available at NAFTA Secretariat Website <http://www.nafta-sec-alena.org/DefaultSite/index_e.aspx?DetailID=394>.

40. *Cross-Border Trucking Services and Investment (Mexico v. United States)* (2001), USA-98-2008-01) (Ch. 20 Panel) [*Cross-Border Trucking*], available at NAFTA Secretariat Website <http://www.nafta-sec-alena.org/DefaultSite/index_e.aspx?DetailID=394>.

41. The actual number is twenty-three out of thirty-three.

42. David Gantz, "Government to Government Dispute Resolution under NAFTA Chapter 20: A Commentary on the Process", *The American Review of International Arbitration* 11 (2000): 501. [Gantz, *Chapter 20*].

43. Debra Steger, "Dispute Settlement under the North American Free Trade Agreement", in *Intergovernmental Trade Dispute Settlement: Multilateral and Regional Approaches*, edited by J. Lacarte and J. Granados (Cameron May, 2004) (citing interviews with Canadian and U.S. government officials).

44. Ibid.

45. *Brooms from Mexico.*

46. In *Cross-Border Trucking*, the initial request for consultations was filed on 21 December 1995. This case is still not resolved.

47. Gantz, *Chapter 20*, p. 526.

48. NAFTA, Article 2002.

49. Gantz, *Chapter 20*, p. 526.

50. William Davey, "Implementation in WTO Dispute Settlement: An Introduction to the Problems and Possible Solutions", RIETI Discussion Paper Series 05-E-013, p. 3 <http://www.rieti.go.jp/en/publications/summary/05030017.html>.

51. On the other hand, the absence of an appeal process in Chapter 20 means that discussions about compliance can begin immediately.

52. R. Leal-Arcas, "Choice of Jurisdiction in International Trade Disputes: Going Regional or Global", *Minnesota Journal of International Law* 16 (2007): 51. Gantz refers to panel decisions as a "strong recommendation". Gantz, *Chapter 20*, p. 497.

53. This figure treats the 107 identical claims by individual members of

the Canadian Cattlemen for Fair Trade as one claim. See Department of State <http://www.state.gov/s/l/c14683.htm> (accessed 18 November 2008).

54. The ICSID Rules are contained in the *ICSID Convention, Convention on the Settlement of Investment Disputes between States and Nationals of Other States*, 18 March 1965, 575 U.N.T.S. 159, 4 I.L.M. 532 (1965) [*ICSID Convention*], and the following rules created by the Administrative Council of ICSID under Articles 6(1)(a) to (c) of the Convention and published by ICSID in ICSID Basic Documents (Washington: ICSID, 2006). *Administrative and Financial Regulations; Rules of Procedure for the Institution of Conciliation and Arbitration Proceedings (Institution Rules)*, and the *Rules of Procedure for Arbitration Proceedings (Arbitration Rules)* [*ICSID Arbitration Rules*].

55. The ICSID Additional Facility for the Administration of Conciliation, Arbitration and Fact-Finding Proceedings was created by the Administrative Council of ICSID on 27 September 1978. ICSID, *ICSID Additional Facility Rules for the Administration of Conciliation, Arbitration, and Fact-Finding Proceedings* [1979] Doc. ICSID/11. Schedule C to the Additional Facility sets out the Arbitration (Additional Facility) Rules [*Additional Facility Rules*]. On 5 April 2006, the Administrative Council approved amendments of the ICSID Arbitration Rules and the Additional Facility Rules. These amendments came into effect on 10 April 2006.

56. UN General Assembly, 31st Session, Supplement 17, p. 46, Chapter V, Section C, *Arbitration Rules of the United Nations Commission on International Trade Law*, approved by the UN General Assembly on 15 December 1976, UN Doc. A/31/17, 1976, reprinted in UN, *UNCITRAL Arbitration Rules* (New York: United Nations, 1977).

57. Additional Facility Rules.

58. ICSID Convention, Article 52.

59. NAFTA, Article 1136(5).

60. Ibid., Article 1131.

61. M. Kinnear and R. Hansen, "The Influence of NAFTA Chapter 11 on the BIT Landscape", *University of California Davis Journal of International Law & Policy* 12 (2005): 101.

62. A publicly accessible register is to be maintained by the NAFTA Secretariat. NAFTA, Article 1126(13).

63. NAFTA, Annex 1137.4.

64. Ibid.

65. FTC, Interpretive Note on Transparency, Foreign Affairs and International Trade Canada <http://www.international.gc.ca/trade-agreements-accords-commerciaux/disp-diff/NAFTA-Interpr.aspx?lang=en> (accessed 18 November 2008).

66. *Pope & Talbot v. Canada*, Amended Procedural Order No. 5, Foreign Affairs and International Trade Canada, 17 September 2008 <http://www.dfait-maeci.gc.ca/tna-nac/documents/Amended%20ProceduralOrder5.pdf> (accessed 18 November 2008).

67. This interpretation of the Additional Facility Rules was recently confirmed in *Aguas Provinciales de Santa Fe S.A., Suez, Sociedad General de Aguas de Barcelona S.A. and Interagua Servicios Integrales de Agua S.A. v. The Argentine Republic* (2006), No. ARB/03/17, ICSID <http://www.worldbank.org/icsid/cases/ARB0317-AC-en.pdf> (accessed 18 November 2008).

68. See, similarly, *ICSID Arbitration Rules*, Article 32.

69. See Joint Statement of Canada, Mexico, and the United States, 16 July 2004 <http://www.dfait-maeci.gc.ca/nafta-alena/JS-SanAntonio-en.asp> (accessed 18 November 2008).

70. *UPS v. Canada, Notice of Arbitration*, filed 19 April 2000 [UPS] <http://naftaclaims.com/Disputes/Canada/UPS/UPSNoticeOfArbitration.pdf> (accessed 18 November 2008); *Methanex Corporation v. United States*, Notice of Arbitration, filed 2 December 1999 [*Methanex*] <http://naftaclaims.com/Disputes/USA/Methanex/MethanexNoticeOfArbitration.pdf> (accessed 18 November 2008); *Canfor v. United States*, Notice of Arbitration, filed 9 July 2002 <http://www.naftaclaims.com/Disputes/USA/

Canfor/Canfor%20Notice%20of%20Arbitration%20and%20 Statement%20of%20Claim.pdf> (accessed 18 November 2008).

71. For example, *ADF Group Inc. v. United States* (2003), No. ARB (AF)/00/1, ICSID, reproduced in *ICSID Review: Foreign Investment Law Journal* 18 (2003), and Department of State <http:// www.state.gov/documents/organization/16586.pdf> (accessed 18 November 2008).

72. NAFTA party states other than the one complained against are entitled, as of right, to make submissions regarding issues related to the interpretation of NAFTA. NAFTA, Article 1128.

73. P. Dumberry, "The Admissibility of Amicus Curiae Briefs in NAFTA Chapter 11 Proceedings: Some Remarks on the Methanex Case, A Precedent Likely to be Followed by Other NAFTA Arbitral Tribunals", *Swiss Arbitration Association Bulletin* (2001): 75.

74. In 1998, the WTO Appellate Body held that panels could receive amicus briefs from non-governmental organizations. See *United States — Import Prohibition on Shrimp and Shrimp Products* (1998), WTO Doc. WT/DS58/AB/R (Appellate Body Report).

75. This expression comes from American usage.

76. *Methanex.*

77. *UPS.*

78. FTC, Statement on Non-Disputing Party Participation, Foreign Affairs and International Trade Canada, 7 October 2003 <http:// www.dfait-maeci.gc.ca/nafta-alena/Nondisputing-en.pdf> (accessed 18 November 2008).

79. NAFTA Article 1136(1) provides that awards "have no binding force except between the disputing parties and in respect of the particular case". Interpretations of NAFTA provisions by the FTC are binding, but the Statement on Non-disputing Party Participation does not purport to be an interpretation of NAFTA. NAFTA, Article 1131.

80. The amendments apply to all Additional Facility Arbitrations and ICSID Arbitrations commenced after 10 April 2006.

81. *UNCITRAL Rules*, Rule 21; ICSID Arbitration Rules, Rule 41; Additional Facility Rules, Article 45.

82. See J.J. Coe, "The Mandate of Chapter 11 Tribunals-Jurisdiction and Related Questions", in *NAFTA Investment Law and Arbitration: Past Issues, Current Practice, Future Prospects*, edited by T. Weiler (Ardsley: Transnational, 2004), p. 238.

83. *Ethyl Corporation v. Canada*, Notice of Arbitration, Foreign Affairs and International Trade Canada, 14 April 1997 <http://www.dfait-maeci.gc.ca/tna-nac/documents/ethyl1.pdf> (accessed 21 November 2008).

84. Ibid.

85. *Waste Management, Inc. v. United Mexican States* (2000), Case no. ARB (AF)/98/2 (ICSID Additional Facility) <http://naftaclaims.com/Disputes/Mexico/Waste/WasteFinalAwardDismiss Jurisdiction.pdf> (accessed 18 November 2008).

86. *UPS.*

87. *Methanex.*

88. *Chemtura Corporation v. Canada* (2008), Confidentiality Order <http://www.international.gc.ca/trade-agreements-accords-commerciaux/assets/pdfs/Confidentialityorder.pdf> (accessed 17 November 2008).

J. Anthony VanDuzer is an Associate Professor at the Faculty of Law Common Law Section, University of Ottawa, Canada.

7
WINNERS AND LOSERS IN ASEAN ECONOMIC INTEGRATION
A Perspective from Vietnam

Vo Tri Thanh

International economic integration has been a profound trend over the past couple of decades. The process took place in almost all parts of the world, with participation from almost all economically active countries and territories with expectations resting on both theoretical and empirical evidence of its benefits. These benefits are, however, largely in net terms. Various benefits of economic integration process are widely acknowledged, such as more efficient allocation of resources, competition-induced efficiency improvement and technological progress, domestic institutional and economic reforms, etc. Yet these benefits come together with challenges and/or costs in several aspects, from promoting sustainable economic growth to reduction of poverty and income gap, for each participating country.

At the regional level, international economic integration might also widen the development gap across participating countries and territories since they have different capacity to effectively grasp the opportunities and mitigate the risks brought about by economic integration, even if their commitments are uniform. For the region of Southeast Asia, widening development gap is among the major risks in economic integration, as the regional countries are vastly heterogeneous in terms of economic development level, culture, social progress, and political system.

This paper discusses the benefits and costs of ASEAN economic integration from the perspective of Vietnam — a member of the Association of Southeast Asian Nations (ASEAN). The paper is structured as follows. Section 1 briefly compares the common theoretical understanding with actual empirical observations of the impact of economic integration. Section 2 then contends that the development gap across ASEAN member countries can be narrowed through economic integration, and makes policy recommendations as to how this can be realized. Section 3 subsequently summarizes the lessons from Vietnam's experience in poverty reduction.

1. Impact of Economic Integration: Theory and Empirical Observations

There is a vast literature on the impacts of deepening international economic integration. Several findings are commonly agreed on. First, trade liberalization is itself a "win-win game", rather than a "zero-sum-game". That is, trade liberalization is not the process wherein the benefits to one economy come totally at the expense of its partners. Instead, trade liberalization leads to welfare improvement for all trading partners. Second, most studies assert that globalizers seem to be winners. Even if trade liberalization is carried out unilaterally, the benefits can be realized since resource allocation becomes less distorted. Third, economic integration is argued to have positive impact on poverty reduction. With wider and deeper trade liberalization, the involved country can better exploit its comparative advantages and allocate resources more efficiently, thereby attaining higher economic growth and lower poverty incidence.

Notwithstanding the general consensus on the impacts of economic integration, actual observation and classification of the impacts embody various dimensions of complexity and difficulty. The meanings of "winners" and "losers" are yet to be clear or widely agreed upon. While the net benefits to each economy can be determined within the framework of economic model, this is not robust to changes in the invoked assumptions and/or model specification. Quite often, the models in use fail to incorporate social and/or political aspects. The documented net benefits, therefore, may be too simple to be a good reflection of the actual net effect that economic integration has on the economy. In this respect, the concepts of "winners" and "losers" can be used with different meanings when comparing between countries and when comparing industries/sectors within any specific economy. Besides, even if all involved economies in economic integration acquire gains in absolute terms, those gains can be different so that some economies outperform others in relative terms. Accordingly, the development gaps within these economies can actually be widened over time. In another aspect, the loss of a small social group might present a political problem. If the political weight of such a group is sufficiently large, the economy may suffer from net loss in economic integration.

Another related problem is how to measure the degree of integration, for adequate assessment of the impacts of integration. The most popular measures of protection, or tendency to refrain from integration, are aggregate measure of supports (AMS) for agriculture and tariff rates for other industries. However, a number of policy instruments can be used as barriers to trade, and the abolition of these instruments in the economy's attempt towards economic integration cannot be properly accounted for. Other economic aspects, such as transportation costs and capital controls, can also be employed as behind-the-border barriers to trade. In fact, the empirical studies on the impacts of economic integration often restrict their focus on the elimination of trade barriers (that is, trade liberalization) and associated impacts. Yet integration now means freer flows of goods, services, investment, capital and people as well as cooperation. Free trade agreements (FTAs) in East Asia, as a profound trend, tend to be comprehensive economic partnerships (CEPs). Failure to identify and quantify all these barriers will prevent good measurement of "integration level".

The interaction between integration and an individual country's domestic reforms also adds a source of complexity to the analytical assessment of the impact of integration. To strengthen competitiveness in the context of integration, any distortions and/or impediments to doing business should be eradicated. Domestic reforms are important measures to achieve this. Unless integration is accompanied by domestic reforms, most benefits will only accrue to trading partners (for example, see Roland-Holst, et al. 2002 for further reference). Besides, the impact on welfare can be either positive or negative depending on several channels, such as relative prices, flexibility of production factor markers, and budget stance.

Last but not least, even if economic integration is beneficial in the long run, its short-term impacts might not be positive in net terms. On the one hand, integration could have a net positive impact on an economy, but also impose the risk for it to fall into the "low cost labour trap" in the long run. The risks associated with increasing inflows of capital and their sudden reversal may leave any economy, whether developed or developing, with enormous challenges. Failure to properly open its capital account may make the economy subject to financial crisis, while deeper integration into the regional and world economy increases its vulnerability to financial crises elsewhere. The short-term impacts can also be overshadowed by the business cycle movements in the economy, raising doubts about the benefits of economic integration and unfavourable associated consequences in economic, social, and even political terms. On the other hand, the future uncertainty about the impact of rising China and India, as reflected by their increasing importance in international flows of goods, services, and capital, and in redistribution of economic power and income, creates both opportunities and challenges to other participants in economic integration.

The actual complexities embodied in assessing the impacts of integration have several implications. First of all, more theoretical studies are needed, so that the channels of effect of integration can be properly identified and captured to a fuller extent. Future studies in the field may also focus on modelling the interaction between economic integration and domestic reforms. Future studies are also vital in identifying and/or suggesting measures to manage foreign capital inflows in the context of economic integration, so that domestic macroeconomic stability can be sustained. Besides, policy-makers and economists need further case studies on the impacts of economic integration. More specifically, these studies should rest on comparison across industries and/or sectors, on the impacts on individual economies, or on the impacts at the micro-level. Finally, developing a scorecard which monitors the integration progress, thereby ensuring the sustainability of regional integration, should be of no less importance.

2. Narrowing the Development Gap within ASEAN from Economic Integration

The institutionalized integration process in East Asia will be less than successful without strengthening ASEAN integration. In turn,

ASEAN integration could fail if the development gap in ASEAN continues to be widened. Table 7.1 presents some evidences of the development gap within East Asian countries in terms of GDP, GDP per capita, human development index (HDI), total trade, trade openness, etc. Regardless of the measure of development level, ASEAN member countries generally lag far behind other East Asian countries such as China, Republic of Korea and Japan.

TABLE 7.1

Some Development Indicators of East Asian Countries

	GDP (current, US$ bil.)	GDP per capita (current, US$)	HDI value	Rank (177)	Total trade (US$ bil.)	Total trade/GDP (%)
Brunei	11.6	30,269.7	0.894	30	9.3	80.44
Cambodia	7.3	511.3	0.598	131	8.4	115.73
Indonesia	364.8	1,635.5	0.728	107	183.8	50.39
Laos	3.4	596.8	0.601	130	2.0	58.19
Malaysia	150.7	5,769.9	0.811	63	291.7	193.60
Myanmar	...	...	0.583	132	6.6	...
Philippines	117.6	1,362.8	0.771	90	100.6	85.57
Singapore	132.2	29,474.0	0.922	25	510.8	386.51
Thailand	206.3	3,252.3	0.781	78	260.0	126.01
Vietnam	60.8	723.0	0.733	105	84.7	139.25
China	2,644.7	2,016.1	0.777	81	1,761.0	66.59
Republic of Korea	888.0	18,340.8	0.921	26	634.0	71.39
Japan	4,368.4	34,193.6	0.953	8	1,230.0	28.16

Source: Author's compilations from various sources.

Within the ASEAN region, the development gap is also huge. More advanced ASEAN member countries such as Singapore, Brunei, and Malaysia enjoy relatively high GDP per capita, high HDIs (in both value and ranking), while these indicators are relatively low for others such as Vietnam, Laos, Cambodia, and Myanmar. Narrowing the development gap within ASEAN should therefore be among the core objectives of the integration process in East Asia in general and in Southeast Asia in particular.

Several approaches can be put forward to address the issue of narrowing the development gap in ASEAN. As suggested by Table 7.1, the first approach to the problem of narrowing the development gap in ASEAN relies on the key "gap indicators" we should think of. Underlying this approach is the idea that development gaps are multidimensional and interdisciplinary, just as the concept of development. An approach of the type is "4-I" — income, infrastructure, integration, and institutional gaps — which is proposed in Bui Truong Giang and Vo Tri Thanh (2007). The basic ideas for the choice are as follows. The income indicators, including HDI, can depict the progress of the country in the catching-up process. Meanwhile, infrastructure, integration, and institution all matter for economic growth and development. Other things being equal, an improvement in each of the indicator reflects a progress towards development. More importantly, improvements in the concerned aspects enlarge the sets of choices available to the people, as well as their capability to exploit benefits from the newer choices.

The above approach has both advantages and disadvantages. Relying upon available indicators, the approach can be used for monitoring the development gap reduction. Besides, it can be used for identifying some (significant) causalities or the areas where the gaps remain prevalently sizeable. Subsequently, the areas and/or policies which need to be prioritized can be identified. Nevertheless, this approach may rely too much on *ex-post* observations of the indicators, with imprecise implications for the future (and the policies). Failure to obtain the required indicators on a timely basis may also hinder the effectiveness of the approach in actual applications. As such, further analyses and, if necessary, modifications to the approach are required.

The second approach to narrowing the intra-ASEAN development gap is about the reforms pursued by each newer member country — Cambodia, Laos, Myanmar, and Vietnam (CLMV), possible cooperation among themselves, and external assistance. Some lessons can be drawn from the reforms in each of these newer member countries. Joining ASEAN and participating in the agreements under the ASEAN umbrella, the newer member countries receive two major types of external assistance. The first one is special and differential treatment (SDT), which allows a longer period of liberalization and/or easier access to other members' markets. The second one is technical assistance. However, the SDT could encourage rent-seeking activities, rather than mere attempts to undertake reforms of the countries in dire need. To catch up with other ASEAN member countries effectively, the CLMV — as transition economies — should also focus on institutional-building and -strengthening.

Notwithstanding its presence, the effectiveness of the Initiative for ASEAN Integration (IAI) remains questionable. The key impediments to its effective implementation are the lack of financial resource, capability, and collaboration/incorporation with other assistance programmes. Narrowing the development gap within ASEAN also relies on the cooperation within CLMV. However, the efficiency and effectiveness of such cooperation are limited. Among the reasons are the inadequate pools of human and financial resources, small market size, while their trade structures are more competitive than complementary. The only advantage that CLMV can take in strengthening their cooperation lies in their ability to learn from and to talk more easily with each other, thanks to their similarities in development levels and issues encountered in joining ASEAN integration.

The above discussion of the approaches gives rise to some policy recommendations as to how the development gap within ASEAN can be narrowed in the context of regional economic integration. First, it is of utmost importance that "narrowing the development gaps in ASEAN" should be a key mission in any community-building strategy/action in the region. In particular, it is important to develop a set of quantitative and qualitative indicators for assessing/monitoring the progress in ASEAN integration and reducing the development gap in ASEAN. In this respect, the Economic Research Institute for ASEAN and East Asia, as a think-tank for regional governments, may play an important role. Besides, more flexibility should be allowed in applying "core" principles of ASEAN while taking into account the interests/benefits of CLMV. Furthermore, regional agreements should incorporate SDT, which should be only temporary and firmly implemented to avoid any distorted incentives.

Second, there appears a need for transformation of the IAI into a new initiative/programme, perhaps the Initiative for East Asian Integration (IEAI). The new initiative for integration at a broader level (that is, IEAI) has a number of tasks/functions to fulfil. On the one hand, the proposed initiative should seek to review the regional development gap, and to recommend major assistance policies. Furthermore, it should incorporate consultations with individual newer member countries for understanding the needs for assistance and, subsequently, for recommending relevant and suitable assistance programmes. In a more or less related aspect, it should have collaboration with other international institutions and donors to ensure effectiveness and efficiency of the assistance programmes. On the other hand, the cooperation scheme "2+1", that is, cooperation between two or more low income countries with financial/technical support from a more advanced country/international institution, needs to be encouraged.

3. Lessons from Vietnam's Experiences

Since the initiation of *Doi Moi* [Renovation] process in 1986, Vietnam has undertaken a market-oriented transition from a centrally-planned economy. In 1988–89, the country undertook a radical and comprehensive reform aimed at stabilizing and opening the economy, and at enhancing freedom of choice for economic agents and competition so as to fundamentally alter its system of economic management. Simultaneously, Vietnam accelerated its proactive international economic integration process and saw this as among the key measures to enhance economic growth and development. Till 2007, the country had been a signatory to a number of trade and investment agreements, at both bilateral and multilateral levels. Vietnam has also concluded necessary multilateral and bilateral negotiations to acquire accession to the World Trade Organization (WTO) in 2007.

Thanks to continuous and comprehensive domestic reforms and proactive economic integration, Vietnam has made numerous socioeconomic achievements during the years 1990–2008. Economic growth has been rapid and continuous, reaching 7.2 per cent per year on average in the 1990s, 7.5 per cent per year on average in 2001–05, 8.4 per cent in 2006, 8.5 per cent in 2007, and roughly 6.2 per cent in 2008. With the trade agreements and trade promotion activities in place, Vietnam's trade has expanded

Figure 7.1

Export, Import, and Trade Balance of Vietnam, 1990–2008

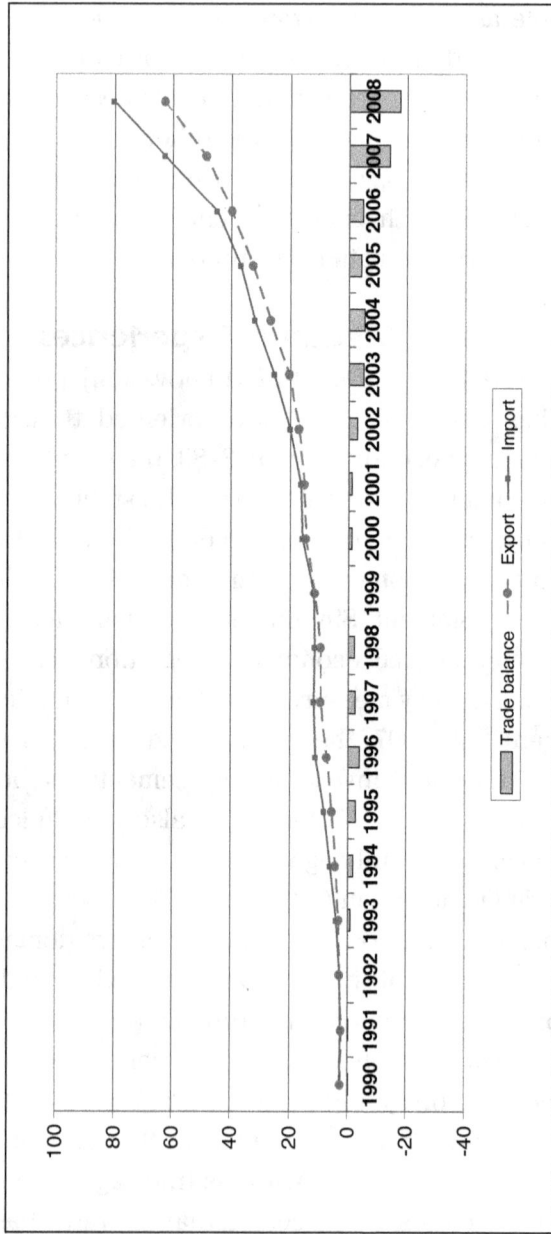

Source: General Statistics Office.

continuously during the period of 1990–2008 (see Figure 7.1). Both exports and imports have risen at impressive paces, with the average growth rate of the former being slower than that of the latter. In 1990–2008, high export growth was a key driver of economic growth in Vietnam, while import helped provide necessary intermediate inputs, machinery, and technology to support export-oriented production. Foreign investment, being relatively stagnant in 1998–2003, started to go up rapidly since 2004, in the number of projects, and registered and implemented capital. The poverty incidence was also reduced from about 70 per cent in the 1980s to 53 per cent in 1993, 37 per cent in 1998, 29 per cent in 2002, 19.5 per cent in 2004, 15.7 per cent in 2007, and 13.1 per cent in 2008.[1]

Nevertheless, the achievements may still be less than outstanding. Despite rapid and continuous economic growth, its sustainability remains questionable. Over the years 1990–2008, there are doubts about the quality of growth, since it has relied on excessive state investment which was inefficient and incorporated sizeable wastages. The bottlenecks in infrastructure, institution, and human resources persist. Without measures to improve its human resources and to move up in the value chain, Vietnam also runs the risk of falling into the so-called "low-cost labour trap" in the long run. Notwithstanding impressive progress in poverty reduction, still, poverty incidence remains substantial in the remote, isolated and ethnic regions. The income and asset gaps have been widening across social groups and across geographical regions. The income gap between urban-rural areas went down continuously, from approximately 2.3 in 1999 to 2.09 in 2006. Meanwhile, that between the geographical regions with highest and lowest average income rose from almost 2.51 in 1999 to 3.15 in 2002, before decreasing to 2.86 in 2006 (for further reference, see Vo Tri Thanh and Nguyen Anh Duong 2009).

The socioeconomic successes in Vietnam in 1990–2008 stem largely from the reforms which the country has sought to enlarge the set of economic and business opportunities for its people and its economic agents. This has been reflected in policy efforts in various directions. First, Vietnam officially acknowledged private ownership and rights of doing business, while eliminating various market entry restrictions. Second, the country has adopted bold and comprehensive market-oriented reforms. Firms' access to land and credit has been significantly improved, thanks to the government's measures to develop markets of production factors. Third, the country has been actively engaged in trade liberalization and integration. Apart from those efforts to enlarge the set of available opportunities, Vietnam has also been determined in strengthening the right choices. While making policy adjustments to ensure macroeconomic stability, the country also undertook longer-term measures to improve the skills of its human resources and institutional capacity.

From Vietnam's experience, the poverty incidence is determined by a number of factors. Growth in GDP per capita has been closely associated with the pace of poverty reduction. Yet the impact of growth on poverty depends not only on the rate of growth, but on the composition of growth and structure of the economy as well. The rapid growth in labour-intensive industries such as textiles/garment, fishery product processing, etc. and its importance in poverty reduction have been a remarkable experience. Such a rapid growth was in turn due to the integration-induced trade expansion of and attraction of FDI inflows into the industries. Conversely, macroeconomic fluctuations and external shocks can have devastating effects on the poor. The surge in inflation, particularly after Vietnam's accession to the WTO, has at times threatened to make certain social groups fall back into poverty. This is among the reasons why Vietnam has striven to maintain macroeconomic stability over the past years. In another aspect, infrastructure development has been crucial to growth and poverty reduction, as it reduces the costs of doing business and/or undertaking economic activities, thereby enhancing the economic participation of the poor. Finally, the specific (targeted) programmes have played a very essential role in reducing poverty, especially the "hard-core" poverty.

Identifying and understanding the reasons for widening income and asset gaps in Vietnam may also be useful for future attempts towards development. Various arguments have been put forward to explain why income and asset gaps seem to get larger over time. The first one is mismanagement in the process of reallocating assets and land of state-owned enterprises (SOEs), which made transition less than different from the mere reallocation/redistribution of SOE assets and land — the key assets owned by the state. Consequently, the richer groups received a larger share of income and assets than the poor, thereby deepening inequality in income and asset distribution. Another argument is the lack of access to new opportunities. In spite of enormous efforts in institutional reforms and infrastructure development, the process failed to keep up the pace with the enlargement of economic and business opportunities. As such, many new opportunities were left unexploited, and this is a more prevalent issue among the poorer ones. Finally, widening income and asset gaps in Vietnam can also be explained by the lack of capability to exploit benefits from newer opportunities. The poor people in Vietnam, being without adequate skills and education, may fail to recognize the opportunities when they come, or fail to realize those opportunities for their own sake.

From the above experience in 1990–2008, Vietnam is seen to make enormous socioeconomic achievements, from economic growth, trade expansion to poverty reduction. However, certain issues remain with, in particular, the quality of growth, widening income and asset gaps, and further reduction of poverty incidence. With its limited resources, the country is unable to deal with all issues, challenges and weaknesses at the same time. Identifying the priorities for development objectives within the contemporary macroeconomic situation has always been critical, and has been done quite well in the country. Together with other policy measures in a broader framework of market-oriented reforms, this has contributed to fulfilling socioeconomic development objectives in Vietnam. With a view to further enhance its own development and reduce the gap with more advanced ASEAN member countries, Vietnam should continue its efforts. In this respect, cooperation with other newer ASEAN members while seeking external assistance has proven to be useful.

Note

1.   With the adjustment of poverty line in 2005, it should be 16–17 per cent.

References

Bui Truong Giang and Vo Tri Thanh. "Approach to Development Gaps in ASEAN: A Vietnamese Perspective". *ASEAN Economic Bulletin* 24, no. 1 (April 2007): 164–80.

Ronald-Holst, D., et al. "Vietnam's Accession to the World Trade Organization: Economic Projection to 2020". *Discussion Papers in Economic Policy Analysis No. 0204*, CIEM-NIAS, 2002.

Vo Tri Thanh and Nguyen Anh Duong. "Assessing Socio-Economic Developments in Vietnam in 1988–2008". Paper prepared for the Asian Development Bank. Forthcoming.

Vo Tri Thanh is the Director of Department for International Integration Studies at the Central Institute for Economic Management (CIEM), Hanoi, Vietnam.

8
WINNERS AND LOSERS IN INTERNATIONAL ECONOMIC INTEGRATION
The Distributional Effects of NAFTA

Dan Ciuriak

1. Introduction

Trade, in its various modes, is the extension of commerce across borders. The basic economics of trade are thus the basic economics of the market economy in general: it is all about the boost in productivity from division of labour and specialization. Based on economic theory, trade is a win-win proposition — which is another way of saying it is a positive sum game. Thus, economic incentives naturally induce trade; absent restrictions, to trade is the norm — not to trade is abnormal.

What is true in the abstract is also for the most part true in the real world. Trade is a win-win proposition, at least at a sufficiently aggregate level and conditional upon a certain minimum level of competence in economic policy and governance. On this point there is little dispute. Hence we observe a trade-intensive global economy.

The disputes arise when it comes to questions of how best to take advantage of trade opportunities (for example, how much, how fast, and with which trading partners a country should liberalize, questions which continue to be debated intensely with respect to developing countries); and whether, under particular given conditions, additional trade is beneficial (a question that is presently under debate in developed countries, and particularly in the United States, about the impact of trade given the extreme differences in wage compensation between the United States and China, Mexico and other developing countries). This is one reason why the political hurdles of advancing multilateral trade liberalization in the context of the Doha Round or regional/bilateral free trade agreements have proven to be so high.

But even if trade liberalization and the international economic integration it promotes is a win-win proposition at the national level, when one drills down from the aggregate national level to the industry level, and further to the firm and household level, it becomes evident that the distribution of costs and benefits is almost inevitably uneven. And this makes international economic integration controversial and politically difficult regardless of the economy-wide benefits.

Liberalization of trade in goods and services in normal circumstances results in a transfer of producer surplus to consumers. But not all consumers benefit equally — given differences in consumption patterns and differentiation in the initial level of tariffs or barriers to services trade, some consumers will benefit more than others. And some may lose if their preferred products are driven out of the market or if prices go up because of terms of trade effects or if competition in their particular local market is reduced through industry consolidation.

Reduction in border barriers intensifies competition for industries in their domestic market but also improves access to foreign markets. Through the operation of comparative advantage, some industries will inevitably gain more than others — and some may lose. The same is true within industries as well: given differences in efficiency across firms, some firms will gain (even in declining industries) while others will lose — and some may be forced to exit entirely. In geographically heterogeneous economies, the impact will vary across regions, between border regions and those more remote, and between urban and rural areas. Adjustment costs will thus necessarily vary across industries, across firms within industries, and across regions.

And, since the incidence of adjustment costs in terms of job impacts tends to be much narrower than the distribution of benefits, there are likely to be significant net distributional effects at the household level.

The benefits and costs will also vary across the economies that are parties to the trade and investment agreements that foster integration — and the impact on third parties will also vary depending on the incidence of trade diversion and creation effects.

There are other lenses as well through which distributional effects can be anticipated — including, *inter alia*, between the environment and the economy (given different intensities of pollution across industries), across genders (given differences in industrial employment patterns of men and women), between social and economic policy outcomes (given impacts on government revenues or regulatory changes through policy harmonization), between labour and capital (and the other broadly defined factors of production, land and technology), between skilled and unskilled workers and, given the length of time that full adjustment can take, across generations as well (an older "adjusted" worker may in fact never work again).

There is, in short, a kaleidoscopic differentiation of impacts flowing from economic integration. Outcomes are not going to meet some norm such as Pareto efficiency, even with successful agreements. In turn, this explains the complex consultative processes that democratic governments use to get "buy-in" to trade and investment agreements, the profusion of measures to deal with "sensitive" sectors, including extended phase-in periods and adjustment support, and the use of side agreements to deal with the side effects of the economic measures being implemented.

These complications should not deter the pursuit of trade opportunities, but they are a reason to prepare well to deal with the differential impacts. And in this regard, the experience under existing experiments in international integration is well worth study.

The North American Free Trade Agreement (NAFTA) which came into force on 1 January 1995, subsuming the Canada-U.S. Free Trade Agreement that had taken effect in 1989, certainly achieved its central objective of expanding trade and investment amongst the parties. At the same time, the agreement remains controversial.

On the one hand, notwithstanding the success in expanding trade and investment amongst the parties, there has been a disappointing lack of convergence in income levels between Canada and the United States. Some in Canada see this as due to failure to realize a fully integrated North American economy, which they blame in part on the static nature of NAFTA — it is just a free trade agreement and lacks institutional levers to address new issues such as movement of people, technology and services which have become more important with the growth of the "new economy".

On the other hand, specific features of NAFTA continue to elicit opposition. One example is the Chapter 11 investor-state dispute settlement regime that grants foreign investors recourse to arbitral tribunals in the member states that is not available to domestic investors. In the United States, a causal link has been drawn between NAFTA and the controversial surge of illegal immigrants. The argument in this case is that the large-scale job reduction in Mexico's agricultural sector and the unexpected failure of increased trade with the United States to drive up Mexican manufacturing wages have been the driving factor behind poor peasants seeking work in the United States, legally or illegally (Uchitelle 2007),[1] with attendant social issues and negative consequences for the U.S. labour market. A possible renegotiation of NAFTA was an issue in the 2008 U.S. presidential election. Similarly, in Mexico, the cliff-hanger 2006 presidential election was in part a referendum on Mexico's trade-oriented policy framework, the centrepiece of which is of course NAFTA. In short, the differential impacts of NAFTA continue to matter very much, long after its inception.

This note considers the evidence on a number of distributional impacts of NAFTA and draws out the implications for policy-makers in ASEAN and elsewhere as they contemplate how best to take advantage of international commerce to enhance economic performance and improve living standards.

2. Short-run Costs and Long-term Gains: What is the Balance?

Canada pursued free trade with the United States for a number of reasons. The narrow objective was to reduce risks from the new protectionism rising in the United States in the 1980s in the form of greater use of trade remedies. At the same time, it was part of a more general shift in economic policy orientation in Canada aimed at increasing economic efficiency through various measures largely focused on the supply-side of the economy, including regulatory and tax reforms, fiscal consolidation, disinflation, and a new opening to foreign investment. In other words, the policy objective was to put the Canadian economy on a faster growth trajectory, which would generate sustained longer-term gains that would cumulatively outweigh any short-run adjustment costs.

In Canada, free trade affected mainly manufacturing, apart from the automotive sector which had earlier been integrated pursuant to the 1964 Canada-United States Auto Pact, a managed-trade rather than free-trade deal (Holmes 1992). In agriculture, continental integration was deepened only in a few sectors as Canada kept its highly protected supply-managed sectors and institutions like the Wheat Board off the table. Issues raised by agricultural integration are addressed below. Services were also little affected by the deal although there was some formal liberalization in the financial sector.[2] Intellectual property measures affecting Canada were, however, included and these likely had a fairly significant impact in distributional terms, as will be discussed below as well.

The Canada-U.S. FTA was implemented at a cyclical peak, just as the North American economy was poised to go into recession. The deterioration of Canada's fiscal situation as the recession developed not only constrained discretionary counter-cyclical stimulus but forced pro-cyclical fiscal consolidation to limit the widening of the deficit. At the same time, the anti-inflationary policy of the Bank of Canada sustained higher valuations of the Canadian dollar than otherwise would have obtained. The adjustment pressures for Canada's manufacturing sector generated by trade liberalization were thus compounded by the macroeconomic context.[3]

Subsequently, helped initially by depreciation of the Canadian dollar and the global cyclical upswing of the mid-1990s, the Canadian economy entered a sustained growth period which featured a significant and sustained improvement in macroeconomic fundamentals. Some of this improved performance is generally credited to the trade reforms and North American integration. In short, there were textbook-like short-run adjustment costs but longer-run macroeconomic benefits. What were the dimensions of these costs and benefits, their incidence and their distributional implications?

The dimensions of the short-run adjustment in manufacturing at the industry level have been assessed, controlling for the prevailing macroeconomic conditions. Trefler (2004) estimates that total manufacturing employment was reduced by 5 per cent (or about 100,000 jobs) while labour productivity in manufacturing rose 6 per cent. In the import-competing manufacturing sectors facing the steepest tariff cuts (which included one-third of all industries at the four-digit standard industrial classification (SIC) level, facing tariff reductions ranging from 5 to 33 per cent and averaging 10 per cent),[4] employment fell by 12 per cent while labour productivity rose by 15 per cent; Trefler estimates that at least half of the productivity gin was due to the exit and/or contraction of low-productivity plants.

The employment losses were not offset by gains in the export-oriented industries which benefited most from U.S. tariff cuts. Trefler's study indicates no significant impact on employment levels in this group of industries; the benefits were realized in the form of a sharp increase in productivity (15 per cent). One unexpected result was that Canadian export-oriented firms that benefitted from U.S. tariff cuts also made significant gains in their domestic business at the expense of Canadian non-exporters.

The manufacturing job losses stemming from the FTA contributed to a steep increase in Canada's unemployment rate in the early 1990s. The unemployment rate rose from 7.5 per cent in 1989 to a cyclical peak of 11.4 per cent in 1993. However, the full impact of unemployment was masked by a sharp decline in the participation rate due to a discouraged worker effect. From a peak of 67.8 per cent in 1990, the participation rate fell to the 65 per cent range from 1994 through 1997. This decline featured the first decline for women's labour force participation in the post-war era and a fall in youth participation to a twenty-year low. Notably, the Canadian participation rate fell below the U.S. rate, which continued to increase in this period, reversing the usual relationship. Taking into account discouraged workers, Canada's actual unemployment rate was probably about 14.5 per cent in 1993, an increase of about 7 per cent from the cyclical low in 1989. Manufacturing sector job losses directly attributable to the FTA accounted for about 0.7 per cent of this, or about one-tenth of the net job loss during this period. Taking into account knock-on effects (supplier industry and service sector jobs dependent on manufacturing), the job loss due to structural adjustment to the FTA was substantially larger at about 170,000, accounting for perhaps 1.14 per cent of the increase in unemployment or roughly one-sixth of the total increase in unemployment during this period.[5]

Canada's labour market eventually recovered. The unemployment rate regained its 1989 low by 1999 and the participation rate its 1990 high by 2007. Accordingly, the labour market impacts can be described as transient. There are reasons to suppose that many of those who bore the adjustment costs in the early part of the post-FTA period might well have subsequently more than made up the short-term losses, in part because the discouraged worker effect was strongest for young people and was mirrored in extended schooling.[6] And, in the overall scheme of things, the Canadian economy that emerged from the structural adjustment was more competitive and productive and created opportunities for subsequent generations that, *ceteris paribus*, most likely would not have been there absent the trade-driven adjustment. Notably, after 1993, the Canadian economy grew faster than the U.S. economy (cumulative growth of 58 per cent versus

53 per cent in the United States over the period 1994–2007[7]), with much less fiscal stimulus, and with an overall shift from a current account deficit to a sustained surplus.

However, the adjustment period was sufficiently long that it is likely that for some individuals who lost jobs in that early period, the losses were permanent. Moreover, given that longitudinal studies show those losing jobs lose fall behind significantly in terms of cumulative income compared to those who retain jobs (Frenette 2007), and in light of the fact that the 1990s featured an increase in long-term unemployment and an increase in the share of employment accounted for by irregular work, it is likely that for many individuals, the transient loss in lifetime earnings could not be made up through subsequent higher-paying work.

As regards the economy-wide balance of long-term gains versus short-run costs, the evidence does not fall neatly into place to support the expected result that the former outweigh the latter.[8] I find two points particularly troublesome in this regard.

First, although as noted above Canada grew faster than the United States during the period of rapid integration (4.0 per cent average annual real growth over the period 1994–2000 versus 3.9 per cent for the United States), the margin was narrow and in any event could hardly be credited entirely to improved competitiveness due to trade liberalization, since this was also a period during which the Canadian dollar trended down. Moreover, while Canada continued to grow faster than the United States in the subsequent period (2001–07) when the Canadian dollar trended up, this period was one of partial de-integration as the United States raised the costs of border transit with its post-9/11 measures.[9] Overall, in the extended period of improved performance (1994–2007), Canada only made up half the ground lost *vis-à-vis* the United States during the period of adjustment (1989–93).

Second, a comparison with Australia, the most similar economy to Canada in terms of trends in exchange rates and impacts of commodity prices, points in the same direction. A Statistics Canada study found that, during the pre-FTA period 1983–88, Canada and Australia had the same average per capita GDP growth of 3.0 per cent (Harchaoui, et al. 2003). Over the subsequent period to 1995 which covered Canada's adjustment to the FTA, Canada's per capita GDP growth slowed to 0.4 per cent while Australia's fell only to 1.6 per cent. Then in the next half decade to 2000, the period of rapid integration, Canada edged out Australia but by only the slimmest margin, 3.0 per cent to 2.9 per cent. Again, the improvement in the post-adjustment phase was not sufficient to make up the lost ground during the adjustment period.

The same study also compared Canadian and Australian productivity trends. Canada has historically realized its growth to a greater extent through labour utilization and less through productivity growth than Australia. For example, in the immediate pre-FTA period (1983–88), Australian labour productivity grew by an average of 1.3 per cent compared to Canada's 0.9 per cent. Canada matched Australia in productivity growth during the period of adjustment of the early 1990s, with both economies realizing 1.2 per cent labour productivity growth (Harchaoui, et al. 2003; p. 4). However, Australia again surged ahead of Canada in the second half of the 1990s by an even wider margin than in the pre-FTA period, outpacing Canada 2.5 per cent to 1.5 per cent.[10] This suggests that the productivity growth in the early 1990s documented by Trefler (2004) was largely a one-time level shift that was for the most part realized through the closure of manufacturing plants with the lowest productivity performance, rather than a shift to a higher growth path for the surviving portion of the economy. Canada's productivity performance compared to the United States thus continues to be a policy issue for Canada (see Figure 8.1).

That the dynamic labour productivity gains were comparatively modest is supported by the evidence concerning the impact of the FTA on manufacturing wages in Canada. Trefler reports an almost negligible 3 per cent rise in wages spread over eight years, although he notes that the more important thing is that wages did not go down as was expected by some analysts prior to the FTA, based on the theory that competition with lower-wage southern United States plants would drive down wages in the more highly unionized labour market (Trefler 2004, pp. 26–27).

3. Trade Deepening and Income Distribution

One of the main concerns with trade deepening is the impact on income distribution. The core economic theory that draws a link between increased trade and changes in income distribution is the theory of comparative advantage. In the original formulation of this theory in the 1800s by English economists Robert Torrens and David Ricardo, comparative advantage was explained largely in terms of the availability of arable land (for example, America was rich in arable land compared to England and thus it paid America to specialize in grain production and England in manufactures). A subsequent formulation of this theory by Swedish economists Eli Heckscher and Bertin Ohlin in the early 1900s based the existence of comparative advantage on differences in endowments of capital and labour across countries.

However compelling the factor endowments theory was to economists, predictions based on this version of the theory of comparative advantage and its corollary of factor price equalization were routinely contradicted by the facts.[11] Accordingly, more

FIGURE 8.1
Canada-U.S. Relative Productivity Level, 1961–2006 (1961 = 100)

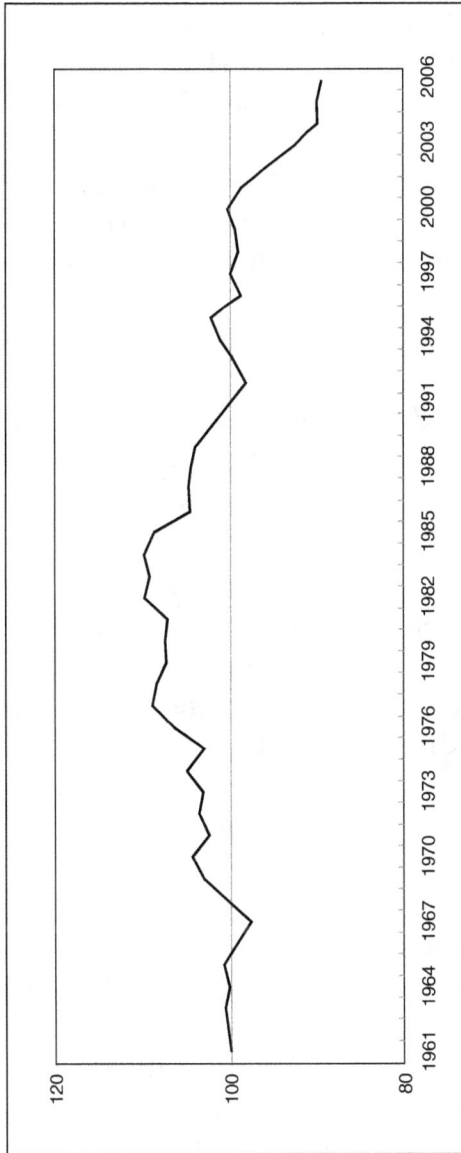

Source: "The Canadian Productivity Review: Long-term Productivity Growth in Canada and the United States 1961 to 2006", Statistics Canada, Catalogue no. 15-206-XIE — No. 013 (2007).

complex articulations of the link between trade and income distribution, which rely on the interaction between trade, technological change (which, it is argued is "skill-biased") and other factors, have been proposed to explain the observed widening in the returns to skilled and unskilled labour in some countries.

Applied to Canada's North American trade, the factor proportions version of the theory of comparative advantage predicts that free trade with the United States should have narrowed wage differentials within Canada, the relatively less skill-abundant economy in this dyad; conversely, it predicts that free trade with lower-wage Mexico should have led to widening wage differentials. The combined impact — widening or narrowing — would depend on the relative strength of the two effects. In short, factor proportions theory falls short of an unequivocal prediction concerning NAFTA's impact on income differentials in Canada.

What does the evidence say? The incidence of low income in Canada did rise during the period of adjustment to the FTA with the United States (see Figure 8.2). This was not, however, unusual given the cyclical rise in Canada's unemployment levels. Nor was the rise unusually strong. Moreover, Canada's Gini coefficient[12] remained stable in the narrow range from about 0.35 to about 0.36 from 1980 through 1995 which covered the adjustment period (see Figure 8.3).

Income differentials in Canada did widen in the second half of the 1990s. As shown in Figure 8.2, Canada's Gini coefficient for all households rose sharply in the post-NAFTA period, moving up to the 0.37–0.38 range in 1996–97 and then ticking up again in 2000–02 to about 0.39 where it has remained in the two years of data since. Between 1995 and 2002, it increased from 0.357 to 0.393. In the view of some this was at least partly attributable to

FIGURE 8.2

Incidence of Low Income and the Unemployment Rate, Canada, 1980–2004

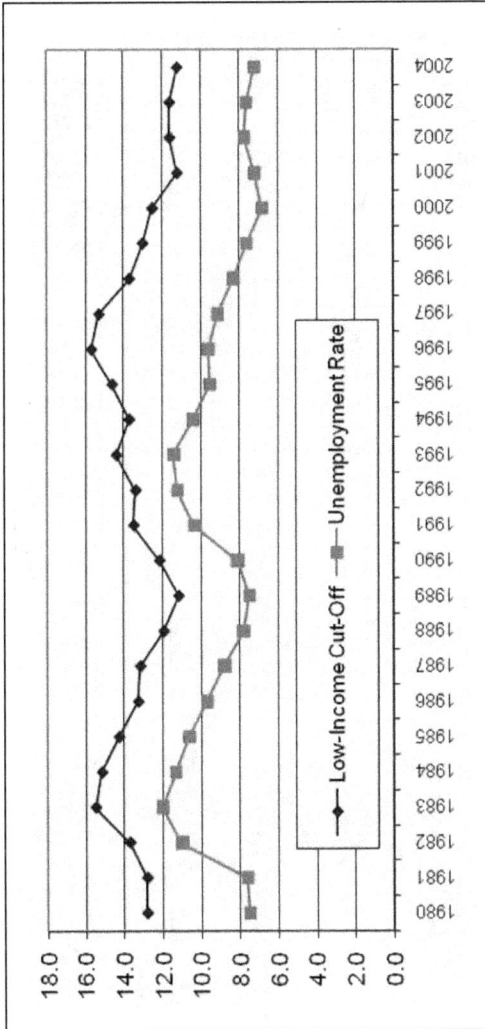

Source: Statistics Canada, *Income in Canada 2004*, 75-202-XIE; and *The Labour Force Survey.* The "low-income cut-off" measures the percentage of all households with income levels at which the percentage of income spent by the household on food, shelter and clothing is 20 per cent more than the share of the average household. It is a conventional measure of relative poverty used in Canada.

FIGURE 8.3

Canada's Gini Coefficient: All Family Units, 1980–2004

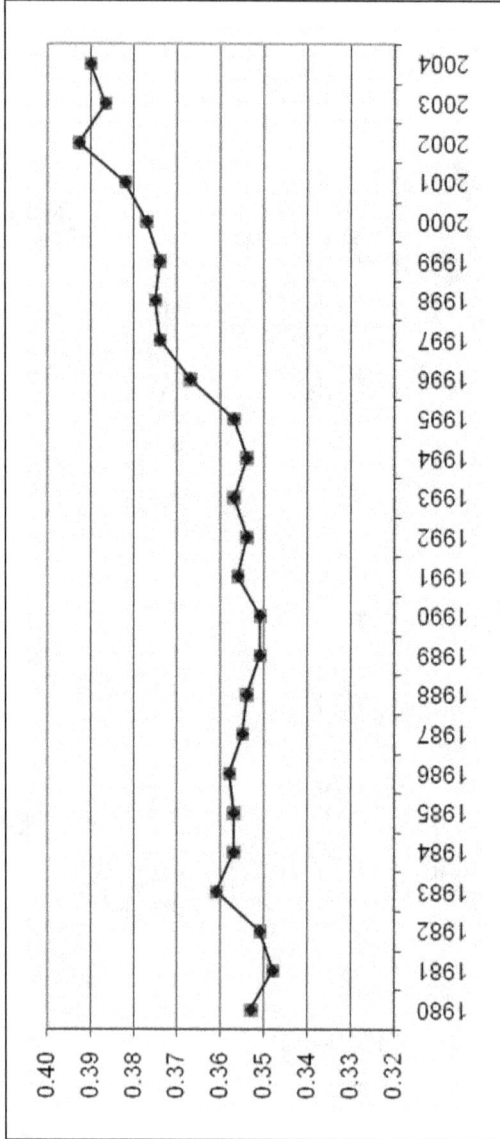

Source: Income in Canada 2004, Statistics Canada 75-202-XIE.

globalization, including North American integration through NAFTA, which included low-wage Mexico.

Canada-Mexico trade did pick up substantially following NAFTA. Romalis (2007) estimated the impact of NAFTA on trade volumes and prices at the six-digit HS classification. He found that the Canada-Mexico trade was boosted by almost 24 per cent by NAFTA, compared to a 5.35 per cent boost to Canada-U.S. trade by the FTA.

However, closer examination of the trends in income distribution points in directions other than increased trade with Mexico for the source of the rise of the Gini coefficient. First, a reduction in benefit levels in Canada's unemployment insurance programme in 1996–97 reduced income support for the quintile of households with the lowest incomes. A partial reversal of these reforms in 2001 resulted in a reduction in low-income prevalence in that year despite an increase in the unemployment rate. Second, a steep rise in the incomes of the top 0.1 per cent of wage and salary earners accounted for the rise in the income share of the quintile of households with the highest incomes. The latter increase has been traced to a steep increase in the generosity of executive compensation based on stock options, a development that was particularly acute in the Anglophone countries (including the United States and the United Kingdom) in the latter part of the 1990s.[13]

Accordingly, the major part of the increased skewness of income distribution in Canada since the mid-1990s was not likely due to NAFTA (or to the implementation of the WTO agreement, which also began in 1995).

Some economists are nonetheless of the view that trade has had a significant impact on income distribution in Canada. For example, Dan Schwanen (2001, p. 177) concludes: "The evidence suggests that increased trade has rewarded the more skilled and experienced workers relative to others. ... Therefore, while trade openness has benefited Canadians in general, it may well have done so at the cost of increased inequality, which impacts social progress overall." Schwanen bases his conclusion on evidence of increased disparity in wages and relies on the notion of skill-bias in technological change to attribute cause to trade. The argument is complicated, however, by two rather key facts: first, not only did wage disparity increase across skill classes but also within skill classes — that is, between "observationally equivalent workers" (Schwanen 2001, p. 175); and second, technological change fails to show signs of skill bias in other countries. On the latter point, Gordon (2001) notes:

> ... proponents of [skill-biased technological change] face the awkward contrast between the U.S. and U.K. on the one hand and Continental Europe on the other. Both the extent of inequality and its change between the 1970 and 1990s are much greater in the U.S. than in Europe, with the U.K. somewhere in between. ... Yet technology flows freely across borders. ... if [skill-biased technological change] was the main cause of rising inequality in the U.S., why did inequality fail to increase in Europe? Clearly, the contrast between Europe and the U.S. causes [skill-biased technological change] to fail even a crude plausibility test, and we must look elsewhere for an explanation (Gordon 2001, pp. 6–7).

4. The Difficulties of Agricultural Trade Integration

For many economies, gaining improved market access for agricultural products is a major trade objective, both to alleviate rural poverty in developing areas and to ease the pressure on urban infrastructure from population shifts into cities. Accordingly, it is important that farmers, especially those on smaller family farms, win from trade liberalization.

This however has often proved to be difficult. Farms are different than factories. They are rural, not urban, and therefore adjustment is much more difficult. They deal with biological matter; nature is not static — it fights back, adapts and innovates. Which in turn raises issues of food safety, transmission of disease, and impacts on the ecology, all of which need to be seen not as random exogenous shocks but as endogenous features of the industrialization of agriculture and agricultural trade. And the political economy of farm sectors tends to be highly idiosyncratic, resulting in often radically different regulatory/administrative frameworks for food production from country to country, including subsidies, price supports, marketing arrangements and so forth.

The climatic and geographic context of Canada and continental United States strongly favours north-south trade over east-west trade, yet there are constant frictions. To pick one example, where the benefits of trade would seem to be easy to identify, consider potatoes. Canada's westernmost province, British Columbia (B.C.) has a small potato industry with about 8,500 acres (3,443 hectares) planted in 2006.[14] B.C. farms meet only about 60 per cent of its potato demand. Conversely, on Canada's Atlantic side, Prince Edward Island (P.E.I.) is a major potato producer with 97,637 acres planted in 2006. B.C. could import potatoes from P.E.I. but it makes more sense to do so from Washington state, which neighbours B.C. and is a major potato producer with some 160,000 acres planted.[15] By the same token, it makes sense for P.E.I. to export some of its crop to the close-by United States. About 10 per cent of P.E.I.'s potato crop is shipped to the United States.

However, there are trade frictions on both sides. The United States Potato Board has a number of market access complaints as it seeks "... the elimination of the anti-dumping duty imposed by British Columbia on fresh U.S. potatoes, the elimination of the Ministerial Exemption (Bulk Easement) restriction on bulk fresh potato exports to Canada and full access for U.S. seed potatoes to Canada".[16] The complaint about the Ministerial Exemption concerns an aspect of Canada's regulatory framework for agricultural produce developed long before the era of free trade to address quality concerns (grading, etc.). As regards the anti-dumping measure, it has been in force since 1984; the tariff is applied seasonally to coincide with the harvest.

At the same time, P.E.I. has had its troubles exporting to the United States. When potato wart virus was identified in a single field on a P.E.I. farm in October 2000, a week later "the United States banned the importation of Island potatoes and demanded severe restrictions on the shipment of Island potatoes even within Canada. The move virtually paralysed the province's multimillion-dollar potato industry and forced many Island farmers into bankruptcy."[17] The United States demanded very detailed farm inspections for several years after, the cost implications of which necessitated federal assistance. P.E.I. farmers suspected this had more to do with protectionism than with the fungus. When another two cases of the wart were identified in 2002, trade was not unduly restricted because of the exacting protocols that were in place — but it is also noteworthy that in the second instance, the United States was having trouble with a different potato disease in eleven of its states.

In short, even when it should be easy, trade in agricultural products can be very hard. The costs are higher than they might appear at first blush — including the costs of periodic disruptions due to outbreaks of disease — and they may be borne by the public purse rather than industry, giving a misleading picture of the actual benefits of trade.

Another example of a type of friction in agricultural trade is provided by wheat. The United States dumps excess agricultural production internationally by giving it away ("food aid"). Canada dumps its excess by selling it on credit to non-creditworthy customers who do not pay back the loan. Canada's method has resulted in the accumulation of a sizeable stock of non-performing loans on the books of Canada's wheat marketing board. These are two different institutional paths to the same objective and neither has anything whatsoever to do with Canada-U.S. trade in wheat. Notably, all Canadian exports to the United States of wheat are on a cash basis and hence do not require debt financing. Nonetheless, the United States conflated the two programmes and countervailed wheat imports from Canada on the basis of food subsidies given by Canada to countries like Iraq.[18] In short, institutional differences are an important hindrance to effective cross-border integration.

Sanitary and phytosanitary (SPS) regimes are amongst the most significant barriers to integration of food markets. This is true even between countries like Canada and the United States which have equally well qualified personnel and overall equivalent regimes. And, of course, they pose much larger barriers when one of the trade partners is a developing country that may not have the infrastructure or cannot afford the costs of the "Cadillac regimes" that are in place in the wealthier industrialized countries. Moreover, even when the SPS hurdles have been successfully overcome, the risk of total disruption of trade always exists. While the example cited above of potato warts is a minor factor in the overall accounting of trade impacts, in some instances the consequences are highly significant for the overall accounts of costs and benefits from trade. A prime example was the outbreak of Bovine Spongiform Encephalopathy (BSE), commonly referred to as "mad cow disease".

The Canada-U.S. FTA provided a modest boost to the integration of the beef industry across the Canada-U.S. border by removing application of quotas and (the already low) tariffs to shipments from the partners (Hahn, et al. 2005). This integration was further boosted by cooperation to reduce trade costs. Under the Restricted Feeder Cattle Project, launched in 1997 on a pilot basis and later rolled out to cover most of the states along the Canada-United States border and Hawaii,[19] Canada and the United States eliminated testing requirements for certain cattle diseases on the basis that national requirements were deemed sufficient. Reflecting geography, the pattern of trade involved Canada shipping beef mostly from western Canadian packers to the western United States, while U.S. beef exports went mostly from the mid-western packers to eastern Canada. As the USDA notes, "In both cases, transportation efficiencies are gained because the other country is the closest major source of beef to a particular regional market." (Hahn, et al. 2005, p. 6).

Yet when BSE was discovered, the integrated market was disrupted completely with a full shutdown at the border — the United States shut its border to Canadian beef when the disease was discovered in Canada and Canada did likewise when BSE was identified in the United States. Of course, both countries faced shutdown of market access elsewhere in the world. This is not a NAFTA issue but it is a market integration issue,[20] and what it shows is that borders that are almost invisible in good times can reappear as major and even impassable barriers when even fairly modest risks emerge.

This point is driven home by the fact that in both cases national markets were handled very differently as governments on both sides of the border sought to contain the damage to the economy while dealing with the health risks to their respective citizenry. Such disasters naturally have varying incidence on producers with the export-oriented producers facing the greatest risk of going under.

The lessons from the above are several. International market integration is difficult under the best of conditions and things are never as good as they look in good times. When calculating the benefits from market integration in agriculture, the likelihood of periodic disruptions due to disease needs to be factored in. Since international trade disruptions are much more severe than national trade disruptions and often require injections of public funds to save the affected industry, which raise distributional issues, it only makes sense to build in insurance mechanisms funded out of the profits from international trade.

Another quite unrelated aspect of agricultural trade integration concerns the impact on family farm incomes of the transformation of the market context in which they function. In North America, extensive consolidation of agribusiness suppliers (including fertilizer, seed providers, grain elevator services, etc.) and buyers, as well as dismantling of farm support programmes has resulted in a combination of increasing input prices and stagnant farm-gate prices[21] and a consequent steep decline in net realized market income for farmers — even as exports have soared. The separation of the trends of exports and farm incomes pre-dated the NAFTA by a decade and a half so it is not a NAFTA issue *per se*; but it is noteworthy that soaring exports have not translated into a more profitable farm sector, despite extensive consolidation of farms. Thus, ironically, Canada, which is the fourth largest agriculture and agri-food exporter in the world, has been in the grip of a politically sensitive farm income crisis for years: 44 per cent of Canadian farms did not cover operating costs in 2005, including a remarkable 71 per cent of those farms with less than $25,000 in gross revenues and the sector as a whole was in the red (Statistics Canada 2007). At the same time, debt levels of Canadian farms have risen to record levels and debt-equity ratios have risen to nearly double those in the United States. Notably, this compression of farm incomes came at a time when corporate profits as a share of GDP were climbing to an all-time high in Canada.

To be sure, within the farm sector, the experience was uneven. The larger farms (with more than $250,000 in gross revenues) which constituted 17 per cent of Canadian farm in 2006, and which accounted for a disproportionate 75 per cent of gross farm revenues (Statistics Canada 2007) tended to be more profitable; however, even amongst the largest farms, those with over $1,000,000 in gross revenues, 14 per cent were in the red in 2005. The global trading environment for agricultural products obviously plays an important role in explaining these developments; the role of regional integration is likely quite small. However, this experience does underscore the difficulty of successfully using trade to improve farm incomes and particularly the lot of small farmers.

5. The Special Case of Intellectual Property Rights

A special feature of the Canada-U.S. FTA is that it included measures that required Canada to strengthen it intellectual property (IP) regime. These measures, which served as a model for the World Trade Organization's Agreement on Trade-Related Aspects of Intellectual Property Rights (TRIPS), resulted in a significant transfer of rents from Canada to the United States.

While a direct estimate of the size of the FTA-induced transfer is not available, it was likely on the order of about half a billion in United States dollars. This order of magnitude can be inferred by comparing two estimates of the impact of the TRIPS agreement. The first estimate, by Philip McCalman (2001), puts the transfer at about US$1 billion from a 1988 pre-TRIPS and pre-FTA basis; and a World Bank (2002) estimate of a US$574 million transfer from a 1995 pre-TRIPS but for Canada post-FTA basis. The difference between the two estimates of about US$500 million reflects in very rough terms the impact of the FTA. These figures should be taken as indicative only of the possible order of magnitude of the transfer, taking into account not only the uncertainties of the methodological approaches used to derive them but also different valuation bases (McCalman's estimate is in 1988 prices while the World Bank's is in 2000 prices).[22]

Note in this regard that this net cost to Canada occurred despite the fact that Canada is actually a net supplier of technology to the world in terms of disembodied technology[23] with receipts of about 1 per cent of GDP, and thus better positioned than most countries to benefit from enhanced IP rights.[24] The vast majority of disembodied technology payments and receipts flow to and from the United States, the European Union and Japan, largely through channels internal to multinational corporations (that is, between parent and affiliate). It is difficult therefore for any other country to make gains through international commerce by granting greater IP protection; at the same time, they face terms of trade losses.

6. The Definitive Role of Geography

For Canada, market integration with the United States makes eminent sense from a geographic perspective because Canada is, for most intents and purposes, a very long, thin border community. Most Canadian GDP originates within several hundred kilometres of the United States border. For most major Canadian cities, the closest large city is in the United States. Even culturally, Canada's sensibilities tend to parallel those of the neighbouring United States border states. By the same token, there is little disruption to Canadian society, in that particular sense, from integration with the United States.

At the same time, the free trade deal with the United States cuts through a set of tangled knots that had come to define Canada's political economy. In fact, Canada had historically come together as a confederation of Britain's remaining North American territories, in part spurred by the abrogation by the United States of the reciprocal trade deal with the then British Province of Canada. Canada's subsequent economic development was shaped by the 1878 National Policy which fostered east-west trade behind a protective tariff wall on the infrastructural backbone of the trans-Canada railroad. This promoted the development of an industrial heartland in central Canada but worked to the disadvantage of more natural north-south economic interactions. Free trade gave rein for north-south regional integration to develop: British Columbia together with Washington and Oregon forming a Cascadia region; Alberta with its resource trade already largely flowing south, Manitoba positioning itself as the northern end of a rail and road NAFTA transportation corridor to Mexico, Ontario deeply integrating into the northern U.S. manufacturing sector, Quebec looking southeast to New England for markets for its natural resources and excess hydropower (Gunderson 2001, p. 361). While some worried about the implications for Canadian unity, the economic evolution post-FTA was in many ways a natural one.

The situation of Mexico stands in sharp contrast. Economically and culturally, Mexico is centred well south of the United States border and is separated from it by vast tracts of thinly populated mountains. Moreover, Mexico's border communities are distinct, sharing a closer cultural and economic history with Texas and California than with Mexico's southern states. Mexico's northern economy is largely concentrated in a string of twin-city locations on the border, the main ones being Tijuana-San Diego, Ciudad Juarez-El Paso, Nuevo Laredo-Laredo, Reynosa-McAllen-Pharr, Matamoros-Brownsville, and Mexicali-Calexico. For the most part, NAFTA-driven integration is for Mexico a story about these border communities and, from the United States perspective, a story about Texas and California.

NAFTA resulted in a boom in the border communities, but a crisis in the poor southern parts of Mexico that did not benefit from the agreement but saw its agricultural base collapse in the face of cheaper imports from the United States. The result was an armed uprising. The regional disparities within Mexico led to a flood of migration towards the north, swelling the border communities but at the same time creating a toxic social setting of uprooted migrant workers, many of whom, having already left their families and homes behind, were more than ready to move one step further and cross into the United States, legally or illegally. The rapid growth of this border economy also outpaced the ability of Mexico to develop the supporting infrastructure with considerable damage to the local environment as a result.

On the United States side, there were also costs, mainly in terms of the pressure on an inadequate infrastructure along the NAFTA corridor, displacement of workers due to the much lower-wage competition just across the border, and the problems of dealing with an escalating drug trafficking problem. However, on balance, Texas and California gained in economic terms.

Texas' exports to Mexico boomed as did California's; in fact for California, Mexico moved up from third largest market into first place. Emphasizing the importance of the border region, "more than three-quarters of all California origin exports are shipped to border states, with the vast majority going to Baja California" (Public Policy Institute of California 2004). As with trade, the direct investment links between California and Mexico are largely close to the border: "More than 72 per cent of Mexican-owned subsidiaries in California are located in Imperial and San Diego Counties, and more than 47 per cent of California-owned subsidiaries in Mexico are located in the border states.... Most Mexican parents are on the border, and nearly all of those border companies are in Baja California" (Public Policy Institute of California 2004).

The irony of course is that, prior to the dramatic shift in Mexico's policy framework, it was Mexico that maintained a wall at the United States border. Now it is the United States building a wall along the border.

7. Conclusions

A number of lessons are to be drawn from the NAFTA experience.

First, timing is, if not everything, very important. The inevitable interpersonal and inter-generational impacts of trade liberalization can be substantially amplified by poor timing or through clustering of reforms which might result in amplification of the costs of adjustment through interaction of the several reform impacts.

Second, while the short-run static gains in efficiency from the "creative destruction" aspect of expanded trade are easy to identify, the longer-run dynamic gains from a shift to a higher growth trajectory through increased productivity growth are much harder to pin down and appear to be at this point disappointingly small.

Third, it is important to understand the degree of heterogeneity of firm productivity levels to anticipate the dynamics of adjustment to trade liberalization — and the scale of adjustment costs. Empirical models of trade usually assume that production is by a representative firm and consumption by a representative household. This of course completely masks the distributional impacts across the populations of firms and households. In the case of firms, models that try and capture productivity gains from trade by building in economies of scale rather than through the market dynamics drive by firm heterogeneity will also yield incorrect answers as to industry impacts. For example, at the industry level, the elimination of the weakest firms drives up average productivity, whereas a model with economies of scale and a representative firm will imply a reduction of productivity in a declining industry. The new generation of heterogeneous firm models are starting to address this issue; however the empirical basis for making assumptions about the distribution of productivity levels of firms is largely lacking. And, of course, the empirical basis for calibrating dynamic productivity gains from trade remains weak.

Fourth, farms are different from factories and the political economy across borders as regards response to risk is very different from the political economy within borders. Since international trade disruptions are much more severe than national trade disruptions, the evaluation of prospective gains from trade from agricultural liberalization needs to take account of the expected costs of periodic crises; moreover, because such crises often require injections of public funds to save the affected industry, it only makes sense to build in insurance mechanisms funded out of the profits from international trade.

Fifth, international market integration changes relative power structures within overall supply chains. The weakest links get squeezed. This is especially important for income distribution concerns with the family farm sector.

Sixth, since the vast majority of disembodied technology payments and receipts flow to and from the United States, the European Union and Japan, largely through channels internal to multinational corporations (that is, between parent and affiliate), and since the location of research & development (R&D) activity is largely driven by the supply of factors of production while the source of intellectual property (IP) profits are driven by the location of protection, it is difficult for any other country to make gains through international commerce by granting greater IP protection; at the same time, they face terms of trade losses.

Finally, geography is very important in understanding how market integration will impact on any given socioeconomic setting. Countries with highly heterogeneous geographic settings need to anticipate the intra-country regional dynamics before setting out aggressively on international market integration.

Vigorous engagement in international commerce is essential for successful development and to sustain growth in a competitive global economy. However, it is not an easy tool to use in a controlled fashion, in such a way as to minimize unexpected results and consequences. It requires political courage to liberalize, but consideration of the complexity of real economies that is not captured in simple trade models may help boost the balance of costs and benefits.

Notes

1. Quite the opposite effect had been expected by the U.S. government: "In 1994, the year NAFTA was put into effect, Attorney General Janet Reno predicted that illegal immigration would fall by two-thirds within six years. 'NAFTA is our best hope for reducing illegal

immigration in the long haul', she declared. 'If it fails, effective immigration control will become impossible.'" Cited in Reiland (2007).

2. The deal removed U.S. banks from the cap on foreign bank shares of Canadian banking system assets but did not open up Canada's major banks to takeover and required Canadian operations of U.S. banks to be organized in the form of a subsidiary that met Canadian regulatory requirements — which in this case included capital requirements and limits on size of loan based on the subsidiary's, not the parent's capital. This meant that growth of market share in Canada required actually building a banking business rather than buying it. History shows this did not interest U.S. banks. As for other financial services sectors, Canada had already opened up its investment brokerage sector to foreign ownership in the 1987 "Big Bang" and the insurance industry was already open internationally. All in all, there was little impact.

3. Mexico also entered into the NAFTA as part of an aggressive policy shift aimed at transforming the Mexican economy. Mexico's policy framework included the use of an exchange rate anchor for monetary policy. The latter policy resulted in the Tequila Crisis which broke out on the eve of the entry into force of the NAFTA agreement. This makes Mexico's experiment even more difficult than Canada's to interpret in terms of differentiating the effects of trade integration from those of macroeconomic policies. It is worth bearing in mind that Mexico's problems were hardly a surprise — as a study by the Bank of International Settlements noted, whereas the credit rating agencies had to downgrade Asian sovereign credits several times within the first seven months of the Asian crisis (because it was a surprise), they did not have to do the same with Mexico: "the Mexico crisis of 1994/1995 only resulted in a single notch downgrade by S&P (from BB+ to BB), and no change at all by Moody's." (Bonte, et al. 1999, p. 21). Since Mexico's policy course was almost self-evidently rash, it is also less useful as a guide to others.

4. As Trefler points out, the true height of protective tariffs was masked by aggregation; at the three-digit industry classification, tariff averages were lower, suggesting only modest overall impacts from tariff elimination. Earlier attempts to assess the impacts of the FTA that found little in the way of tariff effects were based on more aggregated data.

5. Source: Statistics Canada, Input-Output Table Multipliers, 2005. The job ratio of 1.71 total jobs for each manufacturing job is for the manufacturing industries, excluding food. Multiplier effects for manufacturing are two to three times greater than for services. While the data are for 2005, the figure would be representative of the ratio prevailing in the early 1990s.

6. The enrolment rate in post-secondary education in Canada peaked in 1993. See Corak, et al. (2003).

7. For Canada, the growth rate is based on Chain Fisher GDP volume at 2002 prices from *Bank of Canada Banking and Financial Statistics, October 2008*, Table H2. For the United States, the growth rate is based on GDP at chained 2,000 dollars from the Bureau of Economic Analysis, 2008:Q2 national accounts release at <http://www.bea.gov/national/index.htm#gdp>.

8. Hufbauer and Schott (2008, p. 19) provide a rough estimate that "On balance, … the rewards from economic integration far exceed the costs — by a ratio of ten to one or better." They offer a specific estimate of the net gain for the United States: "A rough calculation suggests that NAFTA has added about $60 billion annually to U.S. national income, about $200 per American." The United States did not of course suffer a significant adjustment shock and the reported boost to U.S. GDP, which amounts to about half a percentage point, is not implausible.

9. The U.S. share of Canada's imports of goods and services peaked in 2000 and then fell to its lowest point since 1946 by 2007, more than giving up the gains made during the period of rapid integration. The U.S. share of Canada's exports gave up half the gains made during the 1990s. Patrick Grady (2008) estimates that U.S. post-9/11 border

measures reduced Canadian exports to the United States by about 10 per cent. Another way of looking at this is to note that, in the 1990s, Canadian shipments to the United States exceeded Canada's shipments to Canadian destinations — in other words, Canada became its own second-largest trading partner. However, by the mid-2000s, shipments to the United States again fell below those to Canada. This was not, to be sure, entirely due to the U.S. border measures; part of it was due to the swings in the Canada-U.S. exchange rate which first raised the value of Canadian shipments to the United States as the Canadian dollar fell and then lowered them as the Canadian dollar rebounded.

10.   The comparison with Australia controls for exchange rate trends; both Canada and Australia experienced a comparatively steep depreciation in the second-half of the 1990s, making domestic labour cheaper relative to internationally traded capital goods and thus providing firms an incentive to expand production through greater labour utilization rather than through productivity-enhancing investment.

11.   The factor-proportions version of the theory of comparative advantage has had a decidedly mixed record empirically. The actual pattern of global trade, including extensive intra-industry trade between countries with similar income levels and with similar factor endowments, is not explained well by the factor proportions version of comparative advantage. Nor has the major corollary of the factor proportions theorem — factor price equalization — been consistently supported by the evidence. For example, in contrast to the factor price equalization theorem's prediction that extensive trade with industrialized countries would narrow income disparities in the poor countries, a recent survey of the extensive literature on the impact of globalization on income distribution in developing countries concludes as follows:

> The conclusions thus run the full gamut, from openness having a negative effect on real income of the poor, to raising income of the poor less than income of the rich in relative terms, to

raising both the same (in relative terms, again). Note however, that there are no results that show openness reducing inequality, that is raising real income of the poor by more (in percentage terms) than income of the rich. Let alone raising absolute incomes of the poor by more (Milanovic 2003, p. 4).

12.   The Gini coefficient is the most common measure of income inequality. Invented by the Italian statistician Corado Gini, the coefficient ranges from zero, which represents perfect income equality (all persons have exactly the same level of income), to one, which represents complete inequality (where one person receives all income and others receive nothing). The OECD average for inequality in household income in 2000 was 0.31. To provide some perspective, Denmark and Sweden were the most egalitarian OECD members with coefficients of 0.225 and 0.243 respectively. Turkey and Mexico were the least egalitarian at 0.439 and 0.48 respectively.

13.   See Piketty and Saez (2007). Bebchuk and Grinstein (2005) found that the pay of the top five corporate officers in their sample of 1,500 firms increased by almost twice as much between 1993 and 2003 as could be explained by explanatory variables such as sales, return on assets, and the firm's stock market valuation; this resulted in an increase in the ratio of top five compensation to total corporate profits from 5.0 per cent in 1993–95 to 12.8 per cent in 2000–02. See also Gordon and Dew-Becker (2007). They parse the increased skewness at the very top into three factors: a market-driven rise in "superstar" incomes and the incomes of top lawyers and investment bankers, and a steep rise in the incomes of top executives unrelated to market performance.

14.   Statistics Canada, "Canadian Potato Production", Catalogue No. 22-008, July 2007.

15.   Washington State Potato Commission, "Potato History", 2008.

16.   United States Potato Board, Market Access Priorities, Adopted 14 March 2007 <http://www.uspotatoes.com/550market.html>.

17. *Canadian Press Wire*, "Potato Virus that Devastated Island Farmers in 2000 Found Again", 4 September 2002.

18. Memorandum to James J. Jochum, Assistant Secretary for Import Administration, "Issues and Decision Memorandum for the Final Countervailing Duty Determinations of the Investigations of Certain Durum Wheat and Hard Red Spring Wheat from Canada", 28 August 2003.

19. Originally the programme was called the Northwest Pilot Project.

20. It is possible that the competitive pressures induced by market integration actually contributed to the emergence of BSE in North America, due to the slowness of the authorities to ban the use of the animal feed that had been identified as the cause of BSE.

21. The farm input price index (FIPI) rose 8.6 per cent between 2000 and 2005 while the farm product price index (FPPI) rose only 1.7 per cent (Statistics Canada 2007).

22. For a fuller discussion and citations, see Maskus (2004).

23. Disembodied technology flows involve transfers of technology through a licensing arrangement or through outsourcing of research and development (R&D) which generate payment of R&D fees. By contrast, payment for technology which is embodied in a product is part of the product price. See OECD (2008).

24. The major change in Canada's intellectual property (IP) rights policy was with respect to pharmaceutical products. Canada's regime for compulsory licensing was modified in 1987, prior to the FTA, in part to promote R&D spending in Canada, but also because Canada's regime for compulsory licensing had become "an obstacle to successful completion of the Free Trade Agreement (FTA) between Canada and the United States" (Pazderka 1999, p. 30). The change in IP regime was followed by an increase in pharmaceutical R&D spending in Canada (expenditures roughly doubled in nominal terms compared to a counter-factual trend, or by about CAD$300 million, in 1997). However, whether this was due to the changes in the IP regime *per se*, or to the negotiated commitment of the

industry to increase its R&D spending in Canada to 10 per cent of revenues is less clear. First principles economic reasoning suggests that local protection for IP rights funds global research but does not guarantee local research. The case in point is Switzerland, which is a leading source of pharmaceutical R&D yet historically had weak domestic protection. On this point, see Pazderka (2007). In any event, comparing the scale of increased R&D spending in Canada and the size of the estimated cost to Canada in terms of higher prices for imported drugs, it is still evident that inclusion of IP in the Canada-U.S. FTA had distributional effects internationally.

References

Bebchuk, Lucian A. and Yaniv Grinstein. "The Growth of Executive Pay". *Oxford Review of Economic Policy* 21 (2005): 283–303.

Bonte, Rudi, et al. "Supervisory Lessons to be Drawn from the Asian Crisis". *Basel Committee on Banking Supervision Working Papers*, no. 2. Geneva: Bank for International Settlements, June 1999.

Corak, Miles, Garth Lipps, and John Zhao. "Family Income and Participation in Post-secondary Education". *Analytical Studies Branch Research Paper Series*. Statistics Canada, Catalogue no. 11F0019MIE — No. 210, October 2003.

Frenette, Marc. "Life After the High-tech Downturn: Permanent Layoffs and Earnings Losses of Displaced Workers". *Analytical Studies Branch Research Paper Series*. Statistics Canada, Catalogue no. 11F0019MIE — No. 302, July 2007.

Gordon, Robert J. and Ian Dew-Becker. "Unresolved Issues in the Rise of American Inequality". Paper presented at the Brookings Panel on Economic Activity, Washington, D.C., 7 September 2007.

Grady, Patrick. "How Much Were Canadian Exports Curtailed by the US Border?" Mimeographed, 30 May 2008. <www.global-economics.ca/border_post911.pdf>.

Gunderson, Morley. "North American Economic Integration and Globalization". In *The State of Economics in Canada: Festschrift in Honour of David Slater*, edited by Patrick Grady and Andrew Sharpe. Kingston: Queen's University Press, 2001.

Hahn, William F., et al. "Market Integration of the North American Animal Products Complex". U.S. Department of Agriculture, Economic Research Service, May 2005.

Harchaoui, Tarek M., Jimmy Jean, and Faouzi Tarkhani. "Prosperity and Productivity: A Canada-Australia Comparison". *Analytical Studies Branch Research Paper Series*. Statistics Canada, Catalogue no. 11F0027MIE — No. 018, December 2003.

Holmes, John. "The Continental Integration of the North American Automobile Industry: From the Auto Pact to the FTA and beyond". *Environment and Planning* A 24, no. 1 (1992): 95–119.

Hufbauer, Gary C. and Jeffrey J. Schott. "NAFTA's Bad Rap". *The International Economy* (Summer 2008).

Maskus, Keith E. "Intellectual Property Protection: Is It being Taken too Far?" In *Trade Policy Research 2003*, edited by John M. Curtis and Dan Ciuriak. Ottawa: Foreign Affairs and International Trade Canada, 2004.

McCalman, Phillip. "Reaping What You Sow: An Empirical Analysis of International Patent Harmonization". *Journal of International Economics* 55, no. 1 (October 2001): 161–86.

Milanovic, Branko. "Can We Discern the Effect of Globalization on Income Distribution? Evidence from Household Surveys". World Bank Development Research Group, 22 September 2003.

Organization for Economic Cooperation and Development (OECD). *OECD Science, Technology and Industry Scoreboard 2007*. Paris: OECD, 2008.

Park, Se-Hark and Kenneth S. Chan. "A Cross-Country Input-Output Analysis of Intersectoral Relationships between Manufacturing and Services and their Employment Implications". *World Development* 17, no. 2 (1989): 199–212.

Pazderka, Bohumir. "Patent Protection and Pharmaceutical R&D Spending in Canada". *Canadian Public Policy* XXV, no. 1 (1999): 29–46.

———. "The Effect of Pharmaceutical Patent Term Length on R&D and Drug Expenditure in Canada". *Healthcare Policy* 2, no. 3 (2007): 85–89.

Piketty, Thomas and Emmanuel Saez. "The Evolution of Top Incomes: A Historical and International Perspective". *National Bureau of Economic Research Working Paper 11955* (January 2006).

Public Policy Institute of California. "The Economic Integration of California and Mexico". *Research Brief 89* (August 2004).

Reiland, Ralph. "NAFTA: Winners & Losers". *Pittsburgh Tribune-Review*, 29 January 2007.

Romalis, John. "NAFTA's and CUSFTA's Impact on International Trade". *Review of Economics and Statistics* 89, no. 3 (2007): 416–35.

Schwanen, Dan. "Trade Liberalization and Inequality in Canada in the 1990s". *Review of Economic Performance and Social Progress* 1, no. 1 (2001): 161–82.

Statistics Canada. "The Financial Picture of Farms in Canada", based on the 2006 Census (2007). <http://www.statcan.gc.ca/ca-ra2006/articles/finpicture-portrait-eng.htm>.

Trefler, Daniel. "The Long and Short of the Canada-U.S. Free Trade Agreement". *American Economic Review* 94, no. 4 (2004): 870–95.

Uchitelle, Louis. "Nafta Should Have Stopped Illegal Immigration, Right?" *N.Y. Times*, 17 February 2007.

Valadkhani, A. "Using Input-Output Analysis to Identify Australia's High Employment Generating Industries". *Australian Bulletin of Labour* 29, no. 3 (2003): 199–217.

World Bank. "Intellectual Property: Balancing Incentives with Competitive Access". In *Global Economic Prospects and the Developing Countries: Making Trade Work for the World's Poor*. Washington, D.C.: World Bank, 2002.

Dan Ciuriak is a consulting economist and Senior Associate at the Centre for Trade Policy and Law, University of Ottawa and Carleton University. He was also the Deputy Chief Economist at the Foreign Affairs and International Trade Canada.

9
CROSS-BORDER LABOUR MIGRATION IN ASEAN
Issues and Challenges

Chia Siow Yue

1. Introduction

Liberalization of international labour mobility has progressed more slowly than liberalization of flows of goods, services and investments. In the World Trade Organization (WTO), labour mobility is found only in a trade context under trade in services, that is, General Agreement on Trade in Services (GATS) Mode 4 on movement of natural persons. In regional trade arrangements (RTAs) labour mobility is a key feature of the European Union (EU), but in many free trade areas (FTAs) it is restricted to movement of business persons, traders, intra-corporate transferees and professionals.

In the Southeast Asian region, there is restricted immigration and no free movement of labour across countries, although ASEAN countries grant visa-free entry on visitors from fellow member countries. Employment usually requires work permits and employment passes. The early ASEAN agreements — the ASEAN Free Trade Area (trade in goods), ASEAN Framework Agreement of Services (trade in services) and ASEAN Investment Area (investment) — contain no provisions on cross-border labour mobility. However, "free flow of skilled labour" is incorporated in the ASEAN Economic Community (AEC) to be realized by 2015.

International labour migration (ILM) or cross-border labour migration is an increasingly visible phenomenon in Southeast Asia in recent decades. The region is a net exporter of labour to the rest of the world. Major destinations are the Middle East and Northeast Asia (Japan, Taiwan, South Korea and Hong Kong), with smaller flows to the United States, Canada, Europe and Australia. Within Southeast Asia itself, main labour sending countries are Indonesia, the Philippines and Cambodia, Laos, Myanmar, Vietnam (CLMV); main labour receiving countries are Brunei, and Singapore; while Malaysia and Thailand are both labour sending and receiving countries.

This paper seeks to examine the determinants and patterns of ILM and their macro and micro effects on labour-sending and labour-receiving countries in ASEAN as well as the labour migration policies and issues and regional cooperation challenges.

2. Determinants and Patterns of ILM in Southeast Asia

Southeast Asia has historically been the destination of migration waves from China, India, and the Middle East and these have left strong imprints on the region's demography, society and politics. In the twentieth century, inward migration ended with World War II. In the post-war years, political developments in Southeast Asia have led to controls on cross-border migration inflows (Chia 2008).

(i) Determinants of ILM in Recent Decades

ILM in Southeast Asia in recent decades is a response of individuals and countries to labour surplus/shortage situations arising from differences in economic growth and income levels; different phasings of demographic transitions; demands for professionals and workers by industrial upgrading and presence of foreign multinational corporations (MNCs); demands for workers in informal sectors in some receiving countries, particularly for "3D" work (dirty, dangerous and difficult); porous borders between neighbouring states with strong ethnic affinities; and government policies on foreign workers. Table 9.1 shows the wide differences in per capita GDP and population size among ASEAN countries. In addition, social networks have developed among migrant workers that facilitate migration of their families and friends. The two-way ILM flows have played a significant role in the region's economic dynamism and transformation in recent decades. Demographics will sustain these labour flows.

- Labour-receiving countries in Southeast Asia are the more developed ones that enjoy rapid economic growth and face

TABLE 9.1
Per Capita GDP and Population Size in ASEAN

Country	Per capita GDP (US$)	Population size 2007 2007 (million)
Singapore	35,208	4.6
Brunei	31,076	0.4
Malaysia	6,880	27.2
Thailand	3,740	65.7
Indonesia	1,920	224.9
Philippines	1,653	88.9
Vietnam	837	85.2
Laos	736	5.6
Cambodia	598	14.5
Myanmar	216	58.6

Source: ASEAN Secretariat database.

growing labour shortages. Policies adopted to manage such inflows are usually two-tracked and asymmetric, with liberal policies towards inflows of the professionals and highly skilled, and restrictive policies towards the semi-skilled and unskilled. Also, political-social-cultural considerations led to preferential sourcing from particular regions and countries. At the national level, employers facing labour and skills shortages want access to foreign workers to meet their business needs and to keep a lid on rising wages. However, local labour wants the inflows to be controlled, fearing the increased labour supply would result in loss of jobs as well as of wage bargaining leverage. The general public is concerned with the social impact of a sizeable foreign workforce living in their midst, particularly on the increased demand for public services, rising incidence of disease and crime, and social disruptions.

- In the labour-sending countries of Southeast Asia, government policies toward out-migration range from "*laissez faire*" (for example, the Philippines) to specific policies to promote labour export to ease domestic unemployment and financial and foreign exchange constraints (for example Vietnam and Indonesia). Sending countries benefit from inflow of remittances but face the challenges of a brain drain and potential currency overvaluation. The migrant workers themselves want a freer environment to make decisions to migrate to seek better economic opportunities, but at the same time, expect their governments to protect their rights and welfare. Advances in modern transportation and information and communications technology (ICT) have greatly improved information access and facilitate the choice of destinations, while cultural links and social networks bias migration in favour of certain locations.

- The Middle East oil boom of the 1980s led to a huge demand for foreign contract workers in construction and services and attracted sizeable flow of workers from the Philippines, Indonesia and Thailand among others. The end of the oil boom and completion of major construction projects, the outbreak of the Gulf Wars, as well as the ongoing East Asian economic miracle have increasingly shifted ILM from Southeast Asia towards Northeast Asia and within Southeast Asia itself. In recent times, foreign workers account for over 30 per cent of the total labour force in Singapore and over 20 per cent in Malaysia.

(ii) Labour Flows

There are three ongoing labour migration streams in Southeast Asia. A smaller stream comprises professionals and skilled workers, mainly from Japan and the Asian newly industrialized economies (NIEs) as well as Europe and the United States and linked to the growing MNC presence in the region. A larger stream comprises semi-skilled and unskilled legal temporary overseas contract workers in agriculture, labour-intensive manufacturing, construction and in services such as household maids and care-givers. The labour receiving countries view inflows of semi-skilled and unskilled workers as temporary and impose restrictions on them staying on indefinitely. However, some countries appear to have difficulty in keeping them "temporary", resulting in circular migration. A third stream comprises irregular semi-skilled and unskilled workers who either overstay their tourist visas or enter the countries illegally to seek employment.

Analysis of labour migration in Southeast Asia is hampered by the lack of comprehensive and consistent data from different sources.[1] The World Bank (2006) estimates the size of migrant labour in ASEAN at 3–4 million. The International Labour

Organization (ILO) (2007) estimates (see Table 9.2) the total number of migrants originating from ASEAN at about 13.5 million in 2005, with 5.7 million or 39 per cent in other ASEAN countries, and the rest found in the United States (26 per cent), the Middle East (26 per cent) and EU (9 per cent). Workers from Indonesia, Malaysia, Myanmar, Cambodia, and Laos are found mainly in other ASEAN countries while workers from the Philippines and Vietnam are found mainly in the United States.

Intra-ASEAN migration has played a large role in meeting the labour shortage of ASEAN receiving countries. Intra-ASEAN flows are largely of semi-skilled and unskilled workers and a high proportion are irregular workers who overstayed their visas or entered the destination countries illegally. Migrant workers from ASEAN countries are largely absorbed into occupations such as domestic service, construction, farming and labour-intensive manufacturing. Female labour migrants are growing and concentrated in traditional gender roles of domestic work, healthcare and entertainment services. Intra-ASEAN flows of professionals and skilled workers are rising in response to the rapidly growing trade and investment interdependencies, but remain relatively small. The main receiving countries for intra-ASEAN migration are Malaysia, Thailand (each accounting for 35 per cent of intra-regional migration) and Singapore (21 per cent). The main sources of migrants are Myanmar (27 per cent of total intra-regional migration), Indonesia (23 per cent), and Malaysia (19.5 per cent).

- *Malaysia*: Rapid economic growth led to labour shortages in specific sectors and foreign workers filled the gap in labour intensive industries such as agriculture and plantation, construction and household maid services. ILO

TABLE 9.2
Estimated Migrant Stocks from and to Southeast Asia, 2005

Source/destination	Migrant stock	As % of population	Major destinations/sources
Out-migration from:			
Brunei	12,623	3.4	OECD countries, Philippines
Cambodia	348,710	2.5	OECD countries, Thailand, Laos
Indonesia	1,736,717	0.8	Malaysia, OECD countries, Middle East, Singapore, South Korea
Laos	413,379	7.0	OECD countries, Thailand, Cambodia
Malaysia	1,458,944	5.8	Singapore, Brunei, OECD countries, India
Myanmar	426,860	0.8	Thailand, India, OECD countries
Philippines	3,631,405	4.4	U.S., Middle East, Malaysia, OECD countries, South Korea
Singapore	230,007	5.3	Malaysia, OECD countries, India, Brunei, Thailand
Thailand	758,180	1.2	U.S., Cambodia, Malaysia, OECD countries, South Korea
Vietnam	2,225,413	2.6	U.S., OECD countries, Cambodia, South Korea, Thailand
In-migration to:			
Brunei	124,193	33.2	Malaysia, Philippines, Thailand, Singapore, Indonesia, OECD countries
Cambodia	303,871	2.2	Vietnam, Thailand, OECD countries, Malaysia, Philippines, Singapore
Indonesia	159,731	0.1	not available
Laos	24,646	0.4	China, Australia, Vietnam, Thailand, Cambodia, Myanmar
Malaysia	1,639,138	6.5	Indonesia, Philippines, Singapore, Thailand, South Asia
Myanmar	117,435	0.2	China, South Asia
Philippines	374,458	0.5	U.S., China, OECD countries, Indonesia, India
Singapore	1,842,953	42.6	Malaysia, China, India, Indonesia, South Asia, U.S., HK
Thailand	1,050,459	1.6	China, Myanmar, Laos, Cambodia, Vietnam, South Asia
Vietnam	21,105	0.03	not available

Source: World Bank, *Migration and Remittance Factbook 2008.*

TABLE 9.3

Estimates of Intra-ASEAN Migrant Stocks, 2006

Source	Destination (Number in thousands)										
	Brunei	Camb-odia	Indon-esia	Laos	Malay-sia	Myan-mar	Philip-pines	Singa-pore	Thai-land	Viet-nam	ASEAN
Brunei	–	0	0	0	0	0	1	0	0	0	1
Cambodia	0	–	0	2	7	0	0	0	232	0	240
Indonesia	6	0	–	0	1,215	0	5	96	1	0	1,323
Laos	0	1	0	–	0	0	0	0	257	0	258
Malaysia	68	1	0	0	–	0	0	994	3	0	1,066
Myanmar	0	0	0	0	92	–	0	0	1,382	0	1,475
Philippines	23	1	0	0	353	0	–	136	3	0	516
Singapore	3	1	0	0	87	0	0	–	2	0	92
Thailand	11	129	0	3	86	0	0	0	–	0	229
Vietnam	0	157	0	15	86	0	1	0	20	–	279
ASEAN	111	290	0	20	1,925	0	8	1,226	1,900	0	5,480

Source: ILO, *Labour and Social Trends in ASEAN 2007.*

(2007) estimates that of Malaysia's 2.1 million migrant workers, 60 per cent are Indonesians and a sizeable number are from the Philippines. Manufacturing employs 33 per cent of migrant workers, household domestic service 25 per cent, and construction and agriculture 21 per cent. Malaysia's porous borders with Indonesia and the Philippines have led to large inflows of irregular labour. ILO (2007) estimates that some 70 per cent of Malaysia's estimated 1.5 million workers abroad are in neighbouring Singapore, attracted by its better job prospects and wages.

- **Thailand**: Of Thailand's estimated 1.8 million migrant workers, some 75 per cent are from Myanmar and the rest mostly from Cambodia and Laos. The bulk of Myanmar's 1.6 million workers abroad are in Thailand. Agriculture employs an estimated 24 per cent of migrant workers, manufacturing and construction 49 per cent and services 27 per cent. Large numbers of Thai workers also went to the Middle East during the oil boom years and in more recent years to Japan and the Asian NIEs, with the numbers reaching 162,000 in 2007.

- Thailand and Malaysia are heavily dependent on labour-intensive industries and given the porous borders with poorer neighbouring countries, they experience high levels of irregular migration. Irregular migrant workers comprise 70 per cent of Thailand's migrant workers and 50 per cent of those in Malaysia. Irregular migrants are a serious concern — greater vulnerability to exploitation, abuse of rights and limited access to channels of redress, and potential source of political tension between sending and receiving countries.

- **Singapore**: There are about 755,000 professionals and foreign workers in Singapore, with 110,000 professionals on employment passes and 645,000 semi-skilled and unskilled on work permits out of a total Singapore workforce of 1.8 million. It is estimated that foreigners and permanent residents filled 61 per cent of the jobs created between 2004 and the third quarter of 2008 (*Straits Times*, 20 January 2009). Sectorally, dependency on foreign labour was a high 63 per cent of the workforce in construction, 42 per cent in manufacturing, 28 per cent in community services and 23 per cent in financial and business services. Professionals are largely from OECD economies, while semi-skilled and unskilled are mainly from Southeast Asia, South Asia and China. At the same time, some 150,000 Singaporean professionals are working abroad in Malaysia, Hong Kong, China, North America, United Kingdom, Australia and New Zealand.

- *Indonesia* has 2.7 million officially documented workers abroad representing 2.8 per cent of the Indonesian workforce. Of this, 59 per cent are in ASEAN, mainly in Malaysia. Other major destinations are the Middle East, South Korea and Taiwan. In 2006, out-migration reached 647,000. Ananta and Arifin (March 2008) note that the rising labour outflow is due to the decline in poverty (hence ability to finance out-migration) and rising education levels in Indonesia (hence ability to meet overseas demand), while the substantial number of irregular workers abroad is associated with the cost and bureaucratic process for legal out-migration for employment.

- *Philippines*: Among ASEAN countries, the Philippines has the largest stock and flow of workers abroad. In the 1970s, the Middle East oil boom attracted large numbers of Filipino professionals and unskilled and semi-skilled workers. In the 1980s and 1990s, the economic miracle in Japan, Asian NIEs and Malaysia also attracted Filipinos as entertainers, factory workers, construction workers and household maids. The principal destinations are the United States (3.6 million or 48 per cent of official estimate of 8 million), the Middle East (39 per cent) and ASEAN countries (14 per cent, mainly as contract workers in Malaysia and Singapore). In the first eleven months of 2006, 768,000 Filipino contract workers emigrated.

- **Vietnam**: With the end of the Vietnam War, Vietnam has been sending workers to Eastern Europe. After the collapse of the Soviet Bloc, Vietnam has been exporting workers worldwide, including to Japan, the Asian NIEs, Malaysia, Thailand and Singapore. There are 2.3 million workers abroad, mostly semi-skilled and unskilled, with 48 per cent in the United States and 12 per cent in ASEAN (mainly Cambodia and Malaysia). In recent years about 75,000 workers leave Vietnam annually.

"Brains" generally flow from the less developed to the more developed countries. Many skilled professionals from developing countries first went to Organization for Economic Cooperation and Development (OECD) countries as students and then stayed on after graduation. At the same time, liberalization of the "movement of natural persons" in GATS and growing foreign investment and MNC presence have resulted in significant labour mobility of the professionals and skilled from developed to developing countries as well as flows among developing countries.

There is a general shortage of skills in the ASEAN region. Factors include globalization and technological progress; high economic growth and rapid structural transformation and industrial upgrading; and country specific demographic trends and national education and training policies. Some ASEAN countries such as Singapore and Malaysia now have deliberate policies of attracting brains.

- **Philippines** is the main exporter of large numbers of professional healthcare workers to meet rising demand in OECD countries. However, this exodus has resulted in depleting the Philippines healthcare sector of experienced professionals; at the same time, it has also attracted Filipino doctors and other healthcare professionals to take up nursing qualifications to improve their "exportability". In 2008–09, under the Japan-Philippines Economic Partnership Agreement (EPA) a capped number of qualified Filipino nurses and other healthcare workers have been admitted into Japan as trainees, where they have to pass the Japanese nursing qualifications within a four-year period or face repatriation.
- **Singapore** has a national strategy to attract professionals and executives (including the offer of permanent residence and citizenship) to facilitate economic upgrading and ensure sustainable economic growth. Their actual numbers are not available. Indirect evidence shows that the proportion of permanent residents in Singapore's total population increased to 10.1 per cent in 2005. In 2004–06, an additional 11,000 foreigners were granted Singapore citizenship and 49,000 were granted permanent residence. About 80 per cent of the new Singapore citizens and 60 per cent of the new permanent residents are professionals, managers, executives and administrators.

The majority of ILM in Southeast Asia, both inflows and outflows, are the semi-skilled and unskilled "overseas contract workers"

(OCWs). They are mainly from labour-surplus countries of Indonesia, the Philippines, Thailand, CLMV, as well as from China and South Asia. Receiving countries are mainly the Middle East, Northeast Asia (Japan, South Korea, Hong Kong and Taiwan) and Brunei, Singapore, Malaysia and Thailand in ASEAN. They are found mainly in labour intensive manufacturing, agriculture and plantations, construction, entertainment and domestic services. They involve mainly the young on two- to three-year contracts, with a growing number of females in the entertainment and domestic services. However, while the bulk of OCWs return to their home countries, many of them are either becoming "circular" workers through successive renewal of contracts (due to structural dependency of receiving countries) or becoming irregular workers.

3. Key Impacts and Issues

Data problems have complicated the measurement of the various direct and indirect effects of cross-border labour migration. There are the macro-effects on sending and receiving countries as well as micro-effects on employers, labour, households, and migrants themselves. There are the different effects on the migration of brains versus semi-skilled and unskilled labour and the presence of large numbers of irregular migrants. The bulk of the economic gains accrue at the micro-level to migrants and their families and these gains are often large, as these migrants were either unemployed in their home countries or received wages that were substantially lower than what they are receiving in the host countries.

- At the macro-level, the sending country benefits from reduced unemployment, remittances and spillover effects on economic growth and poverty reduction, and skills and experiences gained by migrant returnees. Out-migration of the economically inactive and unemployed would have no significant negative impact on the country's total output, although in some locales and occupations, the loss of a significant proportion of the labour force can be expected to lead to labour shortages and falls in productivity. It also involves a brain drain. Out-migration is also likely to have significant effects on the labour force participation of remaining household members. Furthermore, out-migration has spawned a thriving labour-migration industry involving employment placement, travel, vocational and foreign language training and related services.

•   For the receiving country and employers, the in-migration relieves the general and specific shortages of labour and contributes to higher productivity and economic growth. ILO (2008) notes that migrant workers can boost productivity and output in receiving countries in several ways — by feeding excess labour demand in rapidly growing sectors, controlling labour costs and maintaining profitability in industries that otherwise would lose comparative advantage; by filling lower productivity jobs, thus allowing higher skilled local workers to find employment in higher productivity jobs; by increasing the current profitability of enterprises; and by augmenting domestic consumption and the multiplier effect of consumption on output.

•   In-migrants fill jobs shunned by local workers and act as buffer during the upswings and downswings of the business cycle.[2] In the intense global competition for FDI, availability of skilled and unskilled labour has become a condition for attracting and retaining FDI. Also, consumers benefit from the cheaper goods produced and more particularly from the availability and affordability of services provided by foreign labour. Negative effects include becoming chronically dependent on foreign labour and delays in structural adjustment, as the availability of cheaper foreign labour made it possible for these countries to maintain competitiveness in labour intensive industries and services despite rapid depletion of the domestic labour supply. Some broader impacts of the foreign worker presence include increased demand for public and social services, impact on population and sensitive ethnic distribution, impact on social structure and social cohesion, and threat to national security and increased incidence of crime and disease. A widely perceived negative effect by domestic labour unions and workers is that foreign workers compete for jobs and depress local wages. On the other hand, when migrant workers take up jobs shunned by local workers, they complement rather than compete for jobs, a point frequently stressed by the Singapore Government to allay concerns expressed by local workers.

- *Singapore*: The contribution of foreign workers to the Singapore economy is evident from an official study[3] that showed foreign labour contributed 29 per cent of the average annual growth of 9.7 per cent during 1992–97. Semi-skilled and unskilled work permit holders enable Singapore companies to overcome the constraint of labour shortage and average down the cost of doing business. Also, foreign professionals help to ease the shortage of talent and skills, breed innovation and entrepreneurship, and facilitate the internationalization of Singapore firms. In May 2008, Singapore prime minister emphasized that "foreign workers help enlarge the economic pie for the country... foreign workers allow the airport, seaports, factories, offices, hotels, restaurants and retail outlets to offer better service and business hours and strengthen Singapore's overall competitiveness; foreign workers can supplement local workers and allow many small and medium enterprises that do not make large profits to continue to operate." [4] Foreign domestic maids allow better educated Singaporean women to enter the labour force and find productive employment and improved productivity.

- *Malaysia*: One study estimated that a 20 per cent reduction in migrant workers would result in a 1.1 per cent decline in GDP, 0.9 per cent fall in exports, 1.4 per cent decline in investment, and 0.8 per cent decline in household consumption, 0.5 per cent rise in average real wage and 1.1 per cent rise in rental price of capital.[5]

- *Thailand*: One study in 1996 concluded that the country's 1.8 million migrant workers contributed about 1.25 per cent of GDP; their contribution could be as high as 6.2 per cent of GDP depending on the average productivity of migrant workers relative to native workers.[6]

(i) Brain Drain and Return Migration

Out-migration of the highly skilled and professionals are commonly viewed as a "brain drain", impacting negatively on the development potential of the sending country, particularly when these skills had been trained at great public expense. Lucas (2005) identified three types of negative effects — productivity losses; loss of key professionals lower the access to healthcare and quality education of future generations; and loss of public investment in education and in tax revenue. The negative effects of skills depletion are exemplified by the Philippines, where success in sending nurses abroad has undermined healthcare in the country and the country has to spend more to produce the same calibre of professionals that will in time also leave the country.

However, the brain drain could also have positive effects on the sending countries that are unable to efficiently employ and utilize them, as emigrants can make a greater contribution to their home country development through their remittances. Prospects of working abroad could also lead to a higher level of human capital formation in the sending country. Also, there are significant gains when the "brains" eventually return, provided that jobs open to the migrants in the receiving countries result in additional skills acquisition; that these new skills are appropriate to the labour market conditions of the sending country; and that upon return the workers will employ these new skills.

The Asian diaspora is increasingly viewed by their countries of origin as a valuable resource to be tapped for national economic development — for their remittances and investments, their experienced entrepreneurial and professional skills, and their business and social networks. Taiwan and South Korea have programmes to encourage a "reverse brain drain". More recently, the "overseas Chinese" communities in Hong Kong and Taiwan and to a lesser extent in Southeast Asia have been major foreign investors in China in the first decade of China's open-door policy.

(ii) Remittances

- The large and growing volume of remittances flows have served as the main redistribution mechanism between labour-receiving and labour-sending countries.
- Data on remittance inflows into ASEAN countries cover contract labour migrants, expatriate professionals, as well the diaspora of permanent emigrants, most of whom have settled in OECD countries. Official records cover only transfers through official channels and exclude the sizeable transfers through various informal channels. They totalled about US$26 billion in 2005, with the Philippines accounting

for 62 per cent, Vietnam 15 per cent, Thailand 9 per cent and Indonesia 8 per cent (Chia 2008). These exclude the substantial remittances through informal channels. Remittances have macro positive effects, as they augment domestic savings and foreign exchange earnings. Table 9.4 from the World Bank 2008 remittance database shows that the Philippines' remittance inflows grew from US$6.2 billion in 2000 to US$17 billion and over 13 per cent of GDP in 2007. In Indonesia, remittances reached US$6 billion by 2007, excluding the sizeable sums sent through informal channels, and reached some 1.6 per cent of GDP. In Vietnam, they reached US$5 billion in 2007, accounting for 8 per cent of GDP. In Thailand, they reached US$1.7 billion in 2007 and less than 1 per cent of GDP.

How effectively have countries used their remittance inflows for development? Tullao (March 2008) argues that the large remittances sent regularly have stabilized the Philippines currency and contributed to household welfare and growth of the national economy. ILO (2007) also highlight positive effects for the Philippines — households with remittances spent about double the share of family income on education compared to households without remittances; children from remittance-receiving households also are significantly more likely to be enrolled at all levels and this compensates to some extent for the outflow of skilled workers; households able to send workers abroad are also able to climb out of poverty; remittances also often have multiplier effects on local economies. However, remittance inflows could also lead to an overvalued currency or the "Dutch disease"; they may also worsen income distribution between regions of the sending country that have sizeable out-migrants compared to those that do not

TABLE 9.4
Remittance Flows to and out of Southeast Asia (US$ million)

Countries	2000	2006	2007
Remittance inflows:			
Brunei	na	na	na
Cambodia	121	298	322
Indonesia	1,190	5,722	6,000
Laos	1	1	1
Malaysia	981	1,535	1,700
Myanmar	104	117	125
Philippines	6,212	15,250	17,000
Singapore	na	na	na
Thailand	1,697	1,333	1,707
Vietnam	na	4,800	5,000
Remittance Outflows:			
Brunei	na	na	na
Cambodia	104	158	na
Indonesia	na	1,359	na
Laos	na	1	na
Malaysia	599	5,560	na
Myanmar	14	32	na
Philippines	93	20	na
Singapore	na	na	na
Thailand	na	na	na
Vietnam	na	na	na

Source: World Bank, *Migration and Remittance Factbook 2008*.

have, and in a particular community between households with and without remittance incomes.

There is growing recognition of the importance of remittances for economic and social development of labour-sending countries.

Governments could try to maximize the effect of remittances on national economic development, by reducing the transaction costs in remittance transfers, and by schemes that could put remittances to productive use. At the micro-level, remittances play a crucial role in reducing the incidence and severity of household poverty; improve household living standards, pay off household debts, increase household "investment" in land, housing, education and health, and enable formation of small and medium enterprises. Evidence from the Philippines shows households with overseas workers spend double the percentage of family income on education than households without remittances; households are also able to climb the income ladder very quickly; remittances also have multiplier effects on local economies.

(iii) Irregular Workers

The ILO has adopted the term "irregular workers" for migrant workers who either overstayed their visas, or else entered the countries illegally, whereas the media and some governments refer to them as "illegal workers". They make up a sizeable component of migrant workers in Southeast Asia, estimated at some two million. Their large numbers reflect the push factor of poverty, unemployment and lack of economic opportunities in their home countries, the pull factor of employment and attractive salaries in the destination countries, procedural difficulties of gaining legal entry and employment in the destination countries, and porous borders that facilitate illegal entries. They pose a major problem for receiving countries.

Thailand and Malaysia have the largest numbers of irregular workers in ASEAN. In 2005 Thailand had an estimated 1.1 million irregular migrant workers, mainly from Myanmar, Laos and Cambodia. In 2006 Malaysia had an estimated 700,000 irregular migrant workers, with 70 per cent from neighbouring Indonesia, the rest from India and China.

There are also sizeable numbers of irregular workers from ASEAN in Japan, South Korea, Taiwan and Hong Kong. As Hugo (2008) notes: "the challenge becomes to develop documented migration systems which meet the labour needs of destinations while being fair and equitable in their treatment of workers so that the documented option becomes more attractive to migrant labourers" (p. 42). National policies on irregular workers are further discussed in the next section.

(iv) Social Issues, Transaction Costs, and Migrants' Welfare

In labour-receiving countries, social consequences of foreign worker presence are a recurrent theme of public debate and media interest. A common perception is that migrant workers contribute to increased crime and disease. There is also an element of racism and cultural protectionism in the objections to a large foreign worker presence in the economy and society. In labour-sending countries, concerns are over the treatment of their overseas workers, such as physical and mental abuse, breach of contract between employer and employee including non-payment of wages. The migrant worker's absence from the family for long periods also affects family life. Because of their lack of information and bargaining power, migrant workers may end up working as irregular workers who are vulnerable to exploitation. International, regional and national non-governmental organizations (NGOs) are concerned over labour exploitation and related human trafficking.

- A major issue in the ASEAN region is the high transaction costs involved in labour migration — passport and visa fees and other charges by government agencies, as well as exploitation and fraud by labour recruiting and placement agencies. At every stage of the migration process — from recruitment at the village level, preparation to travel, transit to destination, to taking up employment — the migrant workers have to make payments for various services and to various gatekeepers. The result is that before the migrant worker actually starts work, he and his family have already incurred a sizeable debt that would take many months of wages to repay. If the migrant worker, for some reason, fails to secure a job on arrival at the destination, or gets retrenched and repatriated within a short time (due to a general economic downturn or specific employer facing business difficulties), or the employer fails to pay his wages, then the migration would result in greater impoverishment for the migrant and his family.

4. National Labour Migration Policies and Practices

Labour policies and practices vary between sending and receiving countries, and for each country it varies between policies and practices toward flows of professionals and the skilled and flows of semi-skilled and unskilled workers. Much of the discussions on the negative impacts of foreign labour refer primarily to the semi-skilled and unskilled, whether legal or irregular.

Labour-sending countries such as the Philippines, Vietnam and Indonesia have proactive government policies aimed at managing the volume and direction of labour flows and protecting worker rights and welfare. Labour-receiving countries such as Singapore, Malaysia and Thailand have proactive labour inflow policies that differentiate between professionals and executives on the one hand and unskilled and semi-skilled workers on the other — controlling the numbers of semi-skilled and unskilled inflows; attracting brain inflows; and controlling irregular inflows.

(i) Managing Labour Outflows and Involuntary Returnees

While the Philippines Government leaves labour migration to market forces and individual decisions, other governments such as in Vietnam and Indonesia have labour export policies aimed at alleviating domestic unemployment, contributing to foreign exchange earnings, and reducing the incidence of poverty. In the Philippines, various government agencies are involved in the migration management programme that encompasses documentation, protection, social services, and human resources development. In Vietnam, the July 2007 Law on Overseas Vietnamese Labour and various implementation decrees aim at a fuller and more comprehensive legal environment for labour exports, covering areas such as procedural simplification, fees and funding, pre-departure training, settlement of administrative violation of labour export businesses. Most Vietnamese provincial governments have set up labour export steering committees and adopted policies and measures to boost provincial labour-export activities. There are also more than a hundred Vietnamese labour-export enterprises licensed to export labour.

Governments of labour-sending countries have sometimes taken proactive action to protect the welfare of their migrant workers as well as try to handle the problems of irregular migrant workers and legal migrant workers who have been retrenched and repatriated by receiving countries. During the Asian financial and economic crises of 1997–98, large numbers of foreign workers were repatriated home as the economies of receiving countries went into severe recession. These involuntary returnees aggravate the unemployment problem in their home economies which were also in recession. The scenario is being repeated in recent months (late 2008 and early 2009) as various Southeast Asian economies experience sharp slowdowns in economic growth as a result of the fallout from the U.S. financial crisis and economic recession.

Some governments wish to discourage the out-migration of their professional and skilled workers to prevent a brain drain, and make special efforts to attract back their diaspora. However, efforts to encourage return migration have not been very successful, unless the home country is experiencing rapid economic growth, expanding employment and business opportunities and rising wage levels, as had been the case with South Korea and Taiwan since the 1980s.

(ii) Managing Labour Inflows and Attracting Brains

Policies and practices vary among ASEAN labour-receiving countries, with many adopting quantitative controls on inflows of semi-skilled and unskilled labour and qualitative controls on inflows of professionals and skilled labour to avoid "over-dependence" on foreign labour, encourage industrial upgrading, as well as protect the domestic job market.

• **Singapore** uses work permits and employment passes. Work permits are issued to semi-skilled and unskilled workers on a temporary basis. Company-specific work permit quotas are allocated to companies according to foreign worker "dependency ratios" that vary with sectors determined by the Manpower Ministry. Companies have to pay a foreign worker levy that varies with the skills of the foreign workers and the dependency ratio of the companies concerned.

Inflows into Singapore of professionals and skilled workers are freely welcomed to augment the domestic talent pool and expand Singapore's population. Measures include liberal issuance of various employment passes, offer of permanent residence and citizenship, and making the working and living environments attractive to foreign expatriates. Foreign professionals with professional or tertiary qualifications and earning salaries of over S$2,000 (about US$1,430) per month are required to obtain firm-specific Employment Passes that are valid for up to five years and renewable; unlike the case of unskilled and semi-skilled foreign workers, there is no foreign worker levy and no dependency ratio ceiling imposed on employing firms. Labour out-migration from Singapore is small and comprises mainly professionals working abroad, reflecting the internationalization of the Singapore economy and Singapore enterprises and the growing number of Singaporeans working for foreign MNCs. However, the inflow of "brains" far exceed the outflow.

- *Malaysia* is both a labour-sending and labour-receiving country but in-migration is almost entirely of low-skilled and temporary contract workers. Malaysia's *"bumiputra"* or affirmative action policy, restricts the employment of foreigners. A number of policy instruments were introduced over the years to control the intake of semi-skilled and unskilled foreign workers — encourage legal recruitment and stem irregular migration; and protect foreign workers. The 1991 Comprehensive Policy on the Recruitment of Foreign Workers covers the recruitment process, terms and conditions of employment and repatriation, introduce an annual levy to offset social costs and discourage the use of foreign labour; the Regularization Programmes legalize the entry and employment of irregular workers without penalty, amnesty and the occasional imposition of the total ban on new recruitment. These measures were complemented by security operations to curb illegal entry and internal surveillance to arrest, detain and deport "undocumented" migrants not responding to the registration exercise.

Malaysian policies have been relaxed to encourage and facilitate the entry and employment of foreign professionals following the national strategy of upgrading to skill and knowledge-intensive industries; they are allowed to work in almost all sectors, except those that impinge on national security and some restrictions are imposed on their numbers in banking and finance, but there are no restrictions for manufacturing firms located in the various Economic Growth Regions. Also, a Brain Gain Scheme was introduced in 1995 to encourage return migration of Malaysian professionals, and in 2001 a "distance service" programme was introduced to solicit the services of Malaysian professionals overseas without the need for return migration.

- In *Thailand*, the growing labour shortage, particularly in agriculture, fishery, construction and domestic helpers led to growing numbers of illegal migrant workers. In order to provide a better control and to manage their very large numbers, a new Alien Employment Act 2008 was enacted. It changed the occupations that permit foreign workers; provides for a levy on occupations; allows foreigners from neighbouring countries who enter by "Border Pass" to seek temporary employment in Thailand; and provides for work permits of two years and extendable by a further two years.

Thailand has also established procedures for entry of expatriates to work in firms promoted by the Board of Investment (BOI). The majority of joint ventures with FDI under BOI coverage are Japanese, British, and America and hence work permits are issued for nationals of these firms. The largest share of occupations of foreign workers who received work permits are managers and executives, followed by elementary occupations and professionals.

(iii) Controlling Inflows of Irregular Workers

Illegal migration is becoming a political and social issue in many receiving countries because of perceived social costs and security risks. To control the growing problem, several labour-receiving countries have introduced policies and measures that penalize these workers as well as their employers and purveyors and tightened border entry and surveillance. In addition to long-standing economic and social problems pose by irregular migrants, there is also the growing national security concerns in the context of global and regional terrorist threats.

Kanapathy (March 2008) argues that managing cross-border labour mobility is exceedingly difficult for Malaysia as it has a fast growing economy in the midst of labour surplus economies, a very long coastline and porous borders, and a multi-ethnic population and cultural similarities with many of the source countries making it difficult to identify and apprehend illegal immigrants, Moreover, migrant workers find ready employment in Malaysia's informal sectors or in remote plantations and forested areas.

- Thailand faces a large influx of irregular migrant workers from Myanmar, Laos and Cambodia to its agriculture and fishery, construction, and services sectors. Foreign worker registrations were carried out periodically, granting lenient treatment and work permits to illegals in various provinces, sectors and occupations. The new Employment Act in 2008 recognizes the hiring of unskilled and semi-skilled workers in occupations and areas specified by the Labour Ministry as well as introduces the imposition of a levy on employers, and registration fee on foreign workers.

Both Thailand and Malaysia have undertaken periodic amnesties and registrations but these have so far failed to resolve the issue.[7] Both countries have also negotiated bilateral arrangements with labour sending countries and its effectiveness is so far unclear. Malaysia has also decreed that workers could be admitted only from twelve designated countries — Cambodia, Indonesia, Laos, Myanmar, the Philippines, Thailand, Vietnam, India, Nepal, Kazakhstan, Turkestan and Uzbekistan. Thailand has signed memorandums of understanding (MOUs) with Cambodia, Laos, Myanmar to allow their nationals to work legally in Thailand provided they go through established procedures for recruitment in their countries of origin, register with Thai authorities, and obtain a Thai identification card.

(iv) Protecting Worker Rights and Welfare

Several labour-sending countries have institutional mechanisms to protect their out-migrant workers through licensing and surveillance of private recruitment agencies as well as country-to-country cooperation, as well as policies to maximize the usage of remittances through various savings and investment schemes. In the Philippines, the government only deploys Filipino workers to countries where the rights of Filipino workers are respected. It provides the mechanism to protect the rights of their overseas Filipino workers (OFWs) to fair and equitable recruitment and employment practices and ensure their welfare under a deregulated condition; develops programmes to ensure quality employment for OFWs; and provides a provident fund for OFWs.

5. Regional and Bilateral Cooperation on Labour Migration

It is the right of every nation state to regulate immigration policies. However, as the ASEAN region contains both labour-sending and -receiving countries, there would appear much is to be gained from regional and bilateral cooperation. Labour-sending countries are keen to have the barriers to ILM lowered or removed, while labour-receiving countries have asymmetrical policies that restrict the inflows of unskilled and semi-skilled workers on the one hand and welcome inflows of professionals and skilled workers on the other.

Nonetheless, there is no free movement of professional and skilled labour. Barriers to mobility include visa requirements and procedures, minimum education/job experience requirements, levies on employment of foreign workers, employment restricted to a specific firm or location, economic needs and labour market tests to justify the need for employment of a foreign professional, and general absence of mutual recognition arrangements on professional qualifications and experiences. Other obstacles include licensing regulations imposed by professional associations. Also, the international market for professionals is mediated by recruitment and head-hunting agencies and overseas employment boards acting as gatekeepers for foreign entry. These various barriers as well as language and cultural differences and social costs of adaptation have to be taken into consideration in labour migration and weighed against the benefits of higher wages and better job prospects.

The 1995 ASEAN Framework Agreement on Services (AFAS) provides *inter alia*, for regulatory convergence and regulatory harmonization, including Mutual Recognition Arrangements (MRAs). These MRAs enable the qualifications of professional services suppliers to be mutually recognized by ASEAN members, hence facilitating easier flow of professional service providers in the region. ASEAN has so far concluded seven MRAs on engineering, architectural, accountancy services, surveying qualifications, nursing, medical practitioners and dental practitioners, and much more remains to be done.

The ASEAN Economic Community (AEC) to be realized by 2015 includes only free movement of skilled labour, as mobility of unskilled and semi-skilled labour remains politically sensitive. The AEC Blueprint highlights the following actions:

- Facilitate issuance of visas and employment passes for ASEAN professionals and skilled labour engaged in trade and investment-related activities.
- Harmonization and standardization to facilitate free flow of services — enhanced cooperation among ASEAN University Network members to increase mobility of staff and students; develop core competencies and qualifications for job/ occupational and trainers skills required in the AEC priority services by 2009 and in other services by 2015.
- Strengthen the research capabilities of ASEAN countries in terms of promoting skills, job placements, and developing labour market information networks among ASEAN countries.

The AEC Blueprint stresses three general categories of actions that need to be undertaken to this end:

(i)   Enhance cooperation among ASEAN University Network (AUN) members to increase mobility for both students and staff within the region;
(ii)   Develop core competencies and qualifications for job/ occupational and trainer skills required in the priority service sectors (by 2009); and in other service sectors (from 2010 to 2015); and
(iii)   Strengthen the research capabilities of each ASEAN member state in terms of promoting skills, job placements, and developing labour market information networks among ASEAN member states.

We would expect that migrant skilled workers flows within ASEAN would increase significantly in the future, especially with increases in intra-regional FDI flows and free flows of services. If mobility of skilled workers is going to be mutually beneficial for all member states, there is a need to develop MRAs for various occupations and qualifications, facilitate foreign registration of qualifications, encourage language proficiency courses, improve transparency and information on labour markets and hiring requirements. In 2008, ASEAN Economic Ministers' (AEM) Meeting deferred the development of a regional qualifications framework until all countries had developed their own national qualifications system. If intra-regional mobility of skilled workers can be regularized effectively, the increasing mobility of ASEAN's human resources is likely to be a new source of comparative advantage in an increasingly competitive global environment. It would also be useful if ASEAN could adopt concerted approaches to improve the efficacy of their education systems in providing the necessary skills for the labour markets.

The ASEAN Declaration on the Protection and Promotion of Rights of Migrant Workers signed in January 2007 is a major step by ASEAN member countries in recognizing the increasingly important role of the region's migrant workers and their responsibility in ensuring the protection of migrant workers' rights. The declaration recognizes the contributions of migrant workers to ASEAN sending and receiving countries and the sovereign right of ASEAN states to determine their own migration policy relating to migrant workers (including determining entry and the conditions under which migrant workers may remain), the legitimate concerns of receiving and sending countries over migrant workers and the need to adopt appropriate and comprehensive migration policies on migrant workers, and the need to address cases of abuse and violence against migrant workers hereby adopted the following principles:

- Both receiving and sending states promote the full potential and dignity of migrant workers in a climate of freedom, equity and stability in accordance with the laws, regulations and policies of respective ASEAN countries.
- Receiving and sending states shall, for humanitarian reasons, closely cooperate to resolve the cases of migrant workers who, through no fault of their own, have subsequently become undocumented.
- Receiving and sending states shall take into account the fundamental rights and dignity of migrant workers and family members already residing with them without undermining the application by the receiving states of their laws, regulations and policies.

Obligations of receiving-state cover: provide migrant workers with adequate access to the legal and judicial system; facilitate the exercise of consular or diplomatic authorities of states of origin where a migrant worker is arrested or committed to prison or custody or detained in any manner.

Obligations of sending-state cover: set up policies and procedures to facilitate recruitment, preparation for deployment overseas and protection of migrant workers, as well as repatriation and re-integration of returnee migrants; establish and promote legal practices to regulate recruitment of migrant workers and adopt mechanisms to eliminate recruitment malpractices.

The declaration also commits ASEAN to the following, in accordance with national laws, regulations and policies:

- Promote decent, humane, productive, dignified and remunerative employment for migrant workers.
- Establish and implement human resource development and re-integration programmes for migrant workers in their countries of origin.
- Take concrete measures to prevent or curb human smuggling and trafficking, for example, by introducing stiffer penalties for those involved.
- Facilitate data-sharing on matters related to migrant workers so as to enhance policies and programmes concerning migrant workers in both sending and receiving countries.
- Promote capacity building by sharing of information, best practices and opportunities and challenges encountered in relation to protection and promotion of migrant workers' rights and welfare.
- Extend assistance to migrant workers of ASEAN countries who are caught in conflict or crisis situations outside ASEAN

in the event of need and based on capacities and resources of embassies and consular offices of relevant ASEAN countries, based on bilateral consultations and arrangements.

- Encourage international organizations, ASEAN dialogue partners and other countries to respect the principles and extend support and assistance to the implementation of the declaration.
- Task relevant ASEAN bodies to develop an ASEAN instrument on the protection and promotion of the rights of migrant workers, consistent with ASEAN's vision of a caring and sharing community and direct the ASEAN secretary-general to submit an annual report on the progress in implementation of the declaration to the ASEAN Summit.
- In the longer term, building a strong and responsive higher education and Technical Vocational Education and Training (TVET) system capable of providing graduates with the skills, knowledge and attitudes required by a competitive economy will be essential. Beyond the education system, governments must support workforce development through lifelong learning and skills training programmes.

Regional and bilateral economic partnership agreements (EPAs) and free trade agreements (FTAs) negotiated by ASEAN and its members also have provisions for labour mobility. For example:

- In the U.S.-Singapore FTA, the United States has liberalized entry of business and professional persons who are Singapore citizens; likewise, Singapore has liberalized entry of legal, architecture, engineering and land surveying professionals from the United States.
- Japan's EPA with Singapore has chapters on the movement of natural persons, specifically for business visitors, intra-

company transferees, and certain categories of investors and professionals. Japan's EPAs with the Philippines, Thailand and Indonesia include provisions for capped entry and employment in Japan of Filipino nurses and caregivers; Thai cooks, care workers, spa therapists and instructors of Thai dance, music, cuisine, language and boxing; and Indonesian healthcare givers.

Some ASEAN countries have also concluded bilateral labour agreements for the protection of migrant workers (Chia 2008). These include:

- The Philippines has signed several bilateral labour agreements. They cover terms and conditions of employment and mobilization of Filipino workers; exchange of trainees; promotion of cooperation on labour, employment and manpower development; protection of the rights of migrant workers including legal assistance; training and certification of migrant workers; exchange of information, materials and experiences; and development of collaborative training. In 2003 a bilateral labour agreement was signed with Indonesia and represented the first successful attempt by the Philippines to consolidate the efforts of other labour-sending countries in the region towards promoting the welfare of migrant workers and protecting their rights.
- The Thailand Government has founded the Friends of Thai Workers Association Office to act as intermediary between Thai government agencies and Thai workers in Singapore, and to provide the workers with psycho-medical, recreational and educational services.
- Malaysia has established bilateral cooperation with its major labour-sending countries covering regular dialogue sessions on labour issues, MOUs on terms and conditions of

employment in Malaysia, practices of recruiting labour agents and the establishment of Joint Working Group to discuss matters arising from the implementation of the MOU.

6. Conclusion

ILM is a growing phenomenon in Southeast Asia. There is converging economic interests of labour surplus and labour shortage countries. However, there are also economic, social and political sensitivities and concerns. In labour-receiving countries, the main concerns are an over-dependence on foreign labour; the competition with domestic labour for jobs and downward pressure on wages; and perceived increased demand for public services; decreased social cohesion; increased crime and disease; and increased security threat. In the labour-sending countries, the main concerns are over better market access for the surplus labour; retrenchments in sending countries aggravating unemployment at home during periods of slow growth and recession; the negative effects of brain drain; absorption of remittance inflows; and protection of the rights and welfare of out-migrant workers.

There are concerns that can be addressed at the national level. These would include policies and measures to promote domestic employment growth to minimize the need for overseas employment for labour-surplus countries; policies to reduce dependence on foreign labour for labour-shortage countries; participation in international labour conventions of the ILO to protect worker rights; controlling the exploitation by labour recruitment and placement agencies; facilitating the inflow of worker remittances; and encouraging the return of the migrants and diaspora.

However, much could be achieved through regional and bilateral cooperative action at the ASEAN level (Chia 2008).

- *Market access and skills recognition issues*: These include liberalization, harmonization and standardization of border barriers of immigration regulations and visa policies; levies and quotas that restrict the entry and employment of foreign workers; regulations governing occupational licensing, qualifications and standards, and different and cultural and language barriers. The liberalization of trade in services and in foreign investment could lead to the lowering of immigration barriers and levies and quotas on employment of foreign professionals and executives. Establishment of MRAs of national qualifications and standards for various occupations, development of common standards and licensing requirements, and help for the less-developed economies to design national qualification frameworks would facilitate cross-border flows of professionals and other skilled migrants. Improving market access for semi-skilled and unskilled labour is more difficult, given the large numbers involved. Pre-employment training could improve their employability and productivity.
- *Cooperation between sending and receiving countries to protect the rights of migrant workers*: The 2007 ASEAN Declaration on the Promotion of the Rights of Migrant Workers represents a major step forward by ASEAN countries. ASEAN governments should ensure that the declaration is executed to maximize the benefits of labour migration for both economic growth and social development.
  - *Possible actions in the recruitment phase*: Reduce the transaction costs and exploitation faced by migrant workers when seeking employment abroad such as — high costs of passports and visas and other fees charged by government agencies; exploitation by recruitment

agencies in both sending and receiving countries that charge high administrative fees; false promises of employment made by labour recruitment agencies in sending countries that leave migrants stranded and without employment on arrival.

- *Possible actions in the employment phase*: Reduce vulnerability to abuses and exploitation at places of employment — these include non-compliance with the labour laws of the receiving country; mistreatment of the workers and non-payment of wages which should receive consular help and legal redress; exploitation in the sending of remittances by unauthorized agents in sending and receiving countries. Social networks for migrant workers can help them with language and cultural assimilation problems. A joint committee should be established to monitor compliance, adjudicate on disputes and if necessary help the migrant workers seek legal redress.

- *Possible actions in the return migration phase*: Improve the employability and adjustment of migrant workers when they return home — acquisition of skills to prepare for eventual return to home countries; placement services and entrepreneurial services in home countries to "resettle" the returnees.

- ***Cooperation to resolve problem of irregular migrants***: These would include improving transparency and lessened bureaucratic and documentary requirements for legal entry and employment; improving information flow on the penalties for irregular entry and employment impose on workers, purveyors and employers; exchange of information between governments on illegal migrants and joint action in the deportation of these workers and their return to their home country; joint surveillance of borders to minimize flows of illegal workers and safeguard national security. The less-developed countries need capacity-building assistance to better handle the issue of illegal migration and human trafficking.

Notes

1. Hugo (2008) lists the following reasons for this — a high incidence of irregular migration; lack of comprehensive and efficient data collection systems; neglect of temporary migration in data collection systems which focus on permanent migration; some destination economies do not divulge data on international migration because they do not wish to be widely known the precise degree of dependence on foreign labour.

2. During the Asian financial crisis of 1997–98, there was massive repatriation of foreign workers thrown out of work by the sharp downturns in economic activity. It was easier for firms to retrench the temporary foreign workers. Likewise, in the current recessions triggered by the U.S. financial and economic crises, the media is reporting growing numbers of foreign workers being repatriated. It should be noted that it is not only the foreign workers that are laid off; there are also massive laid-offs among Japan's temporary workers and among Chinese workers in the Pearl River Delta of China.

3. Economic Survey of Singapore, First Quarter 2004, Singapore Ministry of Trade and Industry.

4. As reported in *Straits Times*, 1 May 2008.

5. Cited in ILO (2008).

6. Ibid.

7. ILO (2008) notes that Malaysia offered amnesty to irregular migrants in a four-month period bridging late 2004 and early 2005, but only

about 380,000 of an estimated 0.8–1.2 million irregular migrants availed themselves of the opportunity. Thailand conducted a registration campaign and offered amnesty to irregular migrants from July–August 2004 with about 1.3 million actually registering.

References

Ananta, Aris and Evi Nurvidya Arifin. "Demographic and Population Mobility Transition in Indonesia". Draft paper for presentation at the PECC-ABAC Conference on Demographic Change and International Labour Mobility in the Asia Pacific, Seoul, 25–26 March 2008.

ASEAN Secretariat. *ASEAN Economic Community Blueprint*, April 2008.

Chia Siow Yue. "Demographic Change and International Labour Mobility in Southeast Asia: Issues, Policies and Implications for Cooperation". In *Labour Mobility in the Asia-Pacific Region: Dynamics, Issues and a New APEC Agenda*, edited by Graeme Hugo and Soogil Young. Singapore: Institute of Southeast Asian Studies, 2008.

————. "Labour Mobility and East Asian Integration". In *Asian Economic Policy Review* (December 2006): 349–67.

Hugo, Graeme. "Demographic Change and International Labour Mobility in Asia Pacific: Implications for Business and Regional Economic Integration: Synthesis". In *Labour Mobility in the Asia-Pacific Region: Dynamics, Issues and a New APEC Agenda*, edited by Graeme Hugo and Soogil Young. Singapore: Institute of Southeast Asian Studies, 2008.

International Labour Office. *Labour and Social Trends in ASEAN 2007: Integration, Challenges and Opportunities*. Bangkok: ILO Regional Office for Asia and the Pacific, 2007.

————. *Labour and Social Trends in ASEAN 2008: Driving Competitiveness and Prosperity with Decent Work*. Bangkok: ILO Regional Office for Asia and the Pacific, 2008.

Kanapathy, Vijayakumari. "Cross-Border Labour Mobility in Malaysia:

Two Decades of Policy Experiments". Draft paper for presentation at the PECC-ABAC Conference on Demographic Change and International Labour Mobility in the Asia Pacific, Seoul, 25–26 March 2008.

Lucas, R.E.B. *International Labour Migration and Economic Development: Lessons from Low Income Countries.* London: Edward Elgar, 2005.

Tullao Jr., Tereso S. "Demographic Changes and International Labour Mobility in the Philippines: Implications for Business and Cooperation". Draft paper for presentation at the PECC-ABAC Conference on Demographic Change and International Labour Mobility in the Asia Pacific, Seoul, 25–26 March 2008.

World Bank. *Migration and Remittance Factbook 2008.*

Chia Siow Yue is a Senior Research Fellow at the Singapore Institute of International Affairs (SIIA).

10
LABOUR MARKET INTEGRATION
WITHIN NAFTA[1]

Don J. DeVoretz

1. Introduction

Many economists, including the famed Robert Mundell, have
made strong trade-related pronouncements to the effect that
trade is a substitute for migration. This proposition was in the
forefront of many United States policy-makers' minds when they
argued for the admission of Mexico into the then Free Trade
Agreement between Canada and the United States. If this
proposition were true in the North American Free Trade
Agreement (NAFTA) context, then it could be argued that
increased trade in goods between Mexico and the United States,
and presumably Canada, would permit factor price equalization
and remove the incentives for unskilled Mexicans to migrate
north for jobs. Of course this proposition only holds under special
conditions, and policy-makers were more circumspect when the
mobility section of the NAFTA agreement was signed.[2] It is
important to note that mobility provisions within NAFTA were
concluded after the core of the agreement was signed to avoid
the contentious issue of granting mobility rights to the unskilled.
In fact, complete labour mobility was only granted to the highly
skilled under the NAFTA accord, and initially only between two
signatories, Canada and the United States.[3]

Thus, even in the very constrained setting of NAFTA, United States and Canadian policy-makers imposed a two-tiered mobility regime on Mexico, their new less developed partner.

2. Model and Theory

In this paper, I will outline a theoretical model drawing on available econometric evidence describing mobility within NAFTA to reflect on the eventual equilibrium size of the flows of both skilled and unskilled immigrants between NAFTA trade partners. This analysis will allow us to determine the equilibrium wage difference between NAFTA countries at unequal levels of development and the degree of labour market integration when migration halts. The equilibrium income difference under which migration halts will be termed the "reservation wage gain". If this reservation income gain is small, then high levels of immigration will occur between states with unequal levels of development, and *vice-versa*, and lead to fully integrated labour markets.

A second and equally important concept to assess labour mobility within the NAFTA context is the "border effect" whereby, given any distance or potential income gain from movement, migration will be lower if the migrant must cross a border, even if mobility is completely unfettered between two international points.[4]

I further assert that the reservation wage and the border effect vary by level of development and across occupations. Thus, theory suggests that, in equilibrium, labour market integration can range from 0 to 100 per cent. An example of a labour market with incomplete but substantial integration is presented in Figure 10.1.

FIGURE 10.1

**Border Effect, Reservation Income Gain and the Degree of
Labour Market Integration in Canada**

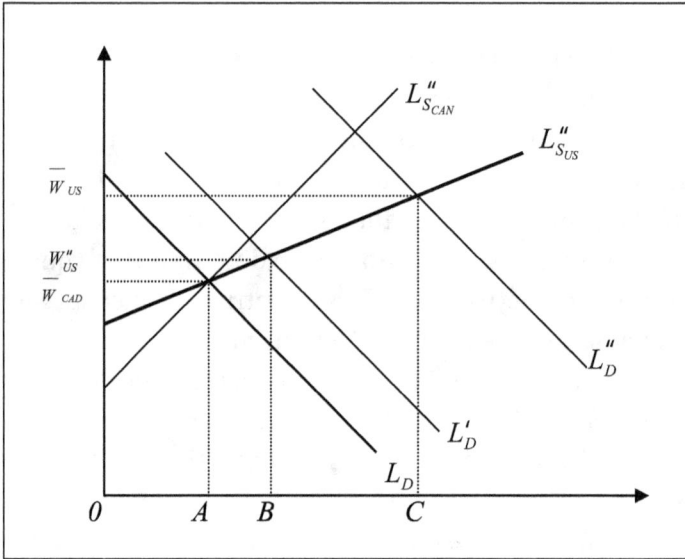

In a closed Canadian economy all OA workers are Canadian, and there are no foreign workers. However, after both sending and receiving countries enter a free trade agreement with mobility provisions, the demand for labour shifts to the right in Canada, the potential receiving country. Now all the increased demand for labour, or AB, is supplied by outsiders from the United States, and this process continues until demand equals supply. How do we arrive at this situation? A quick inspection of the labour supply curves in Canada and the United States provides an answer. For example, United States workers will migrate as demand rises from L_D to L'_D, and now supply all of the new labour (A-B) at a lower wage than their Canadian counterpart. If the border effect is nil for American workers entering Canada and their supply wage is below the Canadian reservation wage, the Canadian labour market achieves equilibrium: AC/OC labour is foreign-born and only OA/OC is domestically supplied.

Figure 10.2 illustrates a similar case, but the United States labour supply curve lies everywhere above the Canadian supply curve for labour in Canada. This is owing to a greater reservation wage for labour in the United States or a sizeable border effect for Americans. Under these conditions, Canadian labour market equilibrium is achieved with zero foreign labour.

Of course, the core question is, which of the two figures applies to which pair of countries? Whether individuals respond to cross-border wage or employment opportunities depends on

FIGURE 10.2

**Border Effect, Reservation Income Gain and Zero Degree
of Labour Market Integration in Canada**

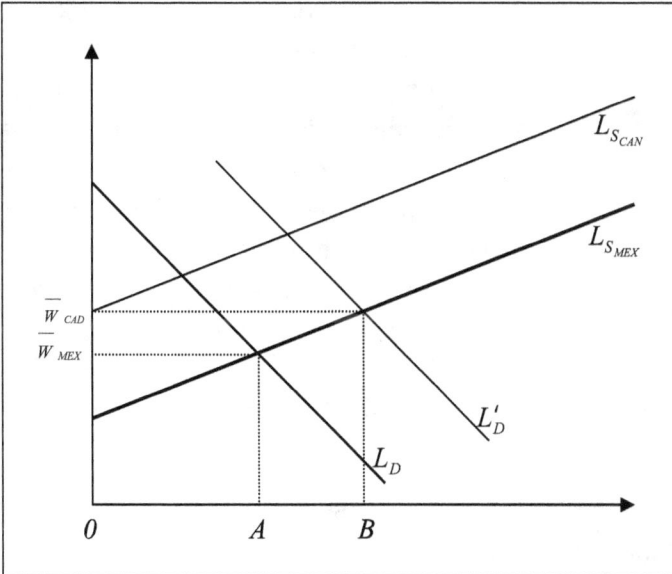

the level of their reservation wage, the size of their potential income gain from migration, and the border effect. In turn, the size of the reservation wage and the border effect, both of which inhibit mobility, arises from the level of development in the sending country and the institutional and cultural variations between the sending and receiving regions. These observations and theoretical paradigms lead me to the following several propositions:

Proposition I: The reservation wage gain is greater for individuals in occupations with greater human capital.

Proposition II: The reservation wage gain is greater for individuals from countries with a large social capital and generous amenities.

Proposition III: The border effect is greater between countries with different institutions and/or language.

Proposition IV: The smaller the border effect the greater the immigrant enclave is in the receiving country.

Proposition V: The border effect approaches zero when the elasticity of migration with respect to any income gain is identical within a country or between two countries.

Proposition VI: In equilibrium the migration flows lead to a level of labour force integration which ranges from 0 to 100 per cent depending on the size of the border effect and the reservation income gain.

3. Stylized Facts and Migration Outcomes

(i) Canadian Highly Skilled Emigres

NAFTA member countries offer several examples to shed light on the propositions listed above. Table 10.1 provides a topology of

TABLE 10.1

**Probability of Moving to High Income Destination from Low-
and Medium-Income Welfare States: The Roles of the Border
and Reservation Income Effects**

	Probability			
Potential labour	Highly skilled		Unskilled	
Welfare levels in sending countries	Low	Medium	Low	Medium
Prime age resident	> .5	< .5	~ 1	~ 0
Border effect	~ 0	~ 0	> 0	> 0
Reservation wage	> 0	> 0	~ 0	> 0

migration cases under a NAFTA-type environment to illustrate
my propositions.

I first posit the existence of at least four equilibrium states in
the proposed regional integration scheme, and two types of labour,
highly skilled and unskilled. Two sending states offer welfare
packages to their residents, with the middle-income country
offering the most benefits under a high-tax environment. One of
the sending states has a low-income environment and the other, a
medium-income environment. The receiving state is a high-income
state with no welfare and a low-tax environment. These assumed
conditions approximate the stylized facts for Canada, Mexico,
and the United States as receiving countries.[5] I now have four
outcomes for the probability of moving for a prime-age resident
from Canada and Mexico to the United States, owing to various
combinations of the border and reservation effects. The probability
to migrate across these cases, is from zero (unskilled from Canada)
to near certainty (unskilled from Mexico).

These outcomes recognize the combined border and reservation income effects. I assert that the border effect between the medium-income country (Canada) or the low-income country (Mexico) and the United States, is nil for the highly skilled, but positive for unskilled migrants to the United States. A minimal border effect arises for the highly skilled since the language and cultural norms *vis-à-vis* the United States are offset by their prior human capital accumulation. Higher education usually equips potential skilled immigrants with English and a broad awareness of cultural norms in the receiving country. This is not true for unskilled workers from Mexico who have limited English language skills, and must live in an immigrant enclave to mitigate the border effect (Chiswick and Hurst 2000).

On the other hand, the reservation wage gain, or the required potential income difference to induce movement, is larger for the highly skilled than for the unskilled immigrants from either sending country. The lower absolute earnings of the unskilled insures that any income gain owing to movement will induce migration if the border effect can be offset.

I now turn to some simulation experiments in actual Canadian case studies to support Propositions I to VI.

The simulations portrayed in Figure 10.3 represent the probability of staying in Canada for labour force members of various ages by marital status, with and without children. Clearly, once a critical age is reached (around thirty-five) where access to social goods matters, the probability of staying rises (to 0.85) for the married highly skilled potential mover in the medium-income welfare state. However, there is little holding effect derived from the social goods for a young skilled person, and the probability of moving is approximately 0.5 at age twenty-five.[6]

FIGURE 10.3

Effects of Gender, Marital Status and Mobility on Predicted Probabilities of Staying in Canada of Labour Force Members by Age Category: 1995–96*

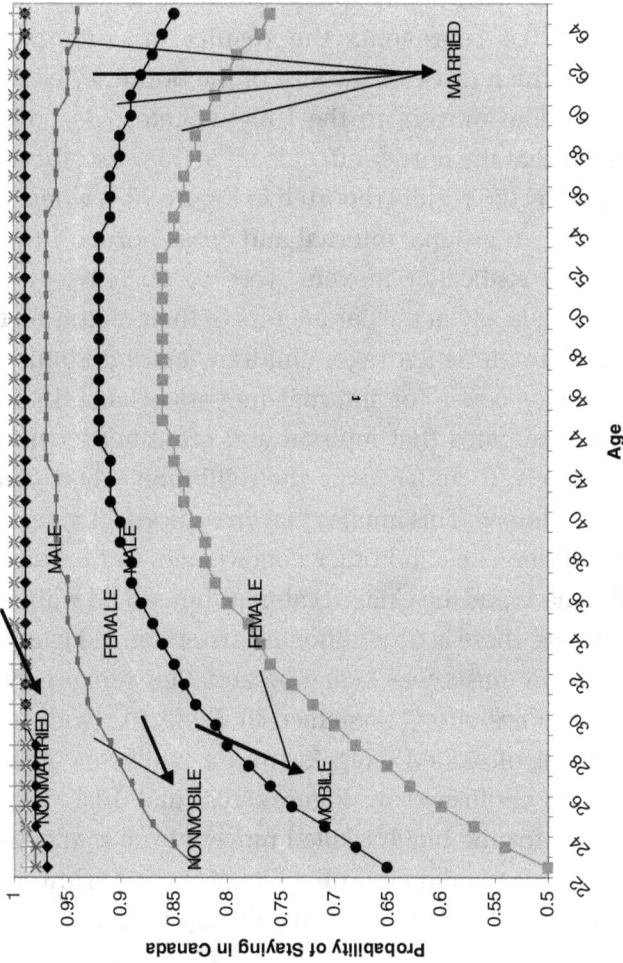

Note: *These are the probabilities as a function of age at the sample means of total income and family.

Sources: 1996 Canadian Census, Public Use Microdata Individual Files and 1995 Current Population Sun Perosn and Family Data Files, U.S. Census Bureau.

In sum, Figure 10.3 allows us to conclude that the income gain effect is critical, and its size can offset the lack of access to social goods for potential movers over their lifetime. I now evaluate the border effect for highly skilled Canadian émigrés.

Figure 10.4 represents the results of a counterfactual experiment which tests for the size of the border effect on highly skilled Canadian movers to the United States. Based on Table 10.1, I assert that the border effect is nil in this case; this assertion is confirmed by the results reported in Figure 10.4, where I divided movers into two groups, internal and cross-border. I then asked how likely cross-border movers were to go between any two points in Canada, given the parameters of their migration function and their characteristics (age, children, marital status, income gain), and *vice-versa* for internal movers (Gaetz 1998, p. 54). Figure 10.4 indicates that internal and cross-border movers are nearly as likely to move over their lifetime when faced with identical conditions. This implies that cross-border movers respond to income differences and other conditioners to the same degree between Canada and the United States as they would within Canada. In other words, there is no additional barrier derived from a border effect if the circumstances facing potential movers are identical.

Thus, the assertions contained in Table 10.1 with respect to the movement of skilled émigrés from a middle-income country (Canada) are confirmed by Figures 10.3 and 10.4. There is no border effect for the highly skilled movers from a middle-income country (Canada), and their probability of moving is lower than 0.5, declines with age, and is insensitive to very large income gains.

(ii) Canadian Unskilled Emigres

Canada's very progressive tax environment, paired with substantial social services, results in the following: the real income for low-

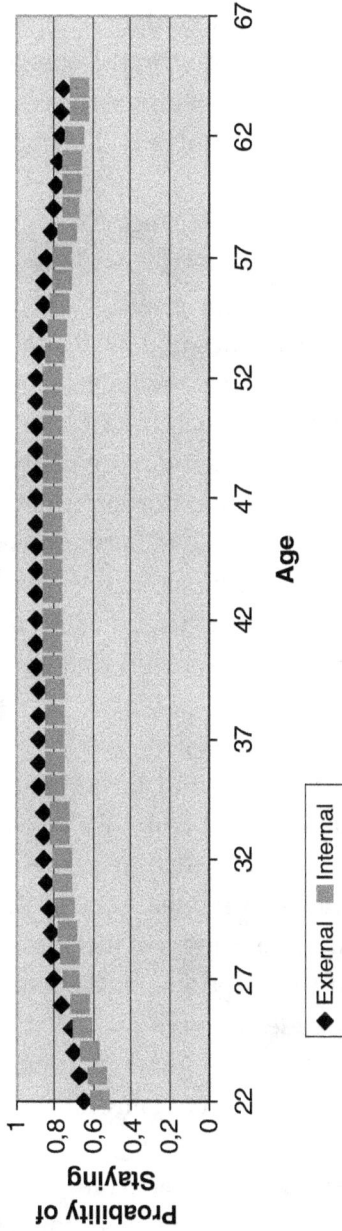

FIGURE 10.4

Counterfactual Experiment: Border Effect

income Canadian earners actually exceeds that of comparable United States workers.[7] Thus, in the absence of a critical income gain to offset any border effect, no emigration of unskilled Canadians to the United States will occur.

(iii) Mexican Unskilled Emigres

Currently scant econometric evidence provides simulation outcomes to portray the equilibrium level of labour force integration between Mexico and the United States. However, both policy measures and some ancillary facts offer hints to support the assertions contained in Table 10.1. In particular, I argue that unskilled Mexican émigrés are more likely to move to the United States since both the actual border effect is low and the critical income difference to induce emigration is not large. The critical income effect between Mexico and the United States has grown during the last decade due to a decline in Mexican agricultural opportunities and the expansion that took place in the United States (Martin 2003). The potential border effect between the United States and Mexico generated by differences in cultural norms, consumption items and language should be high; however, the work of Chiswick and Hurst (2000) indicates the opposite. Chiswick and Hurst argue that Mexicans live in border enclaves in the United States to reduce border effects, and that this, in turn, lowers the deterrent effect of the border. In addition, Chiswick and Hearst note that workers in the enclaves receive a lower wage than the broader class of unskilled United States workers. Chiswick argues that the lower border costs in the Mexican enclaves offset the necessity of any large critical income effect to induce movement.[8]

One contrary fact emerges to measure the substantial degree of the border effect for Mexicans, namely remittances. In the

Lucas and Stark (1985) tradition, remittances can be viewed as part of a co-insurance scheme between immigrants and their family, allowing Mexican émigrés to reintegrate their home community upon return. In sum, the border effect does not act as a significant deterrent for the unskilled Mexicans.

What of the inducement of the job-income effect in the United States? The absolute size of the wage gain can be small, since the home wage in Mexico is low and the rate of return on any modest improvement in expected income will be large. This observation is supported by Martin (2003) who predicted a bubble in unskilled Mexican emigration to California. According to Martin, the post-NAFTA increase in Mexican emigration would be induced by the comparative advantage of California in exporting food and semi-skilled produced goods to Mexico. This in fact occurred and raised employment opportunities for unskilled Mexicans in the United States.

The substantial pull effect of income and a minimal border effect lead me to conclude that south-north unskilled emigration from Mexico will grow.

(iv) Mexican Highly Skilled Emigres

The inclusion of Mexico in NAFTA did not afford the Mexican highly skilled the same mobility rights as their Canadian counterparts in the United States. It will be remembered that substantial mobility rights were granted to a large number of skilled Canadian citizens with the advent of the TN visa. The number of potential skilled émigrés from Mexico who had to apply inland was, however, capped. Until 2004, these restrictions effectively deterred substantial movement, but more highly skilled Mexicans are now likely to move to the United States.[9] The reasons for this are simple. Regardless of where the Mexican highly skilled go to work in the United States, the border effect will be nil. Moreover, the high rate of return arising from subsidized education in Mexico, will hasten the exit of these skilled workers from Mexico.

In sum, both the border effect and size of the critical income are such that the probability of skilled Mexican emigration to the United States will rise.

4. Conclusions

Table 10.1 and the underlying principles embodied in its stylized scenarios allow me to draw some limited lessons from the NAFTA experience for future mobility patterns in other trade blocks. First, the mobility patterns between NAFTA members will depend more on the potential migrants' qualifications than on their country of origin, since the income gain from the move will exceed the border effect. The final degree of labour market integration of foreign workers (see Figure 10.1) will ultimately depend on the slope of the occupational supply curve in the sending country relative to the receiving country. For pairs of countries with potentially large border effects, only the existence of a prior enclave will insure the conditions for substantial foreign-born labour force integration.

In sum, I offer two analytical tools, the border and reservation income gain effects to predict labour mobility in the context of a NAFTA-type trade block.

Notes

1. I thank the Asia Pacific Foundation of Canada under its Canadians Abroad Project for financial support whilst writing this paper. The careful copyediting of Dr D. Coulombe greatly improved the paper.
2. See Markusen (1983) for all the exceptions when this proposition would not hold.

3. The TN visa is valid for one year and renewable indefinitely.
4. Helliwell (1999) first argued this point by noting that, even under free trade between Canada and the United States, there was a greater tendency to trade goods within one country than between two countries, given identical distances separating producers and consumers.
5. Under current U.S. regulations, immigrants are not eligible for most federal programmes.
6. See DeVoretz and Iturralde (2001) for a complete explanation of the simulation methodology.
7. DeVoretz and Laryea (1998).
8. According the 2000 U.S. Census, Mexican immigrants have left enclaves in large numbers for unskilled work in interior U.S. cities. This indicates a further erosion of the border effect in deterring Mexican emigration to the United States.
9. Some restrictions were removed in 2004, but Mexicans still must obtain a TN-2 visa prior to presenting themselves at the border.

References

Chiswick, B. and M. Hurst. "Hispanics and the American Labor Market". In *Hispanics in the United States: An Agenda for the Twenty-First Century*, edited by P. San Juan Cafferty and D.W. Engstrom. New Brunswick: Transaction Books, 2000.

DeVoretz, D.J. and C. Iturralde. "Why do the Highly Skilled Stay in Canada?" *Policy Options* (March 2001): 59–63.

DeVoretz, D.J. and S. Laryea. *Human Capital Transfers: The USA and Beyond*. Toronto: C.D. Howe Institute, 1998.

Gaetz, C.E. "Interprovincial Migration in Canada, 1986–1991: A Multinomial Logit Approach". Unpublished Master's thesis project, Simon Fraser University, Burnaby, Canada, 1998.

Helliwell, J.F. "Checking the Brain Drain: Evidence and Implications". *Policy Options* 20, no. 7 (1999): 6–17.

Lucas, R.B. and O. Stark. "Motivation to Remit". *Journal of Political Economy* 93, no. 5 (1985): 901–18.

Markusen, J.R. "Factor Movements and Commodity Trade as Complements". *Journal of International Economics* 14, nos. 3–4 (1983): 341–56.

Martin, P. "Mexico-US Migration", 2008. <http://www.petersoninstitute. org/publications/chapters_preview/332/08iie3349.pdf> (accessed 1 January 2009).

Professor Don J. DeVoretz is at the Department of Economics of the Simon Fraser University, British Columbia, Canada.

LSEAS   **IDRC ✳ CRDI**   Canadä

ASEAN-CANADA FORUM 2008
Regional Economic Integration:
ASEAN and Canadian Perspectives

25–26 November 2008
Seminar Rooms I and II
Institute of Southeast Asian Studies
Singapore

PROGRAMME

Tuesday, 25 November 2008

8.30 a.m. – 9.00 a.m.   Registration

9.00 a.m. – 9.15 a.m.   **Opening Remarks**

Ambassador K. KESAVAPANY
Director, Institute of Southeast Asian Studies,
Singapore

Mr Richard FUCHS
Regional Director, International Development
Research Centre
(IDRC), Singapore

HE David SEVIGNY
High Commissioner, Canadian High Commission,
Singapore

9.15 a.m. – 9.45 a.m.   **Keynote Address**

Professor Kishore MAHBUBANI
Dean, Lee Kuan Yew School of Public Policy,
National University of Singapore

9.45 a.m. – 10.15 a.m.	Q&A

10.15 a.m. – 10.30 a.m.	Coffee

10.30 a.m. – 12.00 noon **SESSION I:**   **AFTA AND NAFTA: TRADE AND INVESTMENT ISSUES**

Moderator: *Mr Rodolfo C. SEVERINO*
Head, ASEAN Studies Centre,
Institute of Southeast Asian Studies,
Singapore and former ASEAN
Secretary-General

Paperwriters: *Professor Myrna S. AUSTRIA*
Dean, College of Business and
Economics, De La Salle University,
Manila

Professor John WHALLEY
William G. Davis Chair in
International Trade, Department of
Economics, University of Western
Ontario, London, Ontario

12.00 noon – 1.00 p.m.   Lunch

1.00 p.m. – 2.30 p.m.   **SESSION II:**   **INSTITUTIONAL DEVELOPMENT UNDER ASEAN AND NAFTA**

Moderator: *Dr Evan DUE*
Senior Programme Specialist,
International Development Research
Centre (IDRC), Singapore

Paperwriters: *Mr Rodolfo C. SEVERINO*
Head, ASEAN Studies Centre,
Institute of Southeast Asian Studies,
Singapore and former ASEAN
Secretary-General

Professor Richard BARICHELLO
Director, Centre for Southeast Asia
Research, Department of Food and
Resource Economics, University of
British Columbia, Vancouver

2.30 p.m. – 4.00 p.m.	**SESSION III:**	**GOVERNANCE AND ACCOUNTABILITY IN ASEAN AND NAFTA**
	Moderator:	*Associate Professor Locknie HSU* School of Law, Singapore Management University
	Paperwriters:	*Ms Kala ANANDARAJAH* Partner, Rajah & Tann, Singapore
		Professor Paul J. DAVIDSON Department of Law, Carleton University, Ottawa
4.00 p.m. – 4.15 p.m.	Tea	
7.30 p.m.	Buffet Reception hosted by ISEAS and IDRC at The Panorama, 24th floor, Hilton Hotel, 581 Orchard Road, Singapore 238883 (organized by ISEAS Public Affairs)	

REGIONAL ECONOMIC INTEGRATION: A PRIVATE SECTOR PERSPECTIVE

	Presenter:	*Mr George HAYNAL* Vice-President, Government Affairs, Bombardier Inc, Ottawa

Wednesday, 26 November 2008

9.00 a.m. – 9.30 a.m.	**Opening Remarks**
	Dr Rohinton MEDHORA Vice-President, Programs, International Development Research Centre (IDRC), Ottawa
9.30 a.m. – 11.00 a.m.	**SESSION IV:** **DIFFERENT APPROACHES TO DISPUTE RESOLUTION UNDER ASEAN AND NAFTA**
	Moderator:	*Ms Franca CIAMBELLA* Private Consultant

	Paperwriters:	*Associate Professor Locknie HSU* School of Law, Singapore Management University
		Professor J. Anthony VANDUZER Faculty of Law, University of Ottawa, Canada

11.00 a.m. – 11.15 a.m.   Coffee

11.15 a.m. – 12.45 p.m.   **SESSION V:**   **WHO ARE THE WINNERS AND LOSERS IN ECONOMIC INTEGRATION?**

Moderator: *Mr Richard FUCHS*
Regional Director, International Development Research Centre (IDRC), Singapore

Paperwriters: *Dr VO Tri Thanh*
Director, Department for International Integration Studies, Central Institute for Economic Management (CIEM), Hanoi, Vietnam

Dr Dan CIURIAK
Senior Associate, Centre for Trade Policy and Law, University of Ottawa and Carleton University, Canada

12.45 p.m. – 2.00 p.m.   Lunch

2.00 p.m. – 3.30 p.m.   **SESSION VI:**   **LABOUR MOBILITY/CROSS-BORDER MIGRATION ISSUES**

Moderator: *Dr Evan DUE*
Senior Programme Specialist, International Development Research Centre (IDRC), Singapore

Paperwriters: *Dr CHIA Siow Yue*
Senior Research Fellow, Singapore Institute of International Affairs (SIIA)

Professor Don J. DEVORETZ
Department of Economics,
Simon Fraser University,
Burnaby BC, Canada

3.30 p.m. – 5.00 p.m.   **FUTURE RESEARCH:**
BRINGING RESEARCH TO POLICY AND PRACTICE

Moderator: *Dr Omkar Lal SHRESTHA*
Visiting Senior Research Fellow,
Institute of Southeast Asian Studies,
Singapore

Panellists: *Professor Richard BARICHELLO*
Director, Centre for Southeast Asia
Research, Department of Food and
Resource Economics, University of
British Columbia, Vancouver

Professor John WHALLEY
William G. Davis Chair in
International Trade, Department of
Economics, University of Western
Ontario, London, Ontario

Dr Deunden NIKOMBORIRAK
Research Director,
Sectoral Economics Program,
Thailand Development Research
Institute, Bangkok, Thailand

Dr Mia MIKIC
Economic Affairs Officer,
Trade and Investment Division,
UN ESCAP, Bangkok, Thailand

5.00 p.m. – 5.10 p.m.   **Closing Remarks**

Ambassador K. KESAVAPANY
Director, Institute of Southeast Asian Studies, Singapore

Mr Richard FUCHS
Regional Director, International Development
Research Centre (IDRC), Singapore

5.10 p.m. – 5.30 p.m.   Tea

ASEAN-CANADA FORUM 2008
REGIONAL ECONOMIC INTEGRATION:
ASEAN AND CANADIAN PERSPECTIVES

25–26 November 2008
Seminar Rooms I and II
Institute of Southeast Asian Studies
Singapore

MODERATORS, PAPERWRITERS, RAPPORTEURS AND
PARTICIPANTS

Moderators and Paperwriters

1.   Ms Kala ANANDARAJAH
     Partner
     Rajah & Tann LLP
     77 Robinson Road
     #05-00
     Singapore 068896
     Tel: (65) 6507-9566
     Fax: (65) 6438-9622
     Email: kala.anandarajah@rajahtann.com

2.   Professor Myrna S. AUSTRIA
     Dean
     College of Business and Economics
     De La Salle University
     2401 Taft Avenue
     Manila
     Philippines
     Tel/Fax: (63-2) 536-0261
     Email: austriam@dlsu.edu.ph

3.   Professor Richard BARICHELLO
      Director
      Centre for Southeast Asian Research
      Food and Resource Economics
      University of British Columbia
      2357 Main Mall, Vancouver BC V6T1Z4
      Canada
      Tel: (1-604) 822-6213
      Fax: (1-604) 224-0350
      Email: rick.barichello@ubc.ca

4.   Ms Franca CIAMBELLA
      6A Swiss Club Road
      Singapore 288142
      Email: francaciambella@yahoo.com

5.   Dr Dan CIURIAK
      Senior Associate
      Centre for Trade Policy and Law
      Carleton University and University of Ottawa
      Ottawa
      Canada
      Tel: (613) 565-5284
      Email: dciuriak@sympatico.ca

6.   Dr CHIA Siow Yue
      Senior Research Fellow
      Singapore Institute of International Affairs (SIIA)
      2 Nassim Road
      Singapore 258370
      Tel: (65) 6734-9600
      Fax: (65) 6733-6217
      Email: chiasy@singnet.com.sg

7.   Dr CHIN Kin Wah
      Deputy Director
      Institute of Southeast Asian Studies
      30 Heng Mui Keng Terrace
      Pasir Panjang
      Singapore 119614
      Tel: (65) 6870-2433
      Fax: (65) 6775-6264
      Email: chinkw@iseas.edu.sg

8.   Ms Sanchita Basu DAS
        Visiting Research Fellow
        Lead Researcher-Economic Affairs
        ASEAN Studies Centre
        Institute of Southeast Asian Studies
        30 Heng Mui Keng Terrace
        Pasir Panjang
        Singapore 119614
        Tel: (65) 6870-4511
        Fax: (65) 6775-6264
        Email: sanchita@iseas.edu.sg

9.   Professor Paul J. DAVIDSON
        Department of Law
        Carleton University
        Ottawa
        Canada K1S 5B6
        Tel: (1-613) 520-2600 Ext 8062
        Fax: (1-603) 230-1249
        Email: paul_davidson@carleton.ca

10.   Professor Don DEVORETZ
        Department of Economics
        Simon Fraser University
        8888 University Drive
        Burnaby, British Columbia
        Canada V5A 1S6
        Tel: (778) 782-4660
        Email: devoretz@sfu.ca

11.   Dr Evan DUE
        Senior Programme Specialist
        International Development Research Centre (IDRC)
        22 Cross Street #02-55
        South Bridge Court
        Singapore 048421
        Tel: (65) 6438-7877
        Fax: (65) 6438-4844
        Email: edue@idrc.org.sg

12.   Mr Richard FUCHS
       Regional Director
       International Development Research Centre (IDRC)
       22 Cross Street #02-55
       South Bridge Court
       Singapore 048421
       Tel: (65) 6438-7877
       Fax: (65) 6438-4844
       Email: rfuchs@idrc.org.sg

13.   Mr George HAYNAL
       Vice President
       Government Affairs
       Department of Public Affairs
       Bombardier
       50 O'Connor Street, Suite 1425
       Ottawa, Ontario K1P 012 Canada
       Tel: (613) 237-8281
       Fax: (613) 237-9676
       Email: george.haynal@bombardier.com

14.   Dr Denis HEW
       Senior Fellow
       Institute of Southeast Asian Studies
       30 Heng Mui Keng Terrace
       Pasir Panjang
       Singapore 119614
       Tel: (65) 6870-4505
       Fax: (65) 6775-6264
       Email: denishew@iseas.edu.sg

15.   HE KOH Yong Guan
       Singapore High Commissioner to Canada and
       Chairman
       Central Provident Fund Board
       CPF Building
       41st Storey
       79 Robinson Road
       Singapore 068897
       Tel: (65) 6229-3210
       Fax: (65) 6224-5869
       Email: yong_guan.koh@cpf.gov.sg

16.   Associate Professor Locknie HSU
       School of Law
       Singapore Management University
       60 Stamford Road Level 4
       Singapore 178900
       Tel: (65) 6828-0572
       Fax: (65) 6828-0805
       Email: lockniehsu@smu.edu.sg

17.   Ambassador K. KESAVAPANY
       Director
       Institute of Southeast Asian Studies
       30 Heng Mui Keng Terrace
       Pasir Panjang
       Singapore 119614
       Tel: (65) 6778-0955
       Fax: (65) 6778-1735
       Email: kesavapany@iseas.edu.sg

18.   Professor Kishore MAHBUBANI
       Dean
       Lee Kuan Yew School of Public Policy
       National University of Singapore
       469C Bukit Timah Road
       Singapore 259772
       Tel: (65) 6516-3500
       Fax: (65) 6778-1020
       Email: kishore_mahbubani@nus.edu.sg

19.   Dr Rohinton MEDHORA
       Vice-President, Programs
       International Development Research Centre (IDRC)
       Ottawa
       Canada K1G 3H9
       Tel: (613) 236-6163 Ext 2312
       Fax: (613) 567-7748
       Email: rmedhora@idrc.ca

20. Dr Mia MIKIC
     Economic Affairs Officer
     Trade and Investment Division
     UN ESCAP
     Rajadamnern Nok Ave
     Bangkok 10200
     Thailand
     Tel: (66-2) 288-1410
     Fax: (66-2) 288-1027
     Email: mikic@un.org

21. Dr Deunden NIKOMBORIRAK
     Research Director
     Sectoral Economics Programme
     Thailand Development Research Institute
     565 Ramkamhaeng 39
     Bangkok 10310
     Thailand
     Tel: (66-2) 718-5460
     Fax: (66-2) 718-5461
     Email: deunden@tdri.or.th

22. Mr Rodolfo C. SEVERINO
     Head, ASEAN Studies Centre
     Institute of Southeast Asian Studies
     30 Heng Mui Keng Terrace
     Pasir Panjang
     Singapore 119614
     Tel: (65) 6870-4524
     Fax: (65) 6775-6264
     Email: severino@iseas.edu.sg

23. HE David SEVIGNY
     High Commissioner
     Canadian High Commission
     One George Street #11-01
     Singapore 049145
     Tel: (65) 6854-5900
     Fax: (65) 6854-5930

24.   Dr Omkar Lal SHRESTHA
       Visiting Senior Research Fellow
       Institute of Southeast Asian Studies
       30 Heng Mui Keng Terrace
       Pasir Panjang
       Singapore 119614
       Tel: (65) 6870-4531
       Fax: (65) 6775-6264
       Email: oshrestha@iseas.edu.sg

25.   Mr TAN Keng Jin
       Head, Public Affairs Unit
       Institute of Southeast Asian Studies
       30 Heng Mui Keng Terrace
       Pasir Panjang
       Singapore 119614
       Tel: (65) 6870-4527
       Fax: (65) 6775-6264
       Email: kjtan@iseas.edu.sg

26.   Professor J. Anthony VANDUZER
       Vice Dean Research
       Common Law Section, Faculty of Law
       University of Ottawa
       57 Louis Pasteur
       Ottawa, Ontario
       Canada K1N 6N5
       Tel: (613) 562-5800 Ext 3312
       Fax: (613) 562-5124
       Email: vanduzer@uottawa.ca

27.   Dr VO Tri Thanh
       Director
       Department for International Integration Studies
       Central Institute for Economic Management (CIEM)
       68 Phan Dinh Phung Str.
       Hanoi
       Vietnam
       Tel: (84-4) 3845-6903
       Fax: (84-4) 3845-6795
       Email: votrithanh@ciem.org.vn

28.   Professor John WHALLEY
       William G. Davis Chair of International Trade
       Department of Economics
       University of Western Ontario
       Room 4078, Social Science Centre
       London, Ontario, N6N 5C2
       Canada
       Tel: (519) 661-3509
       Fax: (519) 661-3666
       Email: jwhalley@uwo.ca

Rapporteurs

29.   Ms Aparna Bhagirathy KRISHNAN
       Research Associate
       Institute of Southeast Asian Studies
       30 Heng Mui Keng Terrace
       Pasir Panjang
       Singapore 119614
       Tel: (65) 6870-4513
       Fax: (65) 6775-6264
       Email: aparna@iseas.edu.sg

30.   Mr Alex THAM Keng Sum
       Research Associate
       Institute of Southeast Asian Studies
       30 Heng Mui Keng Terrace
       Pasir Panjang
       Singapore 119614
       Tel: (65) 6870-4514
       Fax: (65) 6775-6264
       Email: alextham@iseas.edu.sg

Participants

31.   Ms Vivien CHIAM
       Partnership & Communications Manager
       International Development Research Centre (IDRC)

32.   Mr Terrence COWL
       ASEAN Regional Economic Advisor
       Canadian High Commission

33.   Dr Teofilo C. DAQUILA
        Southeast Asian Studies Programme
        National University of Singapore

34.   Miss Juliana GIAM
        Deputy Director ASEAN
        Singapore Business Federation

35.   Ms Eileen SOO Hoo
        Assistant Manager, Management Development & Consultancy
        MDIS Corporation

36.   Mr Alan TAN W. Wton
        Deputy Director ASEAN & South Asia, Global Business Division
        Singapore Business Federation

ISEAS

37.   Dr Arun BALASUBRAMANIAM
        Visiting Senior Research Fellow

38.   Dr Aekapol CHONGVILAIVAN
        Fellow

39.   Mr Mark HONG
        Visiting Research Fellow

40.   Dr LEE Poh Onn
        Fellow

41.   Dr Daniel NOVOTNY
        Visiting Research Fellow

42.   Mrs Triena ONG
        Managing Editor, Publications Unit

43.   Mr Daljit SINGH
        Visiting Senior Research Fellow

44.   Dr Nasir TAMARA
        Visiting Senior Research Fellow

RULES-BASED GOVERNANCE

Although rules-based governance is often thought of in terms of binding rules backed up by an enforcement mechanism, rules-based governance comprises a much broader spectrum; rules may vary from binding obligations to non-binding commitments. "Rules-based" governance involves the negotiation of rules to govern the cooperation among the actors, and the establishment of mechanisms to achieve compliance with the rules. In the context of a rules-based system, rules define the extent to which obligations exist, and between whom and how redress is to occur. The aim of rules-based governance is predictability and efficiency. The two elements of a rules-based framework — rules and a dispute settlement/compliance mechanism — may be considered as occupying a spectrum representing various degrees of "legalization" as follows:

1. Rule Generation:

    Type of Norm/Rule:

        Non-binding   Binding
        Commitment <- - - - - - - - - - - -> Obligation

    Precision of Norm/Rule:

        Vague   Precise, highly
        Principle <- - - - - - - - - - - - -> elaborated rule

2. Dispute Settlement/Compliance Mechanism:

    Dispute Settlement Mechanism:

        Diplomacy <– – – – – – – – – – –> Formal Court

    Compliance Mechanism:

        Informal <– – – – – – – – – – – –> Formal
        Methods   Methods

The degree of "legalization" of a rule or a system will depend on where the rule or system falls on the spectrum. The possibilities of combinations across these extremes are multiple, ranging from "hard" legalization, through multiple forms of "softer" legalization. There is no clear distinction between "hard" and "soft" law, but rather, the continuum indicates the various degrees of "legalization", from "softer" to "harder", depending on where on the continuum the dimensions of the rule or system fall.

www.ingramcontent.com/pod-product-compliance
Lightning Source LLC
Chambersburg PA
CBHW050704280326
41926CB00088B/2508